Intuition *at* Work

ALSO BY GARY KLEIN, PH.D.

Sources of Power: How People Make Decisions

ALSO EDITED BY GARY KLEIN, PH.D.

Decision Making in Action: Models and Methods
(with J. Orasanu, R. Calderwood, C. E. Zsambok)

Linking Expertise and Naturalistic Decision Making
(with E. Salas)

Naturalistic Decision Making
(with C. E. Zsambok)

Intuition *at* Work

WHY DEVELOPING

YOUR GUT INSTINCTS

WILL MAKE YOU BETTER

AT WHAT YOU DO

Gary Klein, Ph.D.

currency

doubleday

new york london toronto

sydney auckland

A CURRENCY BOOK
PUBLISHED BY DOUBLEDAY
A division of Random House, Inc.
1745 Broadway, New York, NY 10019

CURRENCY and DOUBLEDAY are trademarks of Doubleday, a division of
Random House, Inc.

BOOK DESIGN BY NICOLA FERGUSON

"The Zone of Indifference" reprinted with permission from Leo Cullum, 2002.
"The Alarmist" © 2002 The New Yorker Collection from cartoonbank.com.
All Rights Reserved.

Library of Congress Cataloging-in-Publication Data
Klein, Gary
Intuition at work : why developing your gut instincts
will make you better at what you do / Gary Klein.—1st ed.
p. cm.
Includes bibliographical references and index.
1. Intuition. 2. Work—Psychological aspects. I. Title.

BF315.5 .K57 2003
153.4'4—dc21   2002071409

ISBN 0-385-50288-5

PRINTED IN THE UNITED STATES OF AMERICA

FIRST EDITION: January 2003

SPECIAL SALES

Currency Books are available at special discounts for bulk purchases for sales
promotions or premiums. Special editions, including personalized covers,
excerpts of existing books, and corporate imprints, can be created in large
quantities for special needs. For more information, write to Special Markets,
Currency Books, 280 Park Avenue, 11th Floor,
New York, NY 10017, or e-mail
specialmarkets@randomhouse.com.

1   3   5   7   9   10   8   6   4   2

For Helen

Contents

DECISION GAMES

EXAMPLES

Figures

Tables

Acknowledgments

I've been lucky to have the support and assistance of many friends and colleagues while I wrote this book. Each of them made an important contribution to my thinking and to the final version.

John Schmitt, a former Marine officer and currently a military consultant, was a key collaborator at every step. The work we did for the Marine Corps was the basis for the approach I have taken to train intuitive decision-making skills. John reviewed several drafts, describing at a conceptual level what he liked and what disappointed him, and making critical suggestions for how to improve the manuscript. Further, I was able to turn to John for assistance in the process of rewriting key sections. I am grateful for all of these things, and for his friendship.

I'm also fortunate to have spent the last twenty-three years working in a company that has provided opportunities and capabilities that wouldn't have been available to me in most other organizations. My thirty co-workers continually provide me with a blend of support, criticism, challenges, and new ideas—a combination of academia and business.

Buzz Reed, the CEO of my company, read and reacted to drafts of the manuscript, provided advice whenever I asked, and ran interference in countless ways. I am thankful for having him as a friend and guide.

Several people from a variety of organizations provided opportunities to conduct a series of decision-training workshops in the last year in order to fine-tune some of the decision-training methods: Dick Buckles, Paula Sydenstricker, Alyse McConnell, Jeanne Beauregard, Stephen Blatt, Will Hildesley, Wendy Philleo, Jennifer Holthaus, and Connie Gillan.

Four colleagues were generous enough to recount specific examples of their own intuitive decision making: Jerry Kirby, Lia DiBello, Bob Baker, and Ollie Malone.

Mike McCloskey shared the lessons he learned in training decision-making skills to different groups. For almost a decade, Larry Miller has both encouraged me to find ways to train decision-making skills and has given me opportunities to conduct that training with the firefighting community. Paul Van Riper and Tony Wood had enough confidence in my work to let me develop a decision-training program for the Marines. Pat Sweeney deserves thanks for useful discussions and strategizing about how to train decision making. Bill Breen and Tom Petzinger both helped me conceptualize ways to apply the ideas of intuitive decision making to the corporate sector.

I drew on a number of people who had the patience to review the entire manuscript, the dedication to document their comments, and the trust to share their impressions with me: Jenni Phillips, Laura Militello, Debbie Battaglia, Rebecca Klein, Dale Thoms, and Ann Gabbard. Mike Doherty worked hard (if not always successfully) to keep me from turning this book into a polemic against decision analysis. Steve Gabbard helped me with specific examples throughout the book and also provided a manuscript review. Karl Weick offered his reactions at a critical point in the writing process.

I asked a few people to review and comment on portions of the manuscript, and got very useful suggestions: Ken Boff, David Garvin, Beth Crandall, Devorah Klein, and Rob Hutton.

Barb Law, as usual, stepped in at the end to thoroughly edit the manuscript, catching a frightening number of errors. I have been working with Barb for more than twenty years, and I know she always comes through where needed.

Veronica Sanger is a wonderful production specialist and readily agreed to take on the task of producing the manuscript for publication. Thanks to her unvarying professionalism, competence, and cheerfulness, we came through this with little difficulty. I am grateful for her help.

Gregg Slayton contributed most of the graphics, and Danyele Harris provided me with library support. I also want to thank my agent, Katinka Matson and my publisher, Roger Scholl, for their help in conceptualizing the book. I was worried about the editing process, but

Stephanie Land, at Doubleday, was as much a colleague as an editor and it was a privilege to work with her.

I also want to thank my wife, Helen, for her patience and understanding during a mental "disappearing act" that lasted more than a year. She knew what was in store for her when I started the writing process, and she was as supportive as she always is.

Preface

I never set out to study intuition, and I certainly never expected to write a book about it. There are already enough books on intuition to satisfy anyone's reading habits. But the more research I did, and the more books I read, the more I realized that I needed to write this one. Here is what happened:

Almost two decades ago I conducted my first research project on decision making, studying firefighters to see how they could make high-stakes decisions in just a few seconds despite all the confusion and uncertainty inherent in their work.

I knew that the firefighters couldn't make their decisions by systematically comparing all of the possible ways to put out a fire because there wasn't enough time. I expected that they would only come up with two leading options, and compare these to each other. I was wrong. The firefighters, especially the more experienced ones, some with over twenty years of experience, usually just considered a single option.

In fact, to hear them describe it, they didn't really *consider* anything; they just *acted*. In our interviews with the firefighters, one of the most common statements my research team and I heard was, "We don't make decisions." This amazed us because we watched them routinely making very challenging decisions, many with life-or-death implications—and yet they were unaware they were doing it.

This was a finding I hadn't expected. I had stumbled onto the phenomenon of intuition, although I didn't realize it at the time. In fact, I was frustrated because the data had not come out the way I expected. Although I wasn't looking for intuition, intuition had found me.

My colleagues and I wondered if our results were somehow unique to firefighters but we soon found that people use their intuition to make decisions in every field we studied. Our research led us to the conclusion that we are all intuitive decision makers. Some of us are more skilled than others, certainly, and some are more specialized, but all of us rely on intuition. Even novices rely heavily on their intuitions, though not as frequently as experienced decision makers.

In retrospect, this shouldn't have surprised us. If you think about all the decisions we have to make in our personal and professional lives, it is obvious that we would never get through the day if we had to analyze every decision before we made it. Intuition is an essential, powerful, and practical tool. Flawed though it sometimes may be, we could not survive, much less excel, without it.

Equally important, through our research we came to appreciate that intuition is not a mystical gift that can't be explained. We discovered that the more experience people have in any particular field, the more they rely on intuition, and ultimately we learned that intuition is a natural and direct outgrowth of experience. I define intuition as *the way we translate our experience into action.* Our experience lets us recognize what is going on (making judgments) and how to react (making decisions). Because our experience enables us to recognize what to do, we can therefore make decisions rapidly and without conscious awareness or effort. We don't have to deliberately think through issues in order to arrive at good decisions.

I recall that at first the phrase "intuitive decision making" made me uncomfortable. When I started studying decision making, the concept of intuition was seen as unscientific, so when I began presenting my findings at professional conferences, I avoided using the term "intuition" because it made people want to dismiss my research. Even so, I was criticized for daring to suggest that it might be okay to make decisions without comparing options. I can only guess what the response of my peers would have been had I also thrown in the term "intuition."

Oddly, it was my work with the U.S. Marine Corps, starting in 1995, that helped me realize that intuition was no longer a dirty word. The Marines, as no-nonsense an organization as exists, openly talked about intuition and its importance. They even introduced the term "intuitive decision making" in their manual on command and control, comparing it favorably with analytical decision making. The

Marines sponsored my research and invited me to give presentations in their schools because they wanted to learn how to strengthen their intuitive skills. The lance corporals were comfortable with the idea of intuition, and so were the three-star generals. They weren't worried about terminology—they were driven by the need to make themselves better decision makers. If the U.S. Marines were comfortable with the term "intuition," I decided maybe I could be too.

After working with the Marines, I became more comfortable using the terms "intuition" and "intuitive decision making" to describe my work. These terms made it easier to connect with audiences about the ways they could strengthen their ability to size up situations and recognize what actions to take.

Intuition as I define it may be a very simple concept to understand, but it's often a difficult skill to acquire in practice. And that made the next step predictable—to design a training program. If intuition isn't mysterious, if it is a natural outgrowth of experience, then it should be possible to accelerate the process of gaining it. In 1995, the U.S. Marine Corps asked my company to develop a training program for decision-making skills. The Marines liked what they saw. Soon the Navy and the Army wanted their own training programs. The Los Angeles County Fire Department called us in to help them build intuitive decision-making skills, and so did the National Fire Academy.

Since that initial project with the firefighters almost twenty years ago, my colleagues and I have continued to conduct research studies. We developed special interviewing methods, a type of cognitive task analysis, to carefully examine how people make decisions while handling challenging incidents. To date, we have compiled a database of more than a thousand difficult and critical decisions that we have probed, in over seventy different areas ranging from firefighting to critical care nursing to job seeking. We have completed more than 100 studies using cognitive task analysis methods to understand how people make complex decisions.

In 1998 MIT Press published my first book, *Sources of Power: How People Make Decisions.* The book describes a range of abilities, including intuition, that enable people to make good decisions without having to perform deliberate analyses. One chapter—entitled "The Power of Intuition"—documented how people can make decisions in only a few seconds once they have developed intuitive decision-making skills. I expected that the book would be read by other researchers and perhaps be used in some graduate seminars.

Somehow, the media noticed the book. *The Wall Street Journal* championed our theory that intuition could be a reasonable and trustworthy basis for action, and featured two articles on our work. *Fast Company* carried a lengthy article on the same topic. *O, The Oprah Magazine* mentioned the book in a short article on intuition. *More* magazine did an interview with two of my colleagues. Other outlets picked up from there. Newsletters for auto mechanics, commercial pilots, physicians, business executives, software developers, and others carried articles on our work and the importance of intuition.

This is how, to my surprise, I developed a reputation as an intuition researcher.

The media coverage resulted in calls from corporations asking for training in intuitive decision making for their employees. In response to this demand we began by adapting the training methods we had developed for the Marines. As the demand has continued, in the last few years we have started over again and designed methods specifically geared for managers and executives. Some of these are adaptations of the original methods, but many are brand new. Though there are still some skeptics who doubt that we can identify the basis of our intuition, much less actively work on it, I now firmly believe that it's possible to improve intuitive decision making. My colleagues and I have run dozens of workshops in the past few years, and we have been rewarded by witnessing countless participants respond to the ideas and the methods we teach. In the last workshop I ran, at a global information technology company, a senior executive put one of the tools into effect less than an hour after the workshop concluded. (He used a PreMortem method for spotting potential weaknesses in a plan, as described in Chapter 6.)

The media coverage for *Sources of Power* had one other unexpected outcome—requests that I write a book about how to develop skills in making intuitive decisions. At first I resisted this idea. There are dozens and dozens of books on intuition. Why add to the stack?

Out of curiosity I started reading those other books on intuition.

MAGICAL INTUITION Most of the books I read were advocating a magical view of intuition, claiming that there is a deep level of wisdom residing in each of us, and our job is to make contact with it, to use it as a psychic ability that can guide us over the hurdles of life. Some advocates of magical intuition claim that the best way to make any decision is to get in touch with these unconscious forces. Building expertise, by their way of thinking, is unimportant to the process.

If you are hoping for a magical description of intuition, you have picked up the wrong book. One of my primary motives in writing this book is to offer a different view and to set intuition on firmer ground as a natural outgrowth of experience and preparation.

This book is about how people build up intuitions as they gain experience. It is not about intuition as ESP (extrasensory perception). It is not about Luke Skywalker getting in touch with "The Force." There are other books that treat intuition as a gift, and treat "intuitives" as unique beings with special sensitivity. Those other books will explain how you can become an "intuitive" yourself. In contrast, this book will explain how you can increase your intuitive decision-making skills by putting yourself through a program of mental conditioning to expand your pattern repertoire. It doesn't sound as exciting as turning people into Jedi knights, but it's more realistic.

I realize that people sometimes have hunches that seem to come from nowhere, except perhaps from ESP, but this is because we haven't become aware of the associations and connections that lead to these hunches.

For example, I have interviewed several decision makers—from military and firefighting backgrounds—who believed they had ESP. They recalled concrete incidents that seemed to justify these beliefs. Fortunately, we had a chance to do in-depth cognitive interviews with these individuals to find out what they were noticing and thinking while they were in the process of making their decisions. We were able to show that the decision makers had picked up signs of trouble, without even realizing it, by noticing subtle cues. After going over the evidence, even the decision makers themselves admitted that their intuition did not depend on ESP. Cases such as these show how easy it can be, even for trained professionals, to conclude that their intuitions are based on psychic abilities.

The magical view of intuition has spawned a backlash that doesn't work for me either. These other books, by intuition phobics, condescendingly dismiss the idea of intuition. They're usually written from an academic perspective and contain complicated examples of how intuitions can sometimes be wrong. They advise you to inhibit your intuitions and rely instead on deliberate analyses. These books alarmed me almost as much as those from the first camp because the advice is so wrong. Analysis has its function, and intuition isn't perfect, but trying to replace intuition with analysis is a huge mistake, for reasons I'll explain in detail later.

The more I read, the more dismay I felt. I fear that if we let the field of intuition be dominated by the magical view, urging us to give up analysis altogether, the whole topic of intuition will become disreputable. If we let ourselves be captured by the intuition phobics, we will actually lose ground, trying to make sense of the world by following rules instead of becoming smarter and more seasoned.

And so I found that I needed to write a book on intuition that treats it as a natural extension of experience. This book attempts to chart a realistic course between these two misguided camps.

Let me make it clear that I am not proposing to offer any dramatic solutions or formulas for success. There are no shortcuts that lead to improved judgment. Yes, I believe we can get smarter faster, but there is no substitute for putting in the effort. What I am offering you is a set of tools you can use to become a better intuitive decision maker in whatever field you choose.

MUSCULAR INTUITION I prefer a "muscular" view of intuition that treats our intuitions as skills that can be acquired, as strengths that can be expanded through exercise. The more you exercise—the more repetitions, or "reps," to borrow a term from the gym—the stronger you get. The same applies to intuition. Intuitive decision making improves as we acquire more patterns, larger repertoires of action scripts, and richer mental models. Remember: *Intuition is the way we translate our experience into action.* This approach forms the rationale for this book. Regardless of its limitations, we depend on intuition. Therefore, it is critical that we grow it into a reliable instrument. As with physical exercise, you will get some results if you simply take the time to exert yourself, to do the "reps," but you will get better results faster if you use proper technique and if you have a smart training program with progressive goals—and especially if you can get guidance and feedback on those techniques and goals. Think of it as a fitness program to develop your intuition.

The Three Goals of This Book

The overall objective of this book is to help you strengthen your intuitive decision-making skills. To achieve this objective, this book presents an intuition skills training program aimed at helping readers to develop effective intuitions more quickly, to better apply these intuitions, and to safeguard their intuitions. Instead of passively waiting to acquire them through enough experience, there are steps you can take to speed up the process.

This book has three sections, each with its own goal.

SECTION I. INTUITION: WAYS TO BUILD IT (CHAPTERS 1–4) This section will teach you how to *build* intuition. That means understanding what intuition is. It means learning methods for building skills in intuitive decision making (presented in Chapter 3) and understanding how to blend intuition with analysis (covered in Chapter 4).

SECTION II. INTUITION: WAYS TO APPLY IT (CHAPTERS 5–11) You'll learn to apply your intuitions more effectively in the workplace. These chapters provide tools for using intuition to make decisions, to spot problems, to manage uncertainty, to size up situations, to invent new approaches, and to adapt old ones.

SECTION III. INTUITION: WAYS TO SAFEGUARD IT (CHAPTERS 12–16) I want you to know how to safeguard those skills against the obstacles that often get in the way of intuitive decision making. The chapters in this section show you how to communicate your intuitive decisions more effectively, how to coach others to become more experienced, how to make good use of metrics—quantitative data—and how to recognize and defend yourself against the negative effects of information technologies.

Organizational leaders carry the burden of getting it right when the stakes are high, and therefore I have aimed most of this discussion at managers and executives. I know, however, that many other levels of employees are called on to make decisions, and I think you'll find that the materials and ideas and tools will be relevant to them as well.

Senior executives should be interested in intuition because that is their stock in trade; it's why people seek out their opinions. They are the ones who pick up the early signs of problems or recognize opportunities without having to gather all the relevant data and perform all the necessary calculations. Their decades of experience translate into an ability to confidently make important judgments. Executives also come under pressure to defend their intuitions against criticisms that the world has changed, that their expertise is largely obsolete, that they are stuck in old paradigms. They sometimes have to explain why their conclusions are different from those of the number crunchers. And if they don't understand where their intuitions are coming from, if they can't determine when their intuitions might be misleading, if they can't convince others to take their intuitions seriously, then they may be hard-pressed to justify their authority.

Intuition is relevant to *mid-level managers* because it's what will set them apart from their peers. Their skills at sizing up situations and seeing the big picture may determine whether they move up in responsibility, or spend the next ten to twenty years stuck in a dead-end position. The accuracy of their intuitions helps them become the "go to" people in an organization—the ones others flock to when they run into a dilemma.

New hires, too, should focus on developing their intuition because they don't yet have many intuitions that are trustworthy. The challenge here is to build intuitive decision skills as quickly as possible. This holds true for people who transfer into new roles in an organization, as well as employees fresh out of school. Too often, a new hire's training centers on how to operate equipment or carry out company procedures. There is little, if any, guidance on developing intuitions. As a result, the "newbies" can flounder, get frustrated, and acquire bad habits and poor attitudes.

Organizations that encourage employees to strengthen their intuitions often have a more confident, more adept staff. I remember one interview I conducted with a senior information technologist at a Fortune 500 company. She confided that she had refused to take a promotion in another unit because she couldn't endure the strain of managing computer professionals who had so much more experience on a new system than she did. As a result, she was resigned to keeping her old position, and her organization lost out on a chance to grow a new manager. Fears of inadequacy are a barrier to organizational growth. Therefore, organizations can help themselves by providing skilled employees with ways to more quickly come up to speed in a new area.

All three groups—senior executives, middle managers, and new hires—can take away some useful lessons from this book. Alden Hayashi recently asserted in the *Harvard Business Review* that the higher one goes in an organization, the greater the need for intuition. I believe this is true, but I also know that intuition has to start somewhere. New hires need to start developing intuition skills. Middle managers need to expand and apply their intuition skills. Senior executives need to safeguard their intuition skills and pass them on to the next generations. All of these accomplishments depend on knowing what intuition is and how it works.

In addition, all of these accomplishments depend on improving one's decision-making skills rather than complaining that some people seem to automatically know what to do and others don't. For too long, intuition has been dismissed as unlikely coincidences and lucky guesses. Now it's time to take intuition seriously.

Section I

INTUITION

Ways to

Build It

A Case Study of Intuition

I don't think you can make effective decisions without developing your intuition. To illustrate why intuition is so important, I've selected an incident that contrasts two nurses, each facing the same crisis. One of the nurses has developed intuitive decision-making skills and one is trying to acquire these skills.

The example describes the decision making of nurses working in an NICU. That stands for neonatal intensive care unit, the hospital ward where they keep close watch on newborns in critical condition.

Background

Most of the infants in an NICU have been born prematurely. Some weigh a pound or less, and many are born with underdeveloped respiratory, circulatory, or immune systems.

Each infant is placed in its own isolette or medical bassinet, and attached to little adhesive leads that provide data to a bank of monitors displaying heart rate, blood pressure, respiration, blood oxygen level, and other vital statistics. Nourishment might be provided through an IV (intravenous feed) or through a drip tube snaked down the esophagus directly into the stomach. A thermostat precisely controls the temperature in the isolette.

One of the risks in the NICU is the danger of infection. To gain access in order to see and hold their babies, parents perform a five-minute surgical scrub from hands to elbows. Children are strictly prohibited because they are exposed to so many germs and can easily transmit them to the babies.

Homemade get-well cards and photos of Mom and Dad, brothers and sisters, cousins, and family pets are often taped to the glass walls of the isolettes. A small rubber toy, such as a Mickey Mouse or Winnie the Pooh figure, might be placed in the isolette as a companion, but only after first being sterilized by the nurses, because a stuffed animal might carry dust mites.

Feedings have to be carefully calculated. The goal is obviously to help the baby grow, but it is equally important to make sure the baby does not add body weight faster than heart and lungs can support. Not only is nutrition intake carefully measured, but so is the waste coming out the other end. Every diaper is weighed to gauge the baby's metabolism. Practically every aspect of intensive care in the NICU involves continuous monitoring and adjustments to maintain a precarious balance in these fragile human systems until the babies can grow themselves into stability.

During the day a steady procession of medical technicians comes through to take blood for routine testing, perform sonograms or other procedures, administer respiratory therapy, or deliver medications. But it is the primary NICU nurses who are on the front lines. They are responsible for administering the treatments established by the physicians, monitoring the baby's condition, and being alert to any signs of change.

With infants in these fragile conditions, many things can go wrong, and practically all of them can become life threatening. One of the greatest and most common dangers is sepsis, a systemic infection that spreads throughout the infant's circulatory system. Sepsis can be deadly, especially for low-birth-weight babies. Premature babies come into the world with an underdeveloped immune system, making them particularly vulnerable. The first line of defense against infection is the baby's intact skin and mucous membranes, but in the NICU, that defense has been penetrated by IVs, catheters, and other invasive measures. Sepsis can be detected by a blood culture, but this test takes twenty-four hours and by then the baby might be overwhelmingly infected and beyond help. The onset of sepsis is often accompanied by very subtle changes in the baby's status. The nurses' ability to recognize these subtle changes is the key to early detection of sepsis and appropriate intervention. The nurses in the NICU must be continuously on guard against the potential danger of infection.

Some infants spend only a couple of days in the NICU. Some are there for several weeks or more. And some do not survive. The nurses must also deal with this reality.

Some nurses find the challenges and the mission rewarding and choose to make neonatal intensive care their career. However, many nurses new to the NICU burn out in less than eighteen months, overcome by the complexities and unrelenting stress of caring for the tiny lives in the balance.

"Darlene" was a good example of someone who flourished in this environment. At the time of this incident she had become the assistant clinical coordinator for the NICU. This meant that in addition to working regular shifts on the ward, she was responsible for scheduling, hiring, and firing other nurses. Darlene had a bachelor of science degree in nursing. All of her nursing experience was with babies, and she had spent the last six years working in the NICU.

"Linda" was also an experienced nurse, although she was new to neonatal care and was, therefore, still considered a trainee. She had completed her orientation in the NICU and was working shifts on the floor, mentored one-on-one by Darlene, although they each had responsibility for different infants. The two had been working together this way for several months, so by now Darlene was doing more monitoring than instructing.

A Baby in Crisis

Linda had primary responsibility for an infant girl, "Melissa." By NICU standards, Melissa was not a particularly tough case. Melissa was a "preemie" and tiny like most of the babies in the NICU, but she had no major problems that had to be overcome. She simply needed a little support until she could grow herself out of danger. She was not on a ventilator. She was able to take small amounts of formula in a bottle—up to two ounces at a time—and her young parents had even been able to hold her during feedings. She was putting on weight, and all signs indicated she was on the road to becoming a healthy baby girl.

It was early in the morning, and Linda and Darlene were nearing the end of an uneventful shift. Thankfully, there had been no emergencies. If anything, Melissa had been less fussy than usual. Maybe this was a sign that she was getting better. The ward was quiet and deserted except for the infants and their nurses. Like most visitors, Melissa's exhausted parents had gone home after keeping vigil during the day. The lights on the ward were turned low, except for a small light at each station that allowed the nurse to do her work—an ongoing routine of taking temperatures, changing diapers, feeding, administering medicines, recording readings from the monitors, and adjusting settings on the equipment in accordance with the treatment prescribed by the physician. Frequently an alarm would sound from one of the babies' monitors, but almost invariably it was a false alarm—usually a lead had come loose, interrupting the data input. A nurse would appear, calmly check the situation, and reset the monitor. Occasionally, a baby would fuss, and a nurse would respond. Otherwise, the ward was quiet.

During her scheduled feeding Melissa had seemed a little lethargic, but who wouldn't be at that hour? Linda had regularly checked Melissa's body temperature and found it a little low over several checks, though still well within the normal range. She turned up the thermostat in the isolette each time to make Melissa more comfortable. Late in the shift a medical technician had come in to take a routine blood sample for testing. This had been done by a heel stick, a small prick made in Melissa's heel. The technician had covered it with a small, colorful Band-Aid. A good med tech will make an almost imperceptible heel stick that closes up almost immediately. A sloppy heel stick might bleed for a few minutes. Melissa's heel stick was bleeding a little bit, creating a dark blot on the Band-Aid.

Melissa was Linda's patient. Darlene had talked to Linda several times about her, but by this point in the training she did not routinely check Melissa herself.

But when Darlene walked past Melissa's isolette near the end of the shift, something caught her eye. Something about the baby "just looked funny," as she later put it. Nothing major, nothing obvious, but to her the baby "didn't look good." Darlene had a closer look, now noticing specific details. She noticed the heel stick had not stopped bleeding. To Darlene, Melissa seemed a little "off color" and "mottled," and her belly seemed a little rounded. She noticed this even though every baby had a different complexion and body shape and Darlene was not particularly familiar with Melissa's normal state. A

INTUITION AT WORK

quick physical exam confirmed that Melissa still had an unusual amount of residual food in her stomach, causing bloating. Darlene checked Melissa's chart and noticed that the baby's temperature had dropped consistently over the shift. She called Linda over and asked her if the baby had seemed lethargic during the shift. When Linda replied, "Yes," Darlene immediately raced to the phone and woke the duty physician.

"We've got a baby in big trouble," she said. She explained the symptoms. The physician agreed with Darlene's assessment of a baby in crisis and immediately ordered antibiotics and a blood culture. Twenty-four hours later, the blood culture confirmed sepsis. If they had delayed giving the antibiotic until they had the results of the blood culture it would probably have been too late.

This story has a happy ending. Thanks to an experienced nurse's intuitive sense of a baby who "didn't look good," Melissa would live.

The Contrast

Initially, Darlene was incredulous that Linda had missed the classic symptoms of sepsis, which seemed so obvious. All the new nurses were trained to be alert for signs of it.

In fact, Linda *had* recognized practically all the individual symptoms—but most of them could be reasonably explained in several different ways.

Linda had noticed the decrease in Melissa's temperature. But because the temperature had never dropped out of the normal range, Linda had responded by increasing the heat in the isolette after each reading, four times in a row. This seemed like a reasonable response because, usually, it is a fever that is worrisome to a nurse, not a temperature drop. Darlene, however, knew from experience that a drop in temperature could signal a coming fever.

Linda was aware of the bleeding heel stick, but did not know how quickly the bleeding should stop in a normal baby. Plus, the bleeding could have been the result of a sloppy heel stick. Darlene knew that the continued bleeding was another danger sign.

Linda had noticed that Melissa seemed "sleepy"—she didn't label this as lethargic—but she knew that babies tended to sleep a lot.

She was able to recognize the rounded belly and mottled skin—

possible signs that blood supply to the skin could be shutting down—when they were pointed out to her, but earlier she had not attached any significance to these cues. Linda had already learned that the newborns in the unit sometimes got lighter or darker for no apparent reason, and as their digestive systems matured she expected there would be times when they would become bloated. Darlene, though, had noticed a subtle olive tinge in Melissa's complexion and associated it with a possible infection; Linda could recognize the coloring but hadn't realized its importance.

Ultimately, it was not so much the individual symptoms that were key, but a particular constellation of symptoms. Linda could see all the signs, but she was unable to piece them together into a story that revealed the larger pattern.

During our interview with her, Darlene allowed that it is very difficult to know the signs of sepsis "until you see them."

In our research we found that Darlene was typical of highly experienced NICU nurses who can detect sepsis in premature infants, even before the blood tests pick it up. By noticing the early signs of sepsis these nurses were able to start treatment early and save the lives of babies. Some cues had been recorded previously in the clinical literature, but many of the cues that these nurses could recognize had never even been previously identified (and, in fact, our study resulted in a sepsis handbook for NICU nurses).

What You're Going to Learn

Darlene took one glance and her intuition told her Melissa wasn't okay. What was the nature of this intuition? You'll find out in Chapter 2, Where Do Our Hunches Come From?

Darlene developed her intuitive decision-making skills over many years and many babies like Melissa. You can build these skills more quickly through the techniques introduced in Chapter 3, Intuition Skills Training: Speeding Up Your Learning Curve.

Darlene did not simply rely on her intuition. She also sought information that might confirm or weaken her judgment about Melissa. You will learn how to blend intuition with analysis in Chapter 4, Using Analysis to Support Our Intuitions.

Darlene decided that this was a crisis and that Melissa needed antibiotics. What type of decision process did she use? See Chapter 5, How to Make Tough Choices.

Darlene's intuition enabled her to zero in on the sepsis that was starting to ravage Melissa. You'll understand how to use intuition to detect potential problems while they are still treatable in Chapter 6, How to Spot Problems Before They Get Out of Hand.

Darlene knew which data to seek from Linda, and which data to let go. She did not order tests before bothering the physician—just the opposite. She called the physician to get antibiotics started before getting the results of the blood tests. You will learn how to use your intuition to handle ambiguity in Chapter 7, How to Manage Uncertainty.

With the data she collected, Darlene confirmed that Melissa was in trouble. The ways you can use your intuition to make sense of events are described in Chapter 8, How to Size Up Situations.

Darlene thought that the directions she had given Linda were sufficient. But they weren't. You will learn to effectively convey your intuitions to others in Chapter 12, Executive Intent: How to Communicate Your Intuitions.

Darlene and other NICU nurses report that the subjective nature of the assessment can make it difficult to share with novice nurses. Nurses have trouble articulating in detailed and specific terms what they are noticing intuitively. You can help subordinates come up to speed more quickly by using the guidance offered in Chapter 13, Coaching Others to Develop Strong Intuitions.

Darlene was not misled by the data records. She studied the trend of Melissa's temperature readings, and focused on the feeding charts that suggested that Melissa was having trouble digesting her food. You can use your intuition to actively interpret data instead of passively tending to the records the way Linda did, by applying the advice presented in Chapter 14, Overcoming the Problems with Metrics.

Darlene had learned to look at babies instead of depending on the monitoring equipment. To keep from becoming a slave to information technology, read Chapter 15, Smart Technology Can Make Us Stupid.

Where Do Our Hunches Come From?

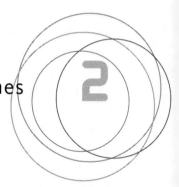

Remember what you were taught about the right way to make important decisions? You were probably told to analyze a problem thoroughly, list all your different options, evaluate those options based on a common set of criteria, figure out how important each criterion is, rate each option on each criterion, do the math, and compare the options against each other to see which of your options best fit your needs. The decision was simply a matter of selecting the option with the highest score.

This is the classical model of decision making, and there is something very appealing and reassuring about it. It is based not on whims or hunches, but on solid analysis and logic. It is methodical rather than haphazard. It guarantees that you won't miss anything important. It leaves nothing to chance. It promises you a good decision if you follow the process properly. It allows you to justify your decision to others. There is something scientific about it.

The whole thing sounds very comforting. Who would not want to be thorough, systematic, rational, and scientific?

The only problem is that the whole thing is a myth. The reality is that the classical model of decision making doesn't work very well in practice. It works tolerably well in the research labs which use undergraduate test subjects making trivial decisions, but it doesn't do so well in the real world, where decisions are more challenging, situations are more confusing and complex, information is scarce or inconclusive, time is short, and stakes are high. And in that environment, the classical, analytical model of decision making falls flat.

That's why people rarely use the classical model—even though they may say they believe in it. And I think the truth is that deep down we all know this. Practically anybody who has even limited experience making tough decisions, in practically any field, realizes that formal analytical decision making doesn't work very well in practice. Most real-life decisions are simply not amenable to this approach. Even when we try to keep an open mind and consider several options, we usually know from the beginning which option we really prefer, so the whole process becomes a charade in comparing what we know we want to two or three other made-up distracters. (And when the process surprises us by giving us a solution we know deep down we didn't really prefer, we tweak the evaluation criteria until we get the solution we wanted all the time. How often have you done that?)

So how *do* we make decisions? Well, largely through a process based on intuition. Think about the times when you had a sense about something, even though you couldn't quite explain it. *Can a subordinate handle a tough project?* You can't imagine it working out without some disaster. Better give the job to someone else. *Why is a customer late with a payment?* You have a hunch that the customer may be having a cash flow problem. *Is a contract going well?* The reports and expenditure rates look fine but you aren't picking up any signs of excitement from the project team. Maybe you should look more deeply into it.

The Process of Intuitive Decision Making

What is it that sets off these alarm bells inside your head? It's your intuition, built up through repeated experiences that you have unconsciously linked together to form a pattern.

A "pattern" is a set of cues that usually chunk together so that if you see a few of the cues you can expect to find the others. When you notice a pattern you may have a sense of familiarity—yes, I've seen that before! As we work in any area, we accumulate experiences and build up a reservoir of recognized patterns. The more patterns we learn, the easier it is to match a new situation to one of the patterns in our reservoir. When a new situation occurs, we recognize the situation as familiar by matching it to a pattern we have encountered in the past.

For instance, a firefighter sees the color of the smoke and the force with which it is billowing, and suspects that toxic chemicals may be burning. A manager sees an increase in small errors from a normally meticulous employee, some loss of speech fluency, less predictable work hours, a slight increase in irritability, and wonders if an employee is having some problems with alcohol or drugs.

Consider the case of the infant with sepsis in Chapter 1. Incidents like this show how differently the world looks through the eyes of a novice and an expert. Darlene knew that a baby's skin could be a good indicator of health, as much as the sensors attached to the infants. She walked down the aisles of the intensive care unit looking at the babies, not at the electronic monitoring devices. Taken together—the skin color, the mottled appearance, the rounded belly—all fit a pattern. The rest of the data fit the pattern and confirmed it. She didn't need to look the symptoms up in a chart.

Darlene's intuition was based on the patterns she had learned from previous cases of babies who had developed systemic infection. She had seen cases where the sepsis had progressed and the symptoms had become more marked. She had seen babies die from sepsis. So she was alert for the early signs in each baby she passed, and was actively looking for signs of problems. Linda had never seen a case of sepsis. All she could do was reliably update her charts and hope her data would alert her to a problem.

Experienced managers often make the same mistake as Darlene, assuming that their subordinates can see the patterns that seem so obvious to them. Sales supervisors may get impatient with new staff members who are so concerned about what to say to a customer that they don't observe the customer's reactions and emotions. Quality control specialists may be frustrated to see trainees studying parts specifications but unable to identify subtle flaws in the product. The ability to detect patterns is easy to take for granted but hard to learn.

Some of the leading researchers in psychology, including the Nobel laureate Herbert Simon, have demonstrated that pattern recognition explains how people can make effective decisions without conducting a deliberate analysis.

Once we recognize a pattern, we gain a sense of a situation: We know what *cues* are going to be important and need to be monitored. We know what types of *goals* we should be able to accomplish. We have a sense of what to *expect* next. And the patterns include routines for responding—*action scripts.* If we see a situation as typical then we can recognize the typical ways to react. That's how we have hunches about what is really going on, and about what we should do about it.

Intuition is the way we translate our experiences into judgments and decisions. It's the ability to make decisions by using patterns to recognize what's going on in a situation and to recognize the typical action script with which to react. Once experienced intuitive decision makers see the pattern, any decision they have to make is usually obvious.

Notice that Figure 2.1 shows that the action scripts "affect" the situation. In many cases they will *change* the situation. However, some of your best decisions may be to let things proceed and *not* make any changes. You want to avoid the trap of intervening at the wrong time.

The more patterns and action scripts we have available, the more expertise we have, and the easier it is to make decisions. The patterns tell us what to do and the action scripts tell us how. Without a reper-

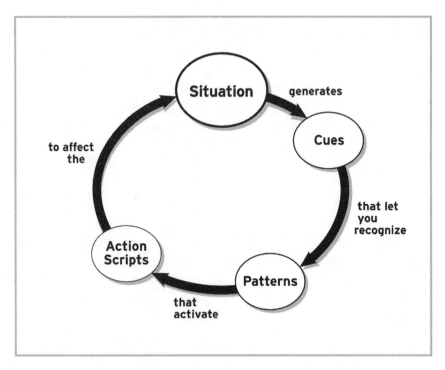

Figure 2.1 The Pattern-Recognition Process
Behind Intuitive Decision Making

toire of patterns and action scripts, we would have to painstakingly think out every situation from scratch.

Because pattern matching can take place in an instant, and without conscious thought, we're not aware of how we arrived at an intuitive judgment. That's why it often seems mysterious to us.

Even if the situation isn't exactly the same as anything we have seen before, we can recognize similarities with past events and so we automatically know what to do, without having to deliberately think out the options. We have a sense of what will work and what won't. Basically, it's at this point that we have become intuitive decision makers.

The Role of Analysis

While I have criticized the idea of replacing intuition with analytical strategies of decision making, I certainly don't believe that intuition can solve all our problems. Analysis has a proper role as a supporting tool for making intuitive decisions. When time and the necessary information are available, analysis can help uncover cues and patterns. It can sometimes help evaluate a decision. But it cannot replace the intuition that is at the center of the decision-making process (although that is precisely what some decision researchers have tried to do). I am only opposed to analysis when it gets in the way of the effective use of intuition. You'll read in Chapter 4 about some ways that we can make effective use of analysis.

Isn't It Obvious?

When I first started giving talks describing how people can make decisions without comparing options, I used to get a lot of skepticism. I still do. But in the last few years I have also started to receive a different kind of criticism: "Of course—isn't that obvious? People use their experience to recognize what to do."

I know that it isn't obvious. It isn't obvious now to all of the hard-core decision analysts who still argue against the notion of intuition. It certainly wasn't obvious ten to twenty years ago, when the leading decision researchers believed that an individual had to come up with a range of options, evaluate these on a common set of evaluation dimensions, then total up the scores to find the winner. According to the decision analysts, any deviation from decision analysis was likely to result in failure. Even today, formal decision analysis is still taught as the ideal in most schools of business and engineering.

In 1978, Lee Beach and Terry Mitchell, two leading decision researchers, took a bold stand to claim that there are times to use analysis, and times when it is appropriate to rely on intuition.

But Beach and Mitchell could not describe what intuition was. They could say what it wasn't—it wasn't performing analysis. Then they got stuck. The best they could do was say that intuition relied on things like flipping a coin, or playing "one potato, two potato," or gut feeling. The field of decision research had not examined the strategies people used when they weren't analyzing situations.

My colleagues and I stumbled on some clues about the nature of intuition in 1985 when we conducted research for the U.S. Army on the decision making of highly experienced firefighters. Our research centered on the commanders who have to make tough calls in the face of a rapidly growing fire or other type of emergency. We thought that under this type of time pressure, the commanders wouldn't be able to compare lots of options. We expected that they would be comparing only two options at each decision point.

We were wrong. Universally, the fireground commanders insisted that they weren't comparing *any* options. They claimed that in most cases, they just came up with a single course of action and carried it out.

This discovery shot down our hypothesis and it raised two puzzles. The first puzzle was how the firefighters could trust the first option they considered. Our research showed that this was what experience had bought them. All of their previous experiences (prior to becoming a commander and after becoming a commander) resulted in internalizing a large set of patterns, as I described in Figure 2.1.

When we are faced with a familiar problem, there is a good chance that the first solution we recognize is going to work. Why? Because in most settings we don't need the best option—we need to quickly identify an acceptable option. Possibly there might be a better one, but if it takes hours to find and evaluate, then there is no practical benefit from searching for the optimal course of action. As the old saying goes, "Better is the enemy of good enough."

The second puzzle was how the firefighters could evaluate an action script—a potential course of action—if they didn't have at least one other option to compare it against. How could they gauge whether a routine or script they had used in the past would work in a specific situation? All the traditional theories of decision making depended on systematically contrasting the strengths and weaknesses of the alternatives. If the firefighters weren't generating alternatives they shouldn't have been able to do any evaluation. The answer is that the firefighters rely on mental simulation, as shown in Figure 2.2.

When we looked at their decision making more closely we discovered that they were evaluating a course of action by consciously *imagining* what would happen when they carried it out. We call this process "mental simulation" because decision makers are simulating and envisioning a scenario—playing out in their heads what they expect would happen if they implemented the decision in a particular case. They build a picture of what they expect, and they watch this picture once, sometimes several times. If they like what they see, they are ready to respond. If they spot a problem, usually they can alter the ac-

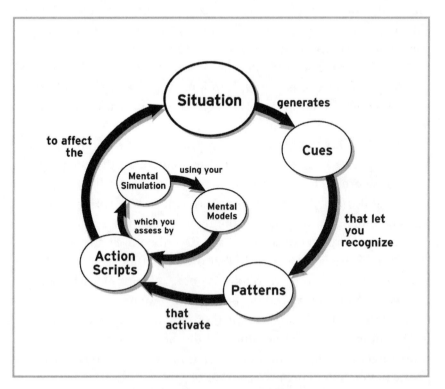

Figure 2.2 Recognition-Primed Decision Model

tion script. If they can't find a way around the problem, they jettison the option and look at the next option in the set without comparing it to any other options.

This two-part process of pattern matching and mental simulation is the "recognition-primed decision" (RPD) model, which explains how people can make good decisions without generating and comparing a set of options. Pattern recognition primes the decision-making process but it needs to be tested through mental simulation.

Mental simulation is the way we evaluate our decisions and figure out what to expect before we implement them so we know later whether the decision is having the desired effect or not.

For example, a marketing representative in a manufacturing company will be called upon to prepare bids for different products. The representative may be able to recognize that a new product described by a potential customer is just like one that the plant built a few years ago. Therefore, the bid that won that job may be just what is needed. This is pattern recognition in action. However, the marketing representative still needs to assess if that old bid will still work. This is where the mental simulation comes in. The rep may build a mental model of how the plant is going to configure its equipment to do the cutting and shaping and assembling, and then the rep may run this model to imagine how the manufacturing tasks are going to be carried out. While imagining how the plant is going to make the part, the marketing rep may realize that a certain aspect of the manufacturing process cannot easily be accomplished—perhaps because a key piece of equipment that was in service a few years ago was damaged and never replaced. That would certainly change the bid.

In order to build an effective mental simulation, we need to have good *mental models* of how things work. This is another aspect of expertise, and another way that experience translates into action. For firefighters to construct a scenario of how an action script will work, they need mental models of the way fires spread, the way different types of construction will withstand exposure to flames, the way heat will react when a hole is chopped into a roof. Nurses dealing with sepsis need mental models of how the infection starts and spreads. In order to prepare accurate bids, marketing representatives for manufacturing companies need mental models of how components are assembled. They have to understand the time and effort needed to modify equipment and they need to know the learning curve for fabricating difficult parts. Otherwise, their bids won't have feasible cost and time estimates. Mental models are our beliefs about how various processes work. They direct our explanations and expectations.

Effective executives understand the importance of helping their subordinates build better mental models. One explained to me how he would never hire a chief financial officer who only had experience in accounting. Once people gain accounting experience, he believed they should switch to operations, as a plant controller or a group supervisor, or to production control, and then move up to corporate controller, followed by a stint managing a division. Only then can they understand the workings of the corporation well enough to become CFO.

To summarize the RPD process, intuitive decision making works like this:

- Cues let us recognize patterns.
- Patterns activate action scripts.
- Action scripts are assessed through mental simulation.
- Mental simulation is driven by mental models.

Our data analysis showed that firefighters used the RPD process for more than 80 percent of their toughest incidents.

After my colleagues and I reported these results in 1986, we wondered if the RPD strategy would be found in other fields as well. In 1989 I documented findings that Army officers used intuition in 96 percent of their decisions during planning. In 1996 my colleagues and I published a study of naval commanders: 95 percent of their decisions were based on intuition and fewer than 5 percent used analytical comparisons of options.

Other researchers have reported the same results working with different populations. Kathy Mosier, in 1991, described a study of commercial aircrews in which "virtually no time was spent in any comparison of options." In 1996, Rhona Flin and her colleagues published a study of decision making in managers of offshore oil platforms—90 percent of the decisions relied on intuition and only 10 percent compared multiple options. Raphael Pascual and Simon Henderson got the same results in their 1997 study of British Army officers and so did Josephine Randel and her team in their 1996 study of U.S. Navy electronic warfare specialists. The RPD model held up in all of these studies. The results consistently showed that, sometimes, decision makers have to invent a new course of action, and rarely, they have to compare one option against another. But most of the time, for about 90 percent of the difficult decisions (and probably many more of the routine ones), the strategy they use is recognition-primed decision making. These findings make a strong argument that even in tough situations, experienced decision makers rely heavily on intuition and rarely use the analytical methods that we have all been taught. Within the last few years, the idea of intuitive decision making has finally started to catch on with the firefighting community, and, to some extent, in the U.S. Army and Marine Corps.

Intuitive decision making is finding its way into the business world as well. Back in 1984, Daniel Isenberg studied managers and executives to see how they solved problems and made decisions. Isenberg reported that executives do not make formal decisions using analytical methods. He explained:

> Senior managers use intuition in at least five distinct ways. First, they intuitively sense when a problem exists . . . Second, managers rely on intuition to perform well-learned behavior patterns rapidly . . . third function of intuition is to synthesize isolated bits of data and experience into an integrated picture, often in an "aha!" experience . . . Fourth, some managers use intuition as a check . . . on the results of more rational analysis . . . Fifth, managers can use intuition to bypass in-depth analysis and move rapidly to come up with a plausible solution. Used in this way, intuition is an almost instantaneous cognitive process in which a manager recognizes familiar patterns . . . intuition is not the opposite of rationality, nor is it a random process of guessing. Rather, it is based on extensive experience both in analysis and problem solving and in implementation and to the extent that the lessons of experience are logical and well-founded, then so is the intuition. Further, managers often combine gut feel with systematic analysis, quantified data, and thoughtfulness.

Isenberg's research has important implications for the way that business managers and executives are trained and advised. The following example illustrates Isenberg's observations about intuition.

This incident in Example 2.1 shows how a CEO could rely on his

Jerry Kirby had a nice forty-three-year run with Citizens Federal Bank, head-quartered in Dayton, Ohio, including a six-year stint with the Federal Reserve, as director of the Cleveland District Board, 1984–1990. Jerry had started as a teller in 1955, fresh out of college—he majored in business with an accounting minor at the University of Michigan. Other than a few stints in the Army (working as a cryptographer), he moved steadily upward and became CEO in 1972 at the age of thirty-seven. At that time Citizens Federal had 100 employees and controlled $200M in assets.

By the time Citizens Federal was sold, in 1998, it had assets of $4B and 1,100 employees. Its stock had gone from $9 per share to $55 per share. That's an appreciation of 1400 percent.

Jerry's management style was team-oriented. For his twenty-five years as CEO he relied on the judgment of the seven officers on his management team. He didn't cede authority to them—he gave himself a bloc of five votes in case his judgment ever conflicted with theirs. But in twenty-five years, he had never had to use this voting bloc. Except for one time.

In the mid-1980s, Jerry felt that Citizens Federal needed to change the way it conducted its mortgage lending. The majority of its assets were in mortgage loans, and up to that time, the bank had conservatively made mortgage loans by originating the mortgage and keeping it on the books until it amortized or the property changed hands. This tied up the bank's assets for thirty years at a time. That's how the banking business worked.

Jerry's intuition, however, was telling him that Citizens Federal needed a more aggressive strategy. After it originated the mortgage, Citizens Federal needed to sell it in a secondary market (e.g., the Fannie Mae and Freddie Mac markets), pocket a servicing fee, and use the proceeds to make more loans. This is called the "mortgage banking" business, as opposed to the conventional mortgage lending that banks do.

Where did Jerry's intuition come from? One source was his bitter experience with recessions. When the economy cycles into recession, deposits are drained out of banks in favor of government securities. This had gotten particularly frustrating after the mid-1960s, when the government's deficits pressed it to compete with banks for savings dollars by raising interest rates. As a result, banks lost their liquidity. Jerry watched another recession in 1973. In the recession of the early 1980s, government interest rates had reached 18 percent. Banks couldn't compete and had to close down their mortgage activities—they didn't have the money to make loans. Besides, few customers were willing to take these loans at interest rates of 18 percent.

After emerging from that recession, Jerry had said to himself that there had to be a better way. By the mid-1980s, the financial environment was strong, prosperity and interest rates were looking good. But Jerry felt it was time to make a fundamental change before the next recession hit. He looked at the mortgage banking companies in a new light. "Why aren't we churning the mortgage loans instead of letting our assets get frozen for decades?" he wondered. "The mortgage banking companies need our assets—why are we keeping them at arm's length?"

There are companies whose business it is to do mortgage banking, but they are not themselves banks. Jerry was familiar with them because they would come to banks such as Citizens Federal to borrow the funds for their activities. Not being banks, they don't have the deposits for making loans. Mortgage banking companies take higher risks than conventional banks, more like stock traders than guardians of the savings and the trust of their depositors. The mortgage banking business has been described as "churning" the loans.

Mortgage bankers experience more failures than conventional banks—but some of the failures occur because they didn't have ready access to funds they could borrow. Citizens Federal could eliminate this problem because the bank itself would back the loans. And, unlike the mortgage bankers, a conventional bank such as Citizens Federal could arrange to collect a servicing fee for the life of the mortgage, providing a continual cash flow. Jerry imagined how he could transform the mortgage lending side of Citizens Federal into a mortgage banking strategy. He didn't see any big pitfalls and he could identify major advantages. At that time there might have been a few banks in the country that also did mortgage banking, but not many, and none that Jerry was familiar with.

Jerry had a second intuition: He didn't think Citizens Federal had the staff to make the strategy work. The bank would have to hire experienced mortgage bankers.

The other members of the management team were strongly opposed to this move. They understood their conventional mortgage loan business, and Citizens Federal had been doing very well over the years. The riskiness of this new strategy worried them—swings in interest can bury you. It was like buying stocks on

cont.

Example 2.1 (cont.)

margin, betting that the price would go up. And the team hated the idea of bringing in outsiders. If Citizens Federal were going to transform into a mortgage banking strategy, wouldn't it be better to let the people from their own mortgage lending department run it? It didn't seem wise to turn over the bank's $3B mortgage portfolio—its crown jewels—to outsiders.

Jerry disagreed. He knew who he wanted to manage this new subsidiary. In working with mortgage banking companies he had been impressed by one group that seemed to really know what it was doing and never seemed to get in a crunch, even in recessions. In particular, he was impressed by their number-one person, not the CEO, but the nuts-and-bolts person who did the work. Watching her in action he realized that the mortgage specialists at Citizens Federal didn't have the mental models needed to make this work. They didn't appreciate the nuances and the challenges. In mortgage banking, you have to bring the loans in the front door, package them, send them out again, and at the right time. You have to understand and anticipate the way interest rates ebb and flow so that you don't make a loan at 8 percent, sit on it too long, watch the prime rate go up, and find that you can't sell that loan. Citizens Federal didn't have staff who had this woman's expertise—or her mental models.

Jerry's intuition told him that with this outside expertise, he could make the new strategy work. He believed then, and believes more firmly today, that if Citizens Federal relied on its own staff the strategy would have failed. It wasn't easy to bring the new mortgage banking specialist on board—he had to hire her CEO as well, knowing the man would soon retire.

In the end, Jerry had to go with his gut feel that this was the right move for his bank. "I was not very popular as CEO," he recalls. His popularity has increased since then. By the time he sold Citizens Federal in 1998, its subsidiary had become the thirtieth largest mortgage banking business in the country.

intuition about how to improve his bank. He could mentally simulate the marriage between a conventional bank taking in deposits and a mortgage banking strategy for recycling loans. His intuition also told him that with the right person in charge, the strategy would work.

We hear much these days about how rapidly the business world is changing. But while speed, flexibility, and adaptability are the buzz-words in many areas, they don't seem to be applied to the critical area of decision making. Ironically, speed, flexibility, and adaptability are precisely the kinds of qualities that can be enhanced by intuitive decision making.

Why are the old ways of doing business, which encourage people to rely on analytical deliberations, so persistent? Why is it so difficult to accept the importance of intuition and give up the notion that all thinking can be tightly controlled?

Barriers to Intuitive Decision Making

The path to developing intuition can be blocked by some significant barriers. Some of the barriers result from organizational policies. Others stem from the increasing pace of change, and even from the widespread adoption of information technologies.

Organizational policies can affect intuition in several ways. One mistake is to count paper credentials more than experience. Another obstacle emerges when global organizations depend on remote teams—it is difficult for remote teams to trade lessons learned and to have members coach each other.

Rapid turnover ensures that staff members will never get much experience at any one task. Organizations promote rapid turnover when they rely on an "up or out" policy for promotions, or even when they promote people too quickly. Adopting a lean staffing strategy makes an organization vulnerable when someone from a team leaves for another position. That vacancy has to be quickly filled, even if the replacement staffer isn't quite ready, and a chain reaction can start in which several employees in succession move to new jobs. Corporate memory is reduced with this drop in the average experience level per job.

The *pace of change* continues to accelerate. Historical ways of doing business are pronounced obsolete, and the experience of seasoned employees is discounted. Tried and true approaches are treated as legacy problems that have to be replaced. The specialists who have mastered these approaches are then part of the legacy problem.

Many organizations attempt to take refuge in *procedures*. This happens when supervisors play it safe and reduce the task to procedures even if those procedures don't really capture all of the nuances and tricks of the trade. Turning a job into a set of procedures makes it easier for new workers to carry out their responsibilities, and it also supports accountability by letting managers more easily verify if the procedures were followed. Unfortunately, this practice can make it even harder to build up intuitions if the procedures eliminate the need for judgment calls. Clearly, we need procedures to help us react quickly to emergencies, or to orient new workers. Once a set of procedures is in place, however, supervisors may not bother teaching the skills workers need to understand or modify the procedures. This is how the expertise that makes a company great gets lost. There is a strong tendency in our culture to proceduralize almost everything, to reduce all types of work to a series of steps. But you cannot reduce intuition to a procedure.

Organizations may try to reduce decisions and judgments to procedures by defining *metrics* (i.e., measurable objectives). Metrics are often seen as a way to replace intuitions. They can be useful as a corrective to relying too heavily on impressions, but if managers try to make decisions based on numbers alone they run the risk of eroding their intuitions.

Finally, *information technologies* are taking their toll. Too often decision aids and smart systems are reducing their operators to clerks responsible for feeding data into the systems. In the Neonatal Intensive Care Unit, nurses are given much more training to operate the monitoring equipment than in how to detect the subtle signs of illness in the infants. Operators come to passively follow what the information technology recommends rather than relying on their intuition.

We have less time and fewer chances to achieve expertise in our current jobs compared to previous generations. And we are faced with the obstacles listed above that further degrade our intuitions. Diminished experience, rapid turnover, little coaching, increased pace of change, reliance on procedures and metrics, widespread use of information technologies to make decisions—all of these create an unprecedented assault on our intuitions.

Why do we tolerate all of these barriers? Because people don't fully understand what intuition is and how it develops. So they're unaware of these barriers and their cumulative effects. The erosion of intuition will continue until we take active steps to defend ourselves.

Business leaders rarely have sufficient data for conducting analysis. As time and budgetary pressures increase, we have fewer chances to try options out to test their feasibility, forcing us to make snap

Intuition Skills Training: Speeding Up Your Learning Curve

3

I will tell you right off that this is the most important chapter in the book. This is where I let you in on the "secret" for improving your intuition. That secret? Three simple words: Practice, practice, practice. Actually, it's slightly more complicated than that, as I will discuss, but that's the essence of it. Just like any skill, you develop your judgment and intuition through practice. The better and smarter you practice the faster you develop your intuition skills. That's what we'll spend this chapter talking about: how to practice better and smarter.

Up to this point I have described how people typically use intuition to make decisions in a variety of challenging real-life situations. The key to using intuition effectively is experience—more specifically, *meaningful* experience—that allows us to recognize patterns and build mental models. Thus, the way to improve your intuitive skills is to strengthen your experience base. The most meaningful type of experience, naturally, is real-life experience. You can't beat the real world when it comes to meaningful experience. It tends to teach the truest lessons and makes the biggest impressions.

There are a couple of problems with relying on the real world for all our experience, though. One is that many of us simply do not get the opportunities to accumulate enough real-life experience in a particular field to develop expertise. Another is that many of us cannot afford to wait until we're doing something for real to learn from our mistakes. That's the paradox: When you take a job, you're expected to be proficient at that job. Naturally. You wouldn't be given the responsibility otherwise. But how can you develop the experience to be proficient at a job before you've actually been in the job for some time? That's where an intuition skills training program comes in.

judgments. At times like these, intuition must replace guesswork. T
is why the loss of intuitive decision-making skills is so detrimental.

The longer we wait to defend our intuitions, the less we will ha
to defend. We are more than the sum of our software programs an
analytical methods, more than the databases we can access, more tha
the procedures we have been asked to memorize. The choice i
whether we are going to shrink into these artifacts or expand beyond
them.

The intuition skills training program is based on a regimen of deliberately practicing the decisions you have to make in your job in order to accumulate the meaningful experiences that are necessary to build up intuition.

As with any conditioning program, you will achieve the best results by establishing a routine. Mental conditioning works best when it is experiential, meaning that it is not based on following some particular set of steps or procedures for making decisions, but rather on learning by doing. It involves "deliberate practice," a term first used by Anders Ericsson and Neil Charness in describing how experts in a number of fields develop their expertise. Deliberate practice means not just practicing to practice, amassing experience randomly, but practicing with specific objectives in mind.

The genesis of the intuition skills training program was a course we put together for Marine Corps rifle squad leaders and officers back in 1996. That program was so well received that it has been institutionalized for the Marines' squad leader training.

Since then, we have expanded the program and presented it to commercial and Navy pilots and to the Los Angeles County Fire Department, specifically to train captains and battalion chiefs. Other fire departments around the country picked it up, including the Albuquerque Fire Department, who labeled it "RPD training," because the objective was to help people use recognition-primed decision making.

We began getting requests to scale-up the training for executive development. During the past few years, we have put on a number of sessions for business executives, including senior managers and vice presidents of global corporations, to improve their intuitive decision-making skills. We have conducted dozens of training sessions, and we have trained hundreds of business leaders.

Specifically, intuition skills training is designed to help you to:

- Size up situations more quickly and with less effort.
- Recognize problems and anomalies more quickly.
- Feel confident that the first option you think of will usually be a good one.
- Have a good sense of what is going to happen next.
- Avoid getting overloaded with data.
- Be calm in the face of time pressure and uncertainty.
- Find alternative solutions when a plan runs into difficulty.

In keeping with the spirit of this book, there is no magic here, no leap of faith. The "secret" is no secret at all. The methods are simple, designed to treat intuitive decision-making skills as you would any other skills that are developed through hard work over time. You define the training objectives, you ensure opportunities for practice, and you conduct feedback sessions to improve in the future.

Furthermore, you don't have to worry about learning new ways to make decisions. The old ways work well enough. What you really need is a richer experience base and stronger mental models to use in making decisions.

If what I'm describing to you sounds anything but revolutionary, you're right. Experts in many fields make sure they have prepared themselves properly before making decisions and competing with others. Chess grand masters spend much more time preparing and studying than they do playing. Athletes spend much more time practicing than competing.

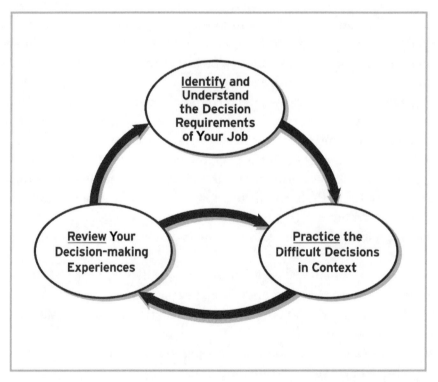

Figure 3.1 The Three Basic Elements of Intuition Skills Training

There are three basic elements of mental conditioning in the intuition skills training program: to identify and understand the decision requirements of your job; practice the difficult decisions in context; and review your decision-making experiences.

Identify and Understand the Decision Requirements of Your Job

Decision requirements are those intuitions, judgments and skills that must be mastered before a job can be reliably accomplished. For example, one of a pilot's decision requirements is knowing when to fly through turbulent weather conditions and when to change routes. Pilots must have the experience base to make that tough decision in order to do their job. In one workshop, a group of pilots had little trouble recounting errors they had made or seen others make. They had little trouble listing the cues and patterns on which they relied. We asked them how new pilots get to learn and appreciate all of these critical cues. The pilots didn't believe that novices would notice or appreciate most of the key items on the list. And therefore, novices couldn't make good decisions about weather no matter how hard they tried—they just didn't have the expertise.

Identifying the decision requirements of a job isn't as easy as you might think. Here's how we proceeded when we began developing a decision skills training program for rifle squad leaders in the Marine Corps. The first thing we did was to ask them to identify their decision requirements by having them make a list of the most difficult decisions they regularly made during field exercises. They grumbled, but being Marines, they complied. In fifteen minutes they had devised a list of about thirty decisions, just for openers. This alone was an eye-opener for them, since they had insisted at the start that as noncommissioned officers they didn't make decisions, but only executed them.

We picked one decision to focus on: calculating how long it took to move the squad from one position to another. "Is this a hard decision?" I asked. They laughed. They explained that they worked with a simple formula: They could move 2.5 kilometers per hour. That was the standard estimate of the time to travel by foot. But they explained that the 2.5 kph rule was useless. It ignored the type of terrain and vegetation, the weather, how muddy the ground was, how much equipment or supplies they were carrying, whether they were carrying any injured Marines, the risk of being detected by the enemy, and a whole host of other factors. In reality, this was a very difficult decision to make. So next I asked them: "If this is an important judgment, and a difficult one to make, how do you train for it?"

It had never occurred to them that this was a trainable skill. The Marines had accepted the 2.5 kph rule because they had accepted that the decision was essentially random and there was no way to get better at it. But once they considered it, they realized how easy it would be to estimate the time needed on every mission in which they needed to move by foot. They could compare the estimate to how long it actually took, figure out why their estimate was off, and try to do better next time. In short, they could treat this judgment as they did any other training requirement. With enough repetitions, they could build up their intuitive feel for time-distance relationships.

We have discovered that many people don't have a good sense of the decisions they routinely must make, what makes those decisions difficult, and what insights might allow them to make those decisions better. Sometimes, just understanding more about your decisions can be a big help.

For an executive at a corporation the critical decisions may be:

* Estimating timelines so you can build a budget or revise a plan
* Selecting one contractor over another
* Picking the opportunities that are most promising for your company and deserve the most resources
* Hiring or promoting people
* Assessing whether a project is progressing well or is derailing

Your decision requirements will be the judgments and decisions that *repeatedly* arise. As you work on improving how you handle them, you'll want to seek out opportunities for feedback. Otherwise, how are you going to learn? You'll also want to identify the outstanding people in your organization who excel at making decisions like the ones you're grappling with.

Decision Requirements Table		
Identify a critical, difficult, and frequent decision or judgment: _____		
What makes this decision difficult?	What kinds of errors are often made?	How would an expert make this decision differently from a novice? *(Identify cues and strategies.)*
How can you practice and get feedback to help you make this decision next time? _____		

Figure 3.2 Decision Requirements Table

One way to organize these types of information is to fill out a decision requirements table. The basic format is shown in Figure 3.2, although as you gain more experience you may find you want to modify it to suit your own needs. It allows you to label the nature of the judgment or decision, fill in why you're having trouble with it, and list the types of errors that you and others may be making. It also has a column to list any tricks of the trade you've learned when talking to experts.

Needless to say, there are many types of decisions you make each day, far too many to list all of them. Instead, pinpoint the ones that matter most to your work, the ones that are giving you the most trouble. After you have identified the decisions that may come up in your work, such as estimating the amount of time needed to accomplish a task, you should ask yourself: What is the real skill I need to learn here? Is it estimating how long a task will take, or is it spotting potential problems that can mess up the schedule? Or is it recognizing when a plan has enough slack built in to give me time to recover from the usual unexpected glitches?

Once you do figure out what you need to work on, you can start hunting for opportunities to make decisions in a setting where you'll get feedback. If a chance for you to test yourself doesn't crop up, you can map out practice sessions with a colleague to build your expertise.

You can also talk to people in your organization who have proven to be good at this type of decision. What are they seeing that you aren't? Try to find a time to talk to them about specific incidents, where they saw a problem one way and you saw it another. Were they aware of things that you weren't noticing? Did they see implications that hadn't occurred to you?

In a workshop for business professionals, I asked the participants to identify some of the tough decisions and judgments that they continually wrestled with. Here are some of the responses:

"Should I make or buy a component I need? I have limited time and resources, and I always seem to underestimate the time it takes to get things done."

"How should I create a budget for a new proposal? I don't have a lot of experience, and it's hard for me to predict how many resources I'll need. In the past I've been too tight with time and money allocated for the subtasks."

"I'm considering entering into a new business area but I don't know a lot about it, and in the past I've overestimated the return on investment."

"Should I accept a request to give a presentation or workshop? I have more work than I can handle, and if I accept too many jobs that don't lead anywhere, I wind up wasting my time."

"How much time and energy should I put into a proposal? I'm supposed to balance revenue needs, existing work demands, and client needs. I've made mistakes before by not consulting with others in my group, and not asking enough questions up front. I've thought we couldn't pass up an opportunity when we could have, thinking we knew more than we did, and underestimating the planning time that I needed."

When I asked the group to think about how they might strengthen their intuition, they came up with some relatively easy methods. One person realized that she could get tips from more experienced proposal writers when she was planning a budget. She also realized that she was getting down into the weeds too quickly, estimating costs for subtasks before she had a good plan for the entire program.

One of the participants figured out that to better evaluate which lectures or workshops were worth accepting he could write down his reason for accepting a project at the time, and then see if that reason was still valid once the presentation/workshop was given. That would help him recognize the ways in which he was deceiving himself.

At another workshop, with an information technology integration company, all the participants agreed that they needed to improve how they handled two major decision requirements in their jobs. One was prioritizing tasks. Their hectic workday consisted of lots of interruptions and requests and they continually had to make snap decisions about whether to continue what they were doing or switch their focus.

The second decision requirement the managers identified was estimating the amount of time it was going to take to complete a project. Just like the Marines who had to judge how long their marches were going to take, the managers had to learn how to make realistic estimates, and not get too idealistic. There are no simple rules for estimating time/effort requirements; fortunately, these are judgment skills that can be strengthened through deliberate practice and feedback. By recording the estimates on a new project, noting the rationale, and then performing the follow-up review once the tasks are completed, managers can sharpen intuitions.

The decision requirements table the managers created for the second decision requirement is on page 34. The items in each column are independent of the neighboring column, so don't look for themes to line up across the rows. The point of the decision requirements table is to get the information down, not to produce an elegant analysis.

The decision requirements table this group produced was a blueprint for the training and preparation they need. They could see, thanks to the "difficulties" column, that they need to spend more time gauging the capabilities of their team members, and to gather more

What makes this decision difficult?	What kinds of errors are often made?	How would an expert make this decision differently from a novice? *(Identify cues and strategies.)*
• It's hard to estimate individual competencies and speeds • Client schedules • No control on resources • Idealism • Newness of this type of project	• Overhead time isn't considered • Not stating client responsibilities clearly in the contract • No experts on the task • Did not consider potential problems • Did not build in extra time • Did not research enough	• Anticipating overhead time • Setting expectancies with the client • Breaking items into manageable chunks (e.g., one component takes *x* amount of time) • Performing background research

How can you practice and get feedback to help you make this decision next time? Record estimates at the time, check the accuracy, diagnose the reasons for inaccuracy.

information from the client about the schedule they want to keep. They need to do more homework about similar types of projects. And they need to negotiate harder about resources before they accept the project.

Looking at the "errors" column they could put together some additional ideas about how they need to prepare, and the types of research they have to do. In thinking through these errors they were building a more sophisticated mental model of how to prepare for future projects.

The third column covered cues and strategies the managers could now try, like building a reserve of time into the plan, and also getting a handle on difficult estimates by breaking tasks into chunks that are easier to estimate.

This is direct training. If the managers go to the trouble of recording their initial estimates, they can later go back and see how accurate they were. If they were not very accurate, they can identify the factors that they failed to take into account—and be ready to do a better job next time.

Practice the Difficult Decisions in Context

Now that you have a better understanding of what challenging decisions you regularly face in your work, the next step is to find opportunities to practice them. This really is the core of mentally conditioning yourself to make better intuitive decisions. It is the all-important phase in which you amass the experiences that allow you to recognize the patterns and build the mental models that are essential to intuition. As I have said, what we're after is not practicing to practice, but deliberate practice.

Sometimes it might be possible to find practice opportunities within your daily experiences—as it was for the Marines, and for the managers who wanted to make more accurate estimates of the time needed to complete a project.

Often, however, it won't be possible to find training opportunities within the daily routine. You'll have to create your own specific decision training. Usually this means devising some sort of training exercise, or "decision game."

Decision games are a centerpiece of a mental conditioning program, simple thought exercises, usually involving paper-and-pencil scenarios, that capture the essence of a typical, difficult decision.

A decision game presents some basic details leading up to a dilemma, typically charged with lots of uncertainty, and challenges those taking the exercise to come up with a plan of action. The materials can include a visual aid such as a map of the area of interest, a process diagram, a profit/loss statement, or an organizational chart. A visual graphic can be a very good way for framing and focusing the issue, although there are some domains in which a visual is just not appropriate. When the military creates decision games, a map of the situation to be analyzed (with the terrain and the relative positions of friendly and enemy units) is the central component.

Well-designed decision games can be surprisingly effective at capturing the essence of a tough decision without many of the costs or other overhead of more complicated simulations or exercises. And, they can usually be done in a much shorter period of time, so you can get more repetitions.

Here is an example of a decision game based on the decision requirements table described earlier. The decision involves estimating the time it takes to complete a task.

➢ DECISION GAME 3.1 CARE PACKAGE FROM THE BOARD

You have recently completed your master's degree in management and have been hired by a consumer products company that has 450 employees. You are working in the research and development group, on new product concepts.

Six weeks ago, on October 25, your supervisor called you into her office and told you that you've just been given a wonderful assignment to lead a small team assessing software packages for your company's accounting department.

It seems that at the last executive board meeting on October 18, one of the members of the board raised a concern that the company was using an outmoded system. This board member had been sitting next to an accounting software specialist on a recent plane trip and got an earful about all the wonderful things that were now possible. Not only will the new packages get the data out faster, but also they will reduce the effort needed. Prices for this new software package have been steadily coming down.

The CEO of your company assured this board member that this opportunity would be carefully studied and a recommendation would be made and briefed at the next executive board meeting, December 13.

And that's how you got the honor. You remind your supervisor that you know nothing about accounting, but she explains that this is just about selecting good software. The head of the accounting department has let the department settle into inefficient routines. It needs an outside look. You point out that you also know nothing about software packages, and she explains that the head of accounting detests the information systems department and would sabotage any report that they issued. No, you are the perfect candidate.

"All you've got to do is take a look at these new software programs and see if our accounting department should adopt one of them to replace the current program, which is pretty limited. We want to show the executive board that we are responsive to their concerns," your supervisor tells you.

(You later discover that your supervisor volunteered you in exchange for the CEO agreeing to unfreeze her travel budget. You also learn that the CEO is waging a desperate power struggle regarding a new acquisition and is doing everything possible to placate the board members.)

You have been assigned a small team of two people from accounting, roughly half time, two from information systems, roughly half time, a writer full time for a week at the end of the effort, and one full-time assistant. After consulting with them, you devised the following schedule:

	TASK	TIMELINE	MONTHS		
			OCT	NOV	DEC
1	Identify relevant accounting software packages	10/29–31	▉		
2	Establish evaluation criteria	11/1–5		▉	
3	Define benchmarks for current accounting tasks	10/29–11/15		▉	
4	Schedule demonstrations of the most promising 3–4 software pkgs.	11/1–2		▉	
5	Conduct the demonstrations presented by the software developers	11/5–9		▉	

TASK	TIMELINE	MONTHS		
		OCT	NOV	DEC
6 Perform the cost/benefit analyses for each software package	11/7–21		▪	
7 Prepare the recommendation to the board	11/11–28		▪	
8 Write a brief report and prepare the CEO's briefing	11/29–12/5			▪
9 Get reviews for the report and the briefing	12/6–10			▪
10 Finalize the report and the briefing	12/11–12			▪

It is now November 21. You have hit every milestone in the plan. Your team selected three software packages to inspect. You found that your six-person team could learn the essentials of each software package in only two pretty intense days. And the cost-benefit analyses were not nearly as complicated as you expected. They only took your full team one to two days per package once you figured out what you were doing—the folks from accounting really knew their stuff.

It appears that one of the software packages is not very good. The other two seem to have clear advantages over the antiquated system that is currently in use, but each of them has its own flaws.

Then your assistant comes bursting into your office with the announcement that a new accounting software package has just been released last Tuesday, November 13. Based on the reviews that accompanied the release, it sounds like just what you need. The assistant has arranged for the company to send a demonstration copy and to run a remote demonstration by walking you through the software using a Web-based tutorial and a team of advisors. They can set this all up next Wednesday or Thursday, after Thanksgiving.

You quickly gather your team together. One of the accounting people can help you out. The other won't be able to spend any

S	M	T	W	T	F	S
			NOVEMBER			
			21	22 Thanksgiving	23	24
25	26	27	28 Make Recommendation	29	30	
			DECEMBER			
						1
2	3	4	5 Draft Report & Briefing	6	7	8
9	10 Reviews of the Drafts	11	12	13 Present Briefing		

more time on the project. One of the software specialists can give you about thirty hours next week. The other has to get back to other projects left hanging—but promises that the group will get you a substitute. Your writer won't be available after December 5 but assures you he will find a replacement.

Your supervisor has left the office for the long drive home for Thanksgiving "with my cell phone turned off for the entire weekend." The CEO has also left for the holiday.

Everyone is looking at you for instructions. What are you going to do?

Take five minutes and determine how you want your team to proceed.

There are no right answers to this decision game. If you continue with the report and claim that the new software was issued too late to be considered, then you run the risk of looking like a slacker. After all, the software was released a full month before the board meeting, and it may be just what is needed. On the other hand, if you try to conduct a quick evaluation you lose some of your team and replace seasoned team members with newcomers. Or, you can cobble together a solution such as reviewing the software and preparing the briefing in time for the board meeting but distributing the report a week or so later. Perhaps you have some other ideas. This scenario could allow you to get into some interesting, and useful, discussions about the real strategic objective in this situation. Is it truly to evaluate new accounting software, or is it to give the CEO what he needs to placate the board in his power struggle? Such factors often underlie challenging real-life decisions.

The decision games you design should be easy to play, be technologically simple rather than complicated, have simple rules, be very flexible and adaptable, and very transportable—in that they should be capable of being played in a lunchroom or during travel layovers.

Decision games have some general features: a name, background, the narrative description of the scenario itself, and usually some sort of visual representation.

The best decision games take the form of compelling stories that build to a climax—a dilemma—putting the participants on the hot seat, forcing them to make a decision to resolve the situation.

It's also important that the game not have a single correct answer. Otherwise, the players cease to offer their own views, and only attempt to figure out the "right" answer. With several reasonable answers available, you open the follow-up discussion to an energetic exchange of opinions. The actual decision is less important than the thinking that went into it. The decision game is merely a vehicle for triggering the decision-making process and then allowing you to reflect on it or talk about it with others.

DEVELOPING DECISION GAMES One way to develop a decision game is to take a personal experience and turn it into a scenario. However, we notice that these types of games often have "right answers." You can't assume that the way a situation turned out in real life is actually the right answer for the game.

An alternative way to design a decision game is to seize on a type of judgment or decision where staff members repeatedly seem to be

INTUITION AT WORK

struggling. The decision requirements tables can give you an idea of the type of dilemma you and your staff may need to practice.

A different strategy for constructing a decision game is to take an upcoming project and turn that into a game, thus helping the staff to anticipate what they are going to have to face. By linking decision games to current projects, you can easily incorporate more history and context and your staff's personality styles. The more familiar a situation, the less detail you need in the scenario description. Many management exercises eliminate the context in order to make the exercises easier to generalize. That doesn't work in this case—we need context in order to exercise our intuition. That's why the best games mirror the realistic challenges you and your team are facing.

When we started to teach the participants in one workshop how to design games, they asked if they could work as teams. They enjoyed working together—each table was a mixture of specialists from different areas, and the cross-functional dynamic was helpful in itself. So we agreed to let each table work collaboratively to make its own game, and then to play it with the members of another table. This turned into a very energetic session.

Each table got to compare notes on what was frustrating them, and how to make life challenging for the others. One table made a game around the common dilemma of starting a project and having the internal client ask for additional work at no additional cost. A second table took out their frustrations with the problem of having to adapt to unexpected staff losses on projects.

This format, pitting one table against another, seemed pretty popular. Several of the participants planned to set up periodic "field days" during long lunch breaks. They thought that routinely having their colleagues make up and play decision games would be a good chance for cross-functional learning, for making connections, and for building intuitive decision-making skills. Having the decision games center around real issues meant that the decision games were directly relevant to their work and provided a way to make sense of problems that were troubling them. They even decided they could bring the games to upper management to help them articulate their frustrations.

USING DECISION GAMES The most important reason for using decision games is to provide simulated experiences, because most of us don't get many opportunities to compile the experience base we need.

Decision games can be used to evaluate or rehearse a plan, to identify potential problems and their solutions before the problems arise. They can be used to build familiarity and mutual understanding within a team, so team members know more about how others are likely to react to certain types of situations. Think about the game we just went through, "Care Package from the Board." Can you predict how your boss would make this decision—or what your subordinates would do? Would there be any benefit in being able to anticipate their reactions to situations like this?

Here is a more complete list of things you can teach with decision games:

- They can reveal the limits of your mental models, and make them richer and broader.
- They can help you appreciate the importance of critical cues and patterns.
- They can fill in the gaps in your experience base.
- They can teach you ways to better handle uncertainty.
- They can give you practice in resolving conflicting goals.
- They can instruct you how to spot leverage points—the starting points for constructing new options.
- They can train you to detect problems.
- They can show you how to see a situation from someone else's perspective.
- They can drill you in allocating limited resources.
- They can help you to learn factual and technical knowledge more quickly, by putting it in a practical context.
- They can offer you practice in giving directions or presenting clear statements of your assessments or intentions.

You can also use decision games to capture corporate memory. Instead of trying to record potentially important observations, and then find a way to store these so that someone someday can locate them (good luck), the observations or incidents can be packaged as a game and put into play immediately or by future groups.

The following example shows how decision games can be an instructional strategy.

> ***Example 3.1* Learning the Wiring Diagram as if Your Life Depended on It**
>
> We were conducting a workshop for pilots, to improve their safety by helping them with decision making. During the workshop, we asked the pilots to recall cases where they had been in riskier situations than they would like. One pilot recalled a time when he was flying a small jet at night and lost his electrical system. Lost it entirely. He managed to blindly struggle to bring the plane down but still felt that he was alive more by luck than because of any skills he had.
>
> The rest of the group could not keep themselves from volunteering things he could have tried, only to realize that their actions required some subsystem that relied on electricity. Eventually, the group realized that this was the way they should have been taught about the electrical system—not by having to memorize diagrams, but by having to confront exactly this type of dilemma, where their mental model of the electrical system would be the difference between life and death.

PLAYING DECISION GAMES Decision games can be played in a solitaire version, like trying to solve a puzzle or a brainteaser. However, decision games are best done in a small group—perhaps six to eight people—to put pressure on the participants by having to perform in front of others, and to give the participants a chance to learn from each other. The dilemma and materials are presented to the group, and the facilitator calls on someone to respond. (I've learned not to ask for volunteers, because then people realize they can disengage. You want people alert and a bit anxious knowing they might be called on.) If the type of decision is time-sensitive, it will be more interesting, useful, and realistic to give participants a time limit instead of letting them carefully ponder the decision (and keep reminding them of it as the clock ticks away). In most of the games we run, people are typically given three to five minutes.

If you run "Care Package from the Board" in a group, you would present the game either by putting the visual aids on a whiteboard and reading the scenario or handing out the description for people to read, going over the highlights of the dilemma. Then, after giving them five minutes to come up with a solution, you would call on one person, probing for the rationale and challenging the person about the weak points and downside of the course of action. You would then ask others to comment on this solution and to present their ideas so that several people get their turn on the hot seat.

Finally, you could have a general discussion about how to avoid or minimize these types of problems. This might be the most useful part of the game—how should the team leader have built the plan or clarified the issues up front? Here, you can apply what you've learned by creating the decision requirements table. For example, the team leader described in the game has neglected to learn more about what the internal clients need. Will the board member be satisfied if the project simply covers all the software that he jotted down during that airplane ride? How likely is it that someone on the board will have heard about the new software package? What counts as success here—finding the best possible software package, or finding a good package that moves the accounting department forward, or maybe just allowing the CEO to say he made the effort? We don't know. The team leader needed to do a more careful job of setting expectancies.

These are not criticisms of the people playing the decision game—they are stuck with the plan. However, the game should have made the players aware of these weaknesses. In retrospect, can they figure out what the team leader should have done?

Keep the decision games simple and easy to run, so that they don't become a dreaded event. Generally, the game should take around thirty minutes, with another twenty to thirty minutes for the follow-up discussion—something that can be done over lunch. John Schmitt, the foremost popularizer of decision games in the Marines, has one main criterion for judging a successful game: The participants are still debating the scenario as they walk back to their offices after the facilitator has called the session to a close. For that reason, John advises against exhausting a situation completely. He likes to end the session when there is still a little something to be gotten out of it.

If you suggest using decision games and someone says, "We already have these," or, "We tried that a few years ago and it flopped," ask the person what they mean: What type of exercise was it and how elaborate did it have to be? When was the last time anyone used it? Did they need to hire an outside company to craft and run the exercise? What type of guidance did people get on building and running these exercises?

Many organizations have some sort of low-fidelity exercise around somewhere. However, they often require too many players. Or else the facilitation is so poor that the exercise falls flat. Sometimes they don't have a way to design the exercises to meet a company's immediate needs, such as preparing staff for a major project that is looming on the horizon. Or the exercises only get implemented once a year, instead of several times a month, which is the repetition rate that really provides payoff. If this is the case, my guess is that you will find that the exercise was far too elaborate, so it wasn't practical to use it except once or twice a year, and with that frequency, the exercises were quickly filed and forgotten.

Should managers and executives simply charge human resources with building and running the exercises? I don't think so. It takes a lot of knowledge about nuances and implications to both construct and to facilitate these exercises. Decision games are a leadership tool. The person who knows the company, the job, and the staff best will usually design and facilitate the best game. Further, you'll learn a great deal by constructing and then facilitating the decision games. One of the reasons John Schmitt says he has enjoyed designing and running military decision games so much (he has designed over 100 different games and conducted hundreds of sessions) is that he learns so much about tactics every time he does.

In running a decision game with a group, you'll need someone to facilitate the session and the follow-up discussion. The best facilitators are those who know the topic, who can enjoy the chance to put people on the spot, who listen carefully for good ideas as well as for unsound plans, and who can listen for the implications in the statements people make. Some facilitators like to be intimidating as a way of adding pressure, and for some facilitators this tactic works. Others keep the session light and lively. In such an atmosphere people are likely to be less guarded and are more apt to give and accept honest and candid feedback.

One of the limitations of decision games is that it is not always easy to arrange for the participants and facilitator to be in the same location. Companies may have their specialists or domain experts in one place, and the employees who need to get up to speed may be in a different office. The expense of getting everyone in the same room can get pretty steep, not to mention the drain on energy for workers who may already be doing too much traveling.

The way to solve these problems is to run the decision games via the Internet. John Schmitt and others have developed a concept called "Decision Net," which is basically a technique for running distributed decision games. We have worked with Decision Net for a few years now, on a variety of projects, and we are impressed by how effective it is.

Regardless of how you conduct the decision game, you aren't restricted to asking people what decision they would make. You can ask them what information they would gather, or what questions they would have, or how they would assess the situation. You can ask them what problems they might anticipate, or what they would expect to happen in the future. You can ask them what guidance they would offer. These are all ways people use their intuitions. The decision games presented in subsequent chapters will use all of these formats.

The follow-up discussion after a decision game can be—in fact, it should be—more valuable than the decision-making exercise itself. Thus, in a group setting you might ask several different people to respond, and then talk about the similarities and differences in their questions and approaches. Often, you will find that one person spots a cue or a pattern that others have missed.

The first five people who played the game "Care Package from the Board" had different solutions. One thought that the team had enough time and capability to evaluate that last software package and include it in the report. Another thought the team should stick to its schedule and not burn out the members trying to do a better job than was necessary. A third took another look at the main goal of the evaluation and realized that it would be sufficient to tell the board that the current software needed to be updated—no need to select the best alternative. A fourth realized you could revise the schedule so that you'd start writing the report while evaluating the last software system, and plug in the findings at the end. The fifth player said he would do a preliminary review of the software package and if it looked good, tell the board that a more serious assessment was in process.

Review Your Decision-Making Experiences

Experience is a powerful teacher, but experience by itself is not the most efficient way to learn. The process can often be painful and time-consuming. To learn as quickly as possible, we must be more deliberate, more disciplined, and more thorough in our approach in order to squeeze as much as possible from each experience. As with everything else about mental conditioning, there is no magic here. We can treat any experience as an opportunity to learn. There are any number of ways to get feedback about our decisions:

Solicit assessments from other, more-experienced decision makers in your field. Talk to people in your organization who have proven to be good at this type of decision. What can they see that you don't? Talk to them about real-life incidents where they saw it one way and you saw it another. Were they aware of things that you weren't noticing? Did they see implications that hadn't occurred to you? If possible, approach your mentors at the beginning of your intuition skills training so they can guide you and comment on your performance during decision games and during actual projects.

Example 3.2 describes effective feedback. It came about by accident and was not the result of a deliberate design.

We often give ourselves feedback, too. It's natural for us to contemplate our decisions after the fact. We often beat ourselves up over bad decisions and congratulate ourselves for good ones. We "what-if" ourselves. I think one of the most valuable things we can do is to take this natural tendency and refine it and discipline it. But instead of passing judgment about whether it was a good decision or a bad decision, we should focus on understanding the decision process, why we decided what we did and how we made the decision.

This type of feedback lets you revise and improve on your intuitions. When you don't have many chances to encounter challenging situations, you have to get the most out of the incidents you have. That means spending time afterward to see what the incident has taught you. This applies both to real experience and decision games.

Reflecting on our decisions is particularly useful when we have encountered some difficulty, including cases of failure. Failures grab and hold our attention, and they are loud signals that our mental models were not good enough. Failures hurt, and that keeps us from forgetting them. One way I have learned to recover from a failure is to figure out what I should have done, and to start hoping I get another chance to try again. Example 3.3 shows how I used feedback to improve my prediction skills.

Research is very clear that we learn a great deal from process feedback—such as reflecting on how we made decisions, how we could

> *EXAMPLE 3.3* LEAN YEARS OR FAT YEARS?

Up until a few years ago, one of my responsibilities was to forecast the revenues for my company. A lot was riding on these judgments. If I was off by too much, it could threaten the existence of the company because our cash flow could be insufficient to make our payments. If we were heading into a lean year, we needed to ramp up our marketing efforts quickly. If we needed to trim costs, we had to recognize it early in the fiscal year in order to do it effectively. If we were facing an avalanche of work, we had to prepare by doing some more hiring or lining up consulting help.

Making a judgment about the company's overall revenues was too difficult, so I broke it down into judgments about my company's chances of winning each of the proposals we submitted, or being tapped for work by each of the potential clients who had contacted us. I had to estimate our chances of getting the project, the size of the project, and the likely start date.

I needed to make my revenue estimates six to eight months before the beginning of the fiscal year. The judgment of anticipated revenues so far in advance was a difficult decision requirement.

Therefore, I spent a lot of time reviewing the results from previous years to learn where my intuitions and judgments were inadequate.

I discovered that there was a certain type of contract that was highly competitive (the agencies funded only 10 percent of all the proposals they received), and too difficult to predict accurately. But over time, my company's success rate was about 21 percent. Therefore, I plugged this historical success rate into my calculations for that class of proposals.

I found that I was overestimating our chances of getting work based on semi-serious client assurances. If I tagged these as having a 3 percent or 5 percent probability, and I dredged up many possibilities, I could paint a picture that was much too rosy. Therefore, I learned to simply list these possibilities on my forecasting sheets but not to count on them.

I realized that I couldn't even count on revenues from contracts that had been signed. Sponsors sometimes ran into their own financial difficulties and requested us to cut down on our effort. Or else a project might get delayed, so that much of the revenues didn't show up until a following year.

Over time, I was able to use feedback to sharpen my estimates. Eventually, I was reaching a point where my estimates at the beginning of a fiscal year were less than 10 percent off of our actual revenues at the end of the fiscal year.

have spotted patterns more quickly—and we learn much less from outcome feedback.

Format for a Decision-Making Critique

The third basic tool in the intuition skills training toolbox is designed to help us review our decisions by getting feedback on the quality of the decisions and the process by which we arrived at them. It's called the "decision-making critique." The goal of this technique is to help you reflect on how you make your judgments and decisions so that you can see what has worked well and what you should have done differently.

Intuitive decision making is the ability to make decisions by using patterns to recognize what is going on in a situation and to recognize which action script to react with. Therefore the decision-making critique has to accomplish several things. It has to help you examine the way you sized up the situation—including the cues and patterns you recognized and those you missed. It has to help you examine the scripts you used to react to the problem—were these effective and were there better ones you didn't consider?

Critiquing works best when it can be very specific. Therefore, I like to conduct a critique of decision making around a specific incident, and then tunnel inside the incident to examine the trickiest judgments, assessments, and decisions that were made, the moments where improvisation might have been needed, where interpretation was required, where missing information had to be filled in.

Usually when I administer a decision-making critique to others, I have them construct a timeline, or even a diagram, depicting where judgments were made about the nature of the situation, and where decisions were made about what to do. Below is a typical format for a decision-making critique that we use, but there is no fixed rule so you should feel free to change this if you find a better way to conduct the critique. The decision-making critique is a framework for a debriefing session. It is guided by curiosity about how people made their interpretations and what patterns they noticed, not by any standard checklist mentality.

When asking why the person found this decision difficult you can build a decision requirements table: How could a person with less experience have made errors, what types of knowledge would have been important, what types of mental models are needed here?

The question about interpreting the situation is aimed at helping you reflect on what cues and patterns should have been recognized earlier. Chapter 8, on sensemaking, expands on this topic and will help you probe more deeply.

The questions about the course of action are intended to help decision makers reflect on the scripts in their repertoires. Perhaps they don't have enough scripts, or a good variety, or perhaps they habitually use the same scripts even when better ones are available. You might wonder why the last question is included, because it seems to encourage option comparison. I think it can be very useful to contrast options *after the fact*.

Some organizations, such as the military, already have lessons-learned sessions. However, we find that the sessions typically get into debates about facts and details, and ignore the intuitive decision-making perspective. In industry, lessons-learned sessions and debriefing sessions are rarely conducted. When they are, they concentrate on the facts of the events, not the ways that the decisions were made. Unfortunately, they turn into "blame-storming" sessions. That's like giving people feedback on their driving by listing the cars they hit,

DECISION-MAKING CRITIQUE

- What was the timeline? Write down the key judgments and decisions that were made as the incident unfolded.
- Circle the tough decisions in this project or episode. For each one, ask the following questions:

    Why was this difficult?

    How were you interpreting the situation? In hindsight, what are the cues and patterns you should have been picking up?

    Why did you pick the course of action you adopted?

    In hindsight, should you have considered or selected a different course of action?

without checking out their vision. In other debriefing sessions the facilitator sometimes tries to maneuver the participants into voicing the one "right" answer.

A good debriefing session may include a discussion of what was done. But it will also help people learn about patterns—for instance, when was a problem first spotted, and were there earlier signs that were ignored? How were people interpreting the situation—were there different ideas of what was going on? What happened to make it clear? Could people have obtained more information earlier to reduce uncertainty? Did they wait too long, in the hope that uncertainty would diminish, and should they have acted more quickly to gain an advantage?

In conducting a review of decision making, you can learn where you need to practice more, either with decision games or in arranging for assignments. You can also learn more about the decision requirements themselves—especially to determine what is difficult about making specific types of decisions.

You can use the decision-making critique to review actual incidents and also to structure the debriefing session following a decision game. In fact, in our training programs we usually introduce the decision-making critique in conjunction with a decision game.

Remember, the reason for using the decision-making critique is to get feedback so that you can improve the quality of your decisions. Without feedback, you cannot expect to strengthen your judgments.

Wrap-up: Turning Experiences into Expertise

If intuition is based on experience, how does that experience get compiled? Merely having experiences is not enough. The experiences have to be transformed into expertise.

To build up expertise, we need to have the following: We need *feedback* on our decisions and actions. We need *actively* get and interpret this feedback for ourselves, rather than passively allow someone to tell us if our decisions were good or poor. We need *repetitions* so that we have a chance to practice making decisions (and getting feedback) and to build up a sense of what should be typical and familiar.

The decision requirements tables help us discover what skills we need so that we can actively apply practice and feedback where they will be most useful. The decision games are a way to practice—to build up the repetitions so that we are ready when we need to use our intuitive decision-making skills—and the decision-making critique is a format for getting feedback about our processes of intuitive decision making.

These three tools are the foundation for the Intuition Skills Training program. But, as you're about to learn, there is much more to the program than practice and feedback. The remainder of this book provides additional tools to help you apply your intuition and cope with the barriers that interfere with your decisions.

POINTS TO REMEMBER

Features of Decision Games

Name:	The decision game should have a name that promotes easy recognition for later reference. The name can refer to the general situation, the physical environment, the dilemma, or some other distinguishing feature.
Background:	The decision game should describe the history of the events leading up to the current decision.
Scenario:	This is the account of the dilemma confronting the players. The decision game should describe where the current situation begins and when the decision needs to be made. The narrative should tell the players who they are, what they are trying to achieve, the environment, the resources they have, and the dilemma. These types of information can be organized in any way that seems appropriate, but usually the flow is from the general to the specific, or in chronological order.
Visual representation:	Where possible, decision games should include some sort of diagram, map, or table to present lots of detail about the environment.

Using Analysis to Support
Our Intuitions

N either analysis nor intuition alone is sufficient for effective decision making. Therefore, we need to explore the connection between them, highlighting what can go wrong if we rely excessively on intuition and what can go wrong if we rely too much on analysis. Ultimately, I want you to learn how to perform analyses that improve intuitive thinking—and what types of analytical decision-making strategies to avoid.

Intuition + Analysis

T he synthesis between intuition and analysis that seems most effective is when we put intuition in the driver's seat so that it directs our analysis of our circumstances. This way, intuition helps us recognize situations and helps us decide how to react, and analysis verifies our intuitions to make sure they aren't misleading us.

Some decision researchers advocate a combination of intuition and analysis, but really aren't comfortable with intuition as such. Their idea of a reasonable compromise is to keep our intuitions under tight control. But this doesn't work. It robs us of our gift to use our intuitions to guide us and give us the big picture.

Bert and Stuart Dreyfus described the type of "deliberative rationality" that I am advocating in their book, *Mind over Machine.*

The hoary old split between the mystical and the analytic will not do . . . for neither pole of that often misleading dualism names the ordinary, non-mystical intuition that we believe is the core of human intelligence and skill . . . analysis and intuition work together in the human mind. Although intuition is the final fruit . . . analytic thinking is necessary for beginners learning a new skill. It is also useful at the highest levels of expertise, where it can sharpen and clarify intuitive insights . . . Detached deliberation and intuition need not be viewed as [opposite] alternatives, as is all too often [the case] in simplistic treatments.

This synthesis is what I described when I introduced the recognition-primed decision model. Pattern matching provides the initial understanding and recognition of how to react to a particular event, and the mental simulation (imagining how the reaction will play out) provides the deliberate thinking—the analysis—to see if that course of action really would work.

A good example of this process at work lies in our visual system. Our eyes contain a fovea and a periphery.

The fovea lets us see fine detail. When we read, we focus the fovea of our eyes on the letters we want to see. In contrast, peripheral vision

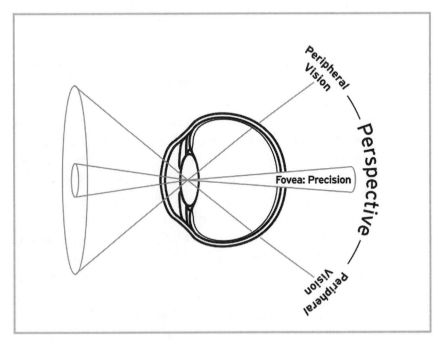

Figure 4.1 Fovea-Periphery Contrast

is useful for providing the overall perspective that lets us keep ourselves well oriented in space.

We need both the fovea and the periphery to carry on our lives. Of the two, the peripheral vision system is more important. Diseases that destroy peripheral vision, such as retinosa pigmentosa, leave the victims helpless, left only with their foveal vision, which is like seeing the world through a straw. The fovea only shows a small amount of the world at a time—if you hold out your arm and focus on your thumbnail, that is about the area covered by your fovea.

If we lose our foveal vision to diseases such as macular degeneration, we have suffered a loss, to be sure; we can no longer read or perform fine-grained visual tasks. But we can still navigate and get around.

Our intuitions function like our peripheral vision to keep us oriented and aware of our surroundings. Our analytical abilities, on the other hand, function like foveal vision to enable us to think precisely. We may believe that everything we think and decide comes from our analytical thinking, the conscious and deliberate arguments we construct in our heads, but that's because we're not aware of how our intuitions direct our conscious thought processes.

Sometimes we need to rely more on intuition and other times we need to draw on analysis. When the situation keeps changing, or when the time pressure is high or when the goals are fuzzy, you just can't use analysis. You have to depend on your intuitions. And when you have a lot of experience, you can just recognize what to do without having to weigh all the options.

In contrast, when your decision involves a lot of computational complexity, such as determining whether there is a cost advantage for purchasing a new color copier instead of leasing one, you can acknowledge your intuitions, but you're sunk if you don't whip out the calculator. If you have to resolve conflict between different people or groups, you can't go with one person's intuitions over those of the other people. To help everyone arrive at a fair compromise you may want to compare the options using a common set of criteria so that everyone can keep track of what he or she is getting and giving up with each option. If you have to find the best option to solve a problem, and not just a workable one, you may want to analyze the strengths and weaknesses of each alternative. And if you have made a decision but are pressed to justify your choice, the most convincing

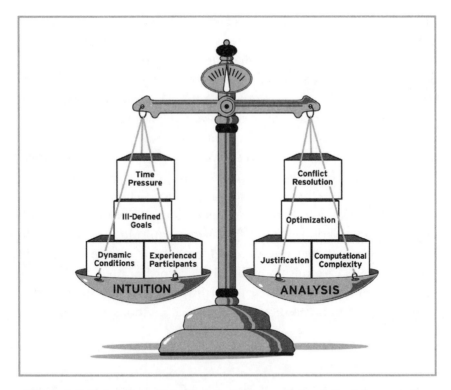

Figure 4.2 Conditions Favoring Intuitive and Analytical Approaches

way is to line up your options and explain why your selection was the wisest choice.

The Limits of Intuition

Why will intuition sometimes prove unreliable? The reasons stem from the types of decisions we face, the opportunities we have to develop intuition, and the inherent nature of expertise.

Complex and Uncertain Tasks Make Intuition Hard to Use

It's hard to develop intuitions based on pattern matching when the situation you are trying to resolve is complicated. Even if you think that you recognize a pattern, you may be fooling yourself. For example, in gambling, roulette wheels are not always uniform—slight differences in wear and tear may give some numbers an edge over others. But the difference is very small. Teams of gamblers have to spend days tabulating frequencies to see if a given roulette wheel does show the signs of imbalance that would give them a sufficient edge to win. The intuitions a gambler forms after watching a roulette wheel for an hour or two are based on random fluctuations, not on reality.

The stock market is also too complex to allow accurate intuitions. No one has the expertise to reliably outperform the market. Stockbrokers have learned the routines of their job. They can provide us with explanations for their recommendations. They can talk knowledgeably about various indices. What they can't do is make reliable forecasts. We may feel intuitive preferences for certain stocks, but most of us who carefully watch the track record of these preferences soon realize that they are not trustworthy. Of course, the stock market is too complex to be predicted by analytical methods either, but that is a different story.

The Decision Makers May Not Have Had a Chance to Acquire Expertise

We may not have a chance to build a strong experience base because we can't get feedback about our judgments. Thus, a personnel department may be judged on how *efficiently* it manages hirings, but not on the *quality* of the workers hired.

Recently, my colleagues and I had a chance to study the job-seeking strategies used by highly intelligent college students. (See Example 4.1.)

When I have described these results to other people, they usually tell me stories about how they have chosen jobs at different stages in their careers. Generally, they acted the same way as our sample of job-seekers. These observations make me uncomfortable. If someone only *gets* one offer, there's nothing more to be done, but many in our sample were selecting the first offer even though they had opportunities to look at more possibilities. A job search isn't really a thorough search if the applicant isn't trying to find a range of options. This type of job-seeker is relying on intuition, but the intuition is not based on solid experience.

This project was an attempt to help our clients figure out how to be more competitive when hiring highly talented workers. We interviewed seventeen people to find out about their job-seeking strategies.

To my dismay, their dominant strategy was to accept the first acceptable offer they received. In only fifteen of forty-five job search incidents did the person compare two or more options. (Most of the interviews covered a series of job searches, not only the first job out of college.)

You might think that I'd be happy to obtain findings that fit with the recognition-primed decision model, which predicts that skilled decision makers usually go with the first option they consider. However, these people were not skilled decision makers. In some cases they had no previous experience at all in choosing jobs and getting feedback about whether they had made a good selection.

Why do the job applicants rely on this strategy? In most cases, the applicants seemed to dislike the process of job seeking. They felt anxious about not having a job lined up. They also disliked having to go through interviews—being evaluated by others, being open to criticism. The sooner they could finish their search, the happier they were.

The Experience Base May Be Distorted

Even if we know how to acquire and evaluate our experiences we still have to worry about whether the feedback we get is trustworthy. An example would be accidental food aversion. When someone contracts a stomach virus shortly after eating a certain type of food, the illness becomes associated with that food even though the connection is accidental. The person will intuitively avoid dishes made with that food even though there's no proof that was the cause of their illness. We see children developing bedtime rituals to stave off the monsters hiding in their closets and underneath their beds. There's no evidence, or feedback, confirming that the monsters really exist and that the precautions are justified, but the rituals reduce anxiety and may persist for a long time. Business practices that are inefficient but are so much a part of the office procedure that people are uneasy about giving them up are also cases in which the feedback isn't reliable.

The Mindset Problem

Think about some of the things expertise buys you. It lets you quickly categorize a situation as typical. It lets you know where to focus your attention, and what to ignore. But sometimes we can become so complacent in what we think we know that we're caught off guard when the unexpected happens as in Example 4.2.

This is the flip side of expertise, a simple demonstration of how expertise can blind us. The mindset problem reveals the errors people make *because* of their expertise, because they have cemented their perception of their world and can't see it in any other way. Expertise gives us the ability to ignore cues and options we don't think are worth attending to, but this same mindset can lead experts to miss relevant but novel cues, to ignore potentially useful strategies, and to fail to notice important opportunities. The industrial accident in Example 4.3 is another illustration of the mindset problem.

We can see the mindset problem in action here. At first everything appeared normal and, therefore, the initial worker, the spotter, and the shift supervisor never considered that the worker collapse might be due to lack of oxygen in the tank. Even with two of his subordinates unconscious, the supervisor didn't question whether anything was unusual with the picture. Only when the new pattern became unmistakably vivid did the rescuers take more precautions.

The mindset problem shows that our intuition is fallible. Even when intuition is based on expertise, that is no guarantee that we haven't overlooked something important. Too often, experienced workers can fall into a routine that blinds them to new possibilities.

OVERREACTING TO THE LIMITATIONS OF INTUITION

The limitations of our intuition are real enough. But sometimes people try to make too much of them. Consider the following statement by Bernard Bass:

> *EXAMPLE 4.2* THE WATER JAR DEMONSTRATION

In 1970, a study was conducted to examine how prior experience can limit people's abilities to function efficiently in new settings. Participants were shown three jars of varying sizes and were told they had an unlimited water supply. Their task was to figure out how to fill a large cistern with the required amount of water using only these three jars. For example, in problem 1, jar A has a capacity of 21 quarts, jar B has a capacity of 127 quarts, and jar C has a capacity of 3 quarts. How would you use the three jars in order to fill a cistern with 100 quarts of water?

Please try to solve this problem, the first in the series, and then continue with the rest of the problems shown.

	Jar capacity in quarts: A	B	C	Fill the cistern with the following amount
1.	21	127	3	100
2.	14	163	25	99
3.	9	42	6	21
4.	23	49	3	20
5.	20	59	4	31

Note that in all five problems the cistern could be filled accurately by filling up jar B, filling jar A from jar B, then scooping out two helpings of jar C. The formula is B minus A minus 2C.

However, problem 4 has a simpler solution: Just fill up jar A, and scoop out jar C. In one study, all of the adult subjects who were initially given problems such as number 4 used the simpler solution of jar A minus jar C. But adults who had first been given the problems with the more complicated solution, in the order I have arranged above, kept on using it, and never noticed that there was an easier way. Only 26 percent of the adults in this condition bothered to continue looking for an easier way, while 74 percent continued with the unnecessarily complicated strategy.

The operators at the Milliken Chemical Company purged a chemical tank with air for twenty-four hours to remove the fumes from the previous production run. When the operation was completed, one of the workers entered the tank, took a few breaths, and collapsed. The spotter saw what had happened, rushed in to help, took a few breaths, and also collapsed. The shift supervisor saw two of his workers in trouble, rushed in to help them, and collapsed.

Other workers standing by finally began to wonder if they were missing something. A fourth worker was lowered into the tank by rope, and was removed when he passed out. The unconscious men were then rescued by workers wearing self-contained breathing apparatus.

The problem was that the hose used to purge the fumes was not connected to an air pipe—it had accidentally been connected to a nitrogen pipe.

The first worker into the tank died; the other three recovered.

Managers, as pragmatists, tend to pride themselves on their intuition, or their ability to "fly by the seat of their pants." Yet, such intuitive judgments have been shown to be fraught with error and to result in outcomes far from optimum when completely depended upon . . . for example . . . given five seconds in which to estimate the product of $1\times2\times3\times4\times5\ \times6\times7\times8$, the median estimate is 512 and for $8\times7\times6\times5\times4\ \times3\times2\times1$, the median estimate is 2,250. The true calculated answer, however, is 40,320.

Bass is attacking a straw man. No one could suggest we should turn in our pocket calculators and rely on intuition when doing complex mathematical calculations. But many times mathematicians do rely on an intuitive sense of what the answers to a problem ought to look like. This leaves them alert to the possibility of a calculation error if their answer doesn't ring true. Good mathematicians also need an intuitive sense of how to attack a difficult problem in order to uncover new types of solutions. And how do they build that intuition? Through their experience in solving countless mathematical problems and building up strong mental models about relationships and structures.

There is a slippery slope of nervous reactions to intuition. It's easy to start with "intuition is not infallible" to "you can never completely trust your intuitions" to "intuition is basically untrustworthy" and come out the other end with "avoid intuitions at all costs." The statement by Bass illustrates this progression—he is suggesting that if we can't trust our intuitions about arithmetic calculations, we should similarly reject intuition in all other cases.

I don't buy into this logic. Our eyes aren't perfect—they have blind spots, they sometimes have floaters that create blurriness, they often require lenses to correct for distortions. Yet we aren't rejecting the information we receive from our eyes. Just because intuition is fallible that doesn't mean we can't make good use of it.

Decision researchers such as Bass are uncomfortable with the idea of intuitive decision making. They see intuition as an accidental, nonscientific source of confusions and superstitions. These researchers point to research that shows how intuitive judgments are usually wrong. (They ignore the analytical judgments that are also wrong.) They point to examples where decisions led to disasters, such as the United States' entry into the Vietnam War, and the British appeasement policy with Hitler prior to World War II. They argue that with more careful analyses, politicians might have avoided these blunders. (They ignore the intuitive decisions that worked, such as MacArthur's landing at Inchon in the Korean War, Reagan's intuition that the Soviet Union could be vanquished, Mandela's intuition that his resistance to apartheid could make a difference, and Martin Luther King, Jr.'s intuition that passive resistance could work against segregation policies in the United States.) They laugh at the intuitive decisions at Ford that led to the Edsel. (But they drove Mustangs and Caravans, two cars that originated in the intuitions of Lee Iacocca when he worked for Ford.)

Based on examples like the ones above, their conclusion is that you cannot trust intuition, that your only hope is to base your decisions on solid analysis. The argument takes the extreme view that analysis alone can be sufficient, and that intuition will only muddy the waters. But under close scrutiny, analysis, too, has its share of drawbacks.

The Limits of Analysis

e can define analysis as the process of trying to understand a problem by breaking it down into its components and then performing logical and/or mathematical operations on these components. Analytical methods such as deductive logic will help us arrive at sensible conclusions. One of the risks of relying upon analysis, though, is that we'll distort the problem when we deconstruct it so that it won't make sense when we try to put the pieces back together.

One of the most common methods taught for analyzing a decision is to create a Rational Choice model—a method of comparing options to see how they stack up on a common set of yardsticks. Many people like this method because it's general (it can be used in all kinds of fields), reliable, comprehensive, and quantitative.

For example, if you are going to buy a used car, you might consider several models, and evaluate each one by comparing it to the others using the same set of criteria.

Table 4.1 shows an example of such an analysis, which you can think of as a fancy way of listing pros and cons. The comparison is between a Mercury, Chevrolet, and Honda. To keep things simple, the analysis relies on only four criteria: color, estimated maintenance costs, roominess, and price. The left-hand column shows that the buyer cares more about the price than the others—this criterion has a weight of 4 in the evaluation.

Now that the ground rules are set up, the decision maker just has to fill in the matrix, using a scale from 0 to 100 for each feature. Thus, for this buyer, the color silver gets a score of 90, whereas black gets a value of 70 and white only gets a score of 50. These are multiplied by 3, the weighting of the color criterion, to give a color score for each of the four cars being considered. The example shows the rating and score for each of the cars on each of the criteria. The Mercury gets the highest score of all—840.

Let's look more closely at the decision strategy used in this Rational Choice method. Intuition has to be used throughout the analysis: in recognizing the problem, in decomposing it, in setting up the rating scales, in assigning the numerical values, in estimating probabilities. We cannot perform analysis without relying on intuition.

Further, we may *subvert* the method in order to make it come out

Table 4.1 Rational Choice Model of Decision Making

Criteria	WEIGHT	OPTIONS								
		MERCURY				CHEVY				
		Feature	Score	Wt.	Total	Feature	Score	Wt.	Total	
Color	3	Silver	90 x	3 =	270	Black	70 x	3 =	210	
Maint. Costs	3	Low-Med.	50 x	3 =	150	Low	40 x	3 =	120	
Roominess	2	High	90 x	2 =	180	Med.	70 x	2 =	140	
Price	4	$15,000	60 x	4 =	240	$12,000	90 x	4 =	360	
TOTAL					840				830	

the way we want. If you really want to buy a Honda, but the analysis comes out in favor of the Mercury, then you might go back and change the individual values of your criteria. Let's say the Honda ranked high on estimated maintenance costs, but that criterion only had a weight of 3; if you give it a weight of 4, and drop roominess to a weight of 1, then the Honda will come out as the better choice. Or you can change the way you evaluate colors, so that "white" becomes preferable (better visibility, after all). You can add more categories— the Honda may have a good prognosis for resale value so you might add that as a fifth criterion. Eventually you would be able to arrange it so that the Honda gets the highest score. Then you would announce to the world that you are a rational decision maker even though you have cooked the numbers to make them come out the way you wanted.

Another difficulty is that it takes a fair amount of *time* to set up the comparisons. If you don't have a half hour or more to fill in the matrix, or if the situation keeps changing so that your estimates are often out of date, then you will have trouble using this method.

The problem of *distortion*, too, can come into play when you break down the decision task. Perhaps it made sense to weight color almost as much as cost in the example, and perhaps we can express a clear preference for silver over white, but are we really going to pay $1,000 more for the Mercury than for the Honda just because we are not enthusiastic about the color of the Honda? The way we assigned weights and then assigned ratings resulted in a bizarre decision.

Further, the setup assumes you only care about four dimensions, and that each dealer only has one car of interest to you. Imagine that you were comparing ten cars, not three, using fifteen evaluation criteria, not four. The calculations become more *complicated* and your confidence in your choice might go down.

Another problem is that to compare the options, the evaluation criteria have to be *general* and abstract so that the different options can be measured using the same standards. Why should you have a general preference for the color silver over white? Wouldn't the color white look better in one type of car than another? For that matter, why is color given a weight of 3? Color can matter more with one make of car than another.

It's a mistake to reduce decisions to quantitative exercises. In contrast, the strategy people typically use for evaluation, the mental simulation discussed in Chapter 2, is sensitive to *context*. When you use mental simulation you are evaluating an option by seeing if it will work in the situation.

Still another problem is that the Rational Choice format, illustrated in Table 4.1, assumes that decision makers can't be trusted to make fair and accurate comparisons between the options, yet the method depends on their ability to make fair and accurate judgments on all the small estimates. This seems *paradoxical*, because the smaller judgments, assessing an option on an abstract evaluation criterion, can be harder to make. Thus, you may have a better sense of whether you want to buy a Chevy or a Honda than whether you prefer silver over white.

Finally, we run into the problem I call the *zone of indifference*. If you had to compare two options, one of which is outstanding and the other of which is terrible, you wouldn't need to do any analysis. It would be an easy choice. As the two options get closer and closer together in their attractiveness, the decision gets harder. The method shown in Table 4.1 is best suited for the hardest choices, where the options are just about equal in attractiveness. However, at this point, it really doesn't much matter which one you choose (see Figure 4.3). In the example of purchasing a used car, we can see that the three options are all very close—they each have comparable strengths and weaknesses. There just isn't much that differentiates them. The options were so close together that simply flipping a coin would have been sufficient.

Considering all these drawbacks, it's not surprising that decision researchers haven't been able to demonstrate that analytical methods actually help people make better decisions. In fact, decision analysts working in the commercial sector admit that the benefit of analytical methods such as the one I've outlined is really not to help people make decisions, but rather to explore the issues at stake and get a better sense of what to take into account *before making a decision*.

There are even several studies that show that the use of analytical methods results in worse decisions. The reason is that these methods seem to interfere with intuition.

Jonathan Schooler at the University of Pittsburgh demonstrated that when we encourage people to be analytical we are usually pres-

(Reprinted with permission of Leo Cullum, 2002)

Figure 4.3 The Zone of Indifference

suring them to redefine the decision task in a way that can be put into words, and this can be enough to distort the task.

From the perspective of intuitive decision making, conscious analysis is the bottleneck. The idea of trying to do all of our thinking by using conscious deliberation seems misguided. Consciousness can only illuminate one thing at a time—the thing we are conscious of— and therefore makes it hard to track several activities going on simultaneously. Consciousness does let us perform analyses to compare options, but that is not usually sufficient for making decisions.

And now I would like to introduce you to EVR. This is the code name for a patient described by Paul Eslinger and Antonio Damasio. The case of EVR illustrates the limitations of trying to make decisions without using intuition.

Scientists who argue that we can't trust intuition, that we should

INTUITION AT WORK

EVR had had an uneventful life. He was a very good student, had many friends, and got married soon after high school. He became an accountant for a home-building firm, was the father of two children, and was active in church affairs. He quickly rose to become comptroller of his company, and was seen as a role model by others. All this changed when he was diagnosed with a cerebral tumor at the age of thirty-five. The tumor pressed in on both frontal lobes of his brain. The tumor was removed, and EVR returned to work. But he wasn't the same. He entered into an unwise partnership, lost all his savings, had to declare bankruptcy, was hired and fired from a series of jobs, divorced, and finally moved back in with his parents.

Follow-up testing showed that EVR was still very intelligent. His IQ was in the 97–99th percentile, reaching 120 and 140 on some of the scales.

But his personal deterioration continued. "Deciding where to dine might take hours, as he discussed each restaurant's seating plan, particulars of menu, atmosphere, and management. He would drive to each restaurant to see how busy it was, but even then he could not finally decide which to choose. Purchasing small items required in-depth consideration of brands, prices, and the best method of purchase." These are the types of decisions we handle without much thought, using the patterns and action scripts we have learned to recognize what we want and how to get it.

When Eslinger and Damasio evaluated EVR, they didn't find any abnormal personality traits. However, brain scans did turn up some damage in the frontal area. Apparently, this damage had been enough to undo EVR's life. When asked abstract questions, EVR showed that he knew the correct ways to respond to situations. When he was in those situations, however, he wasn't able to use the abstract knowledge. He had forgotten his daily routines, his intuitions about how to react. He had lost touch with the emotional impulses he needed to organize his life: "he rarely acted on impulse, spending instead an inordinate amount of time reviewing detailed and not necessarily pertinent aspects of a proposition without keeping the whole problem in perspective."

try to rely entirely on scientific thinking and analysis, would do well to ponder the tragedy of EVR, a man who embodies a life in which decisions are made with nothing but analysis. People who complain about how emotions get in the way of reason should remember EVR. We know which critical parts of their frontal lobes to destroy, to free them from their intuitions. Would they like to volunteer?

Making Good Use of Analytical Strategies

Most decision researchers appreciate that we need both analysis and intuition. They do not detach emotion from analysis. The challenge, rather, is to find ways to use analysis appropriately.

Here are some recommendations about ways you can use analysis to augment intuition, and also some practices that you might want to avoid. Many of the suggestions can be used in conjunction with each other.

START WITH INTUITION, NOT WITH ANALYSIS. If you begin by analyzing a decision, you are inevitably going to suppress your intuition. You're best off starting by getting a sense of your intuitive preference—a gut check of your immediate preference, identifying your intuition before it gets clouded. If you're having trouble sensing your intuitive preference, you can pull numbers out of a hat or flip a coin, anything to give yourself a chance to check your emotional response. Are you satisfied or frustrated with the result? Now you know in which direction your intuition is leading you.

Then, if you still can't immediately make up your mind, do some analysis. Doing it the other way around, first breaking the situation down, then looking at the pros and cons surrounding your choice, will compromise your intuition.

ACCEPT THE ZONE OF INDIFFERENCE. We usually think that the goal of decision making is always to pick the best choice. There are few decisions more important than on the battlefield or on the fireground, where lives are at stake. Yet military leaders and fireground commanders recognize that it is better to make a good decision fast and prepare to execute it well rather than agonizing over a "perfect" choice that comes too late. We can rarely know what is the best choice, and the quest for a best choice can drive us to obsess over inconsequential details. How often do we get ourselves trapped into splitting hairs, to find the very best option out of a set of perfectly good choices? Better to make your goal one of selecting a good option that you can live with. If one option emerges as the clear winner, fine. If two or more options wind up in the zone of indifference, that's fine too—just pick one of them and move on. If you can accept the impossibility of making the "right" choice, you can free yourself from unnecessary turmoil and wasted time.

MAP THE STRENGTHS AND WEAKNESSES OF OPTIONS WITHOUT ATTACHING NUMBERS. Analytical methods can help us make sense of complicated decisions. We can learn a lot simply by listing the options and considering each one. We don't have to assign weights to the evaluation criteria or make numerical ratings. The method I am advocating was first described in Benjamin Franklin's letter to Joseph Priestley. Franklin counseled Priestley to list the advantages and disadvantages of each option, on separate sides of a page, in order to compare them.

Franklin begins with the observation that our memories are often selective. You know this yourself. When we are happy with someone, we remember all the good times we had together. When we become angry, we recall all of the times they took advantage of us, and don't remember the pleasant events. Therefore, Franklin's strategy is designed to work within the constraints of our psychological makeup, rather than adhering to mathematical formulae. His next step is to group the factors on each side that appear comparable, to see whether the remaining factors fall in one column or the next. Again, he does not aim at precision. This method is not trying to carefully account for all the advantages that could exist. Rather, he wants to provide an overview, a big picture so that, on one page, you can review the major issues contributing to the decision.

I suspect most of us rely on this type of method when we get stuck in choosing between options. I recall one set of discussions with some sponsors at Procter & Gamble. They wanted to have my company perform a demonstration project, and they identified three possible consumer decisions we could investigate. To structure the conversation I used a whiteboard to list the advantages and disad-

> *EXAMPLE 4.5* HOW TO MAKE A DECISION

To Joseph Priestley   London, Sept. 19, 1772

Dear Sir,

In the affair of so much importance to you, wherein you ask my advice, I cannot, for want to sufficient premises, advise you *what* to determine, but if you please I will tell you *how*. When those difficult cases occur, they are difficult, chiefly because while we have them under consideration, all the reasons *pro* and *con* are not present to the mind at the same time; but sometimes one set present themselves, and at other times another, the first being out of sight. Hence the various purposes or inclinations that alternately prevail, and the uncertainty that perplexes us.

To get over this, my way is to divide half a sheet of paper by a line into two columns; writing over the one *Pro*, and over the other *Con*. Then during three or four days consideration, I put down under the different heads short hints of the different motives, that at different times occur to me, *for* or *against* the measure. When I have thus got them all together in one view, I endeavor to estimate their respective weights; and where I find two, one on each side, that seem equal, I strike them both out. If I find a reason *pro* equal to some two reasons *con*, I strike out the three. If I judge some two reasons *con* equal to some three reasons *pro*, I strike out the five; and thus proceeding I find at length where the balance lies; and if, after a day or two of further consideration nothing new that is of importance occurs on either side, I come to a determination accordingly. And, though the weight of reasons cannot be taken with the precision of algebraic quantities, yet, when each is thus considered, separately and comparatively, and the whole lies before me, I think I can judge better, and am less liable to make a rash step; and in fact I have found great advantage from this kind of equation, in what may be called *moral* or *prudential* algebra.

Wishing sincerely that you may determine for the best, I am ever, my dear friend, yours most affectionately,

Ben Franklin

vantages of each option. The process helped us clarify the issues we needed to take into account in selecting the project. That was more helpful than identifying the "best" option—in fact, the option we eventually pursued was different from the one we ranked highest at the meeting.

USE MENTAL SIMULATION TO EVALUATE THE OPTIONS. Once you have identified a few good options you can spend some time imagining how each possible approach would play out, for better or for worse. This way, you can see why one approach might be risky, and form a sense of whether the approach can be salvaged if you run into an obstacle. If you try to imagine a worst-case scenario, but find that you have trouble thinking of a way that one of your options could turn out poorly, that may be a sign that you are not sufficiently experienced to be making this important decision. It shows that you just haven't encountered enough over time to pick up the patterns that a more experienced person would be able to envision. You should either defer the decision until you can get more information, or bring in some experts, or just admit defeat and try to find the option with the lowest level of risk and commitment.

SIMPLIFY THE COMPARISONS. One way of simplifying a decision is through a "face-off" strategy, in which you compare options two at a time, gauge which seems best, discard the loser, and bring in a new challenger. This helps you rely on your intuitive preferences while still comparing options.

BRING IN THE INTUITION OF AN OUTSIDER TO CHECK ON YOUR ANALYSES. Charles Abernathy and Robert Hamm suggested that "a certain proportion of the time intuition can catch the errors of analysis." Surgeons may find it useful to check their analyses intuitively—does the analytical result make sense? Like surgeons who consult with their colleagues before operating, sometimes you can benefit by bringing in an objective party to provide an intuitive gut check. The outsider has not participated in the analytical process and can therefore provide a fresh judgment.

DON'T TRY TO REPLACE INTUITIONS WITH PROCEDURES. Your intuitions are not accidental. They reflect your experience. If you persist in rejecting your intuition, you are turning yourself into EVR. You might as well lop off the offending portions of the frontal lobe of your brain.

Admittedly, in many circumstances, procedures are essential. We don't want commercial pilots to ignore the procedures on their checklists. We also don't want them to believe that as long as they follow the checklists they don't have to worry about how the airplane is handling. Research has shown that experts not only know the routines, they know when and how to depart from those routines. You cannot devise a system of procedures that is so comprehensive it can substitute for expertise.

Some people might argue that we just have to add to the procedures in order to make them foolproof. However, the more comprehensive you make a system of procedures, and the more contingencies you include, the more complex and bewildering the whole thing becomes. You reach a point where the excessive procedures straitjacket intuitions. Kim Vicente at the University of Toronto tells of an incident when he and his team were observing a highly skilled control-room team in a nuclear power plant. The one weakness of the team was that they would sometimes take shortcuts rather than compulsively following all the steps in the procedure manual. During evaluations, the team was sometimes written up for these shortcuts. As they prepared for one evaluation exercise, all the team members agreed that they would follow every step, no matter what. Midway through the exercise, facing the simulated malfunctions that the examiners had devised, the team members realized that they were in a loop that was not intended in the task description. They would carry out step *A*, which led to step *B*, and then to *C*, and back to *A*. Remembering their pledge, they merrily continued around and around in this loop until the examiners called a halt and directed them to discontinue the session. And, of course, the examiners wrote them up again—this time for "malicious procedural compliance."

If you try to substitute a procedural system in exchange for your expertise and intuition, you will slow down your learning curve and mire yourself in a set of brittle rules.

Expertise itself has limits, but it's the basis for most of what we accomplish. The less experience we have, the weaker our intuitions will be and the less useful our analyses.

By not trusting our intuition, we may miss opportunities to develop it. The less it develops, the less trustworthy it becomes. The longer we wait to strengthen our intuition, the stronger we make our habits of performing the tasks strictly according to procedures.

For an example of people who constantly balance between intuition and conscious deliberation, consider chess grand masters, who spend all their energy ferociously trying to find the "best" choice. Yet

> *EXAMPLE 4.6* HOW GRAND MASTERS OPTIMIZE

In the game of chess, each move should be as strong as possible. This is particularly true at the grand-master level, where even one or two slack moves—not blunders but simply weak moves—can lead to defeat. Therefore, we would expect that chess grand masters would be using all the methods developed by the decision analysts.

They do not. The idea of generating a set of options and evaluating them on a common set of criteria (potential for attack, potential for defense, and so forth) misses the strength of chess grand masters. It isn't even used by Deep Blue, the powerful computer chess program.

The grand masters do want to find the best possible move, and they do examine more than one move, but the way they do this tells us a lot. They use their intuition to recognize the promising moves that they should examine more closely. They shift to an analytic mode by looking at the moves as they will play out in the context of the game, and rely on their ability to mentally simulate what will happen if they play a move. In the course of these mental simulations, some of the moves drop out because they are found to contain weaknesses. By the end of their mental simulations, the grand masters are usually only left with a single move they consider playable.

In the cases where they have two or more moves they consider playable, the choice seems to depend on an intuitive sense, an emotional reaction of how they felt about the board position as they were doing the mental simulations. The move that triggers the most positive emotional reaction is chosen.

grand masters are not using the methods of decision analysis. In studying Adriaan deGroot's influential book *Thought and Choice in Chess*, I came upon Appendix A in which deGroot provided the results of a study where he asked five famous grand masters and other strong players to think aloud while they tried to find the best move in a difficult chess position. When I worked through the responses of the grand masters I found that as a group they had considered around forty different moves. But in only five places in the records was there any indication that the grand masters were even trying to compare the strengths and weaknesses of one move over another, and none of these cases relied on a common set of evaluation dimensions. Yet clearly the grand masters were analyzing the board positions. Their form of analysis was to identify the moves worth studying and to appreciate how those moves affected the board position.

If this type of strategy is good enough for chess grand masters, it should be good enough for the rest of us.

POINTS TO REMEMBER

Strategies to Coordinate Analysis with Intuition

- Start with intuition, not with analysis.
- Accept the zone of indifference.
- Map the strengths and weaknesses of options without attaching numbers.
- Use mental simulation to evaluate the options.
- Simplify the comparisons.
- Bring in the intuition of an outsider to check on your analyses.
- Don't try to replace intuitions with procedures.

Section II

INTUITION

Ways to

Apply It

How to Make Tough Choices

What can you do when you really have to choose between two valid options? Often, the process can be painful. How many times have you rushed a decision simply because you couldn't bear wrestling with it any longer?

The recognition-primed decision (RPD) model I introduced in Chapter 2 explains how people can use their experience to size up a situation and use that experience to know how to react. The model was *not* designed to explain how people choose between options.

Let's start with a decision game that will provide us with some examples of tough choices. Try your hand at the following challenge.

> ### DECISION GAME 5.1 SETTING THE AGENDA

You are an executive for a global construction company, Fabrications Ltd., and are in the midst of making a set of site visits of major global business units. Your next stop is the Southeast Asian headquarters. You arrive in the late evening and have a breakfast meeting the next day with an old friend who is the vice president for operations. At the end of breakfast, while you are enjoying coffee, he receives a call on his cell phone. His voice takes on a very serious tone, and when he finishes the call, he informs you that his mother has had a stroke and that he has to fly to Europe immediately. In fact, he has to head home to pack and make arrangements to catch the next flight, which is in a few hours.

Just before he leaves, he asks you for a last-minute favor. He explains that there is a critical meeting that morning at 9:00 A.M. It's been very difficult to schedule this because of the hectic pace of travel for everyone in his business unit. He believes it can run without him, and it's urgent that the meeting take place because there are four major decisions that have to get made. Since time is short, he doesn't want to cancel the meeting.

The favor he requests is this: Will you please chair the meeting? You won't have to make the decisions, merely keep the discussions on track. Now, because of time pressures, the meeting can only last for one hour. Your job is to make sure that each decision gets made before the meeting ends. Then he reaches into his attaché case and hands you a piece of paper with the four decisions that will need to be settled. With that, he excuses himself and rushes out of the room.

Here are your instructions:

1. Select a site for building a waste treatment plant in the Philippines. There are two sites to choose from. Numerous studies have been performed and have shown that both sites seem adequate. The decision is an important one, with about $100M riding on it. Proponents for each site seem to be evenly lined up, and the strengths and weaknesses of the two sites seem pretty well balanced. One site offers some potential for cost savings, but carries slightly higher risk for schedule delays. No one has been able to find a decisive reason to select either one.

2. Pick a subcontractor for the project to build the waste treatment plant in the Philippines. There are five possible companies from which to choose. A team has studied the strengths and weaknesses of each, and has disseminated a report with their findings. The team will give a ten-minute report showing how the subcontractors line up on common criteria. But they refuse to give their opinion. The whole committee will have to make this decision together.

3. Green-light a proposal. A team reporting to your friend has worked for several months to prepare a bid in excess of $160M for a major construction project in Australia. However, doubts have been expressed about the competence of the team he has put together. There are concerns that the team may have ignored some potential problems and that the contract may lead to financial losses. You have to decide whether or not to issue the bid.

4. For a project in Indonesia, a major supplier who is a local government monopoly has been providing both the necessary supplies and the shipping to bring in those supplies. The company has announced it is doubling its rates. They need a revised contract from you in one week or else they will refuse to provide any more service. The additional cost will be $10M per year. Should you accept this change?

You realize that in order to get these decisions made within one hour, you have to estimate how much time to spend on each decision, and perhaps even identify the method the group should use to make each decision. If you spend too much time on the first decision or two, then you won't be able to finish or do justice to the later decisions. But the first decisions are too important to rush.

How much time will you schedule for each of the four decisions you have to cover? How do you plan to orchestrate the team to make each of the decisions?

As in all decision games, there are no right answers. When I've run this game with managers, I have encountered a variety of solutions. Some people take the easy way and split up the hour into four fifteen-minute blocks, assigning one decision per block. Others try to judge which decisions are going to require the most discussion, and give these the most time.

If it were me, I'd do it this way: Decision 1 = 2 minutes, Decision 2 = 28 minutes, Decision 3 = 5 minutes, and Decision 4 = 25 minutes. You'll see why as I outline how I'd approach each decision. I am not, by the way, claiming that this is the right answer, only the best solution I come up with based on my experience. You may have more experience than I do with these types of decisions, or a different, equally valid perspective, and you may choose a different path.

Each of the four decisions falls into a different category. Each one is likely to need a different approach. Here's what I suggest:

Decision 1 is about choosing between two sites for the waste treatment plant. The potential sites are virtually identical in terms of strengths and weaknesses. Therefore, this seems like a classical case of the zone of indifference. The teams have been hashing this over for months. This is *not* the place for intuitive decision making. There is probably nothing you can say in an hour that will add anything new to the argument.

The group should realize that the small edge of the site with lower projected costs is insignificant compared to the higher risks of the approach. If you must, list all the shaky assumptions and areas of uncertainty, so the group can see how much the unknowns dwarf the miniscule advantages one option might hold over another.

In this case, I wouldn't let the group vote, because that takes up time, and because it fosters the illusion that one option may be better than the other, and that the group's collective wisdom can ferret it out. Better to bring forward the lead advocate for each site, have them flip a coin, and let them call it. Then move on. Flipping the coin dramatically makes the point that neither option is better than the other. Action is needed, and it's time to get this project moving.

Decision 2, selecting one subcontractor from a set of five options, calls for a comparison. This is the kind of decision that is most suited for deliberate analysis.

You'll have to think about the reputation of the subcontractors, the costs of their bids, the approaches they are taking, the quality of the people they are assigning, the backlog of work each seems to have, and so forth. When there are a large number of factors, you cannot rely on overall intuitions about what to do. You can rely on your intuitions about specific factors, though, such as reputation, quality of the people, soundness or riskiness of the contractors' suggested way of approaching the project. For making the overall decision, the number of factors to consider, and their complexity, goes beyond anyone's patterns and intuitions.

If you approach this decision using a traditional analytical approach, you would list all of the key evaluation dimensions, assign a weight to each according to its importance, have each member of the group rate each subcontractor on each criterion that your group has decided is crucial, add up the results, and see which one comes out on top. There is nothing wrong with this type of strategy, as long as you remember that the weights and the ratings are both subjective. Don't feel trapped by your analysis—treat it as a starting point for further discussions.

When using a rational choice strategy, people tend to overemphasize factors that are more easily calculated. It's easy to line up the proposed bids from lowest to highest and see which bidder is offering you the best price. But if you try to rate the bidders on reliability you could find that everyone is rated "somewhat better than average." So even though reliability is an important quality to consider in a subcontractor, with no way to distinguish them this criterion is tossed away during the final decision making.

One advantage of this analytical method—comparing options on a common set of criteria—is that it helps to make sense of a complicated decision and it helps to gain consensus in a group where different people might have different preferences. If there is disagreement about how to weight each of the dimensions, you can drop that part of the process.

Another suggestion: Try to keep the decision makers' intuitions in play by asking the group members for their preferences before you start any of the analyses. Then, regardless of the method you use to analyze the subcontractors, you'll know where people stand.

Decision 3, the suspicious bid of $160M, is going to be based on intuition. This is a case where expertise does exist. Your most experienced team members are uncomfortable with the quality of the bid. Their intuition is making them uncomfortable. They are worried about the chances for overlooking something important that could have grave financial and legal implications. If you don't heed their advice, why bother asking them at all?

In many cases, though, we do feel reluctant to let prior expenditures (money, time, energy) go to waste. We trap ourselves. Or else we fear the political backlash of changing our minds. So in this context, some in the group might be reluctant to waste the effort of the proposal team—they would rather run the risk of huge losses down the road. This type of reasoning is known as the "sunk cost fallacy," trying to get some return for resources that have already been spent. Your job is to prevent this. Forget about the amount of work that went into the proposal. If the end result isn't reliable, drop it.

Decision 4, should you agree to a revised contract with an increased cost of $10M per year? It's a good bet that no one is going to simply accept a rate hike without a fight, so the natural thing to do is shift into a problem-solving mode and discuss ways to negotiate.

You can expect that the group has a lot of intuitions about what prompted this demand, and what it will really take to satisfy the supplier. It's a good bet that people have been through this drill before and have learned routines for handling this type of crisis.

Perhaps your group can suggest political considerations that need to be addressed or tempting counteroffers that can be made, or even simple compromises. A short meeting is not enough time in which to craft a negotiation strategy with the assembled group so use the time to see who has the time and the connections to lead the negotiations. At a minimum, you must identify the key players, determine who is capable of getting a strategy in place, and come up with a fallback position if that strategy doesn't work. Remember, you only have one week to respond to the supplier's request for a revised contract, so you may want to engage a team in a parallel effort to prepare the revised contract for the additional rates while the task force tries to delay the deadline and find a compromise. Notice that you are not making the final decision at this meeting—there is no reason to rush into a judgment at this point.

I have taken you through these four decisions to show that not all decisions are created equal. On the surface, each one called for a tough choice. However, once we looked more carefully, we could see that the nature of the decision making was very different for all four cases. If you only have the Rational Choice method in your repertoire, you might not get past Decision 1 in the example. But by becoming skilled at categorizing decision types, you can save yourself a lot of work and a lot of frustration. The four decision categories illustrated by this example are zone of indifference choices, choices requiring comparison, intuitive choices, and choices that turn into problem solving.

Maybe you would have tackled this decision game differently than I did. That's fine. It is less important to figure out which is the right approach than to see how different the choices were. It doesn't matter if you have a completely different set of categories from the one I have presented. Being able to differentiate between types of choices is the short cut to responding more adaptively to decisions.

To develop an ability to categorize decision types, as part of an intuition skills training program, you can start practicing by taking notes during your meetings for the next few days. Jot down what decisions are being discussed. Try to categorize them. See if you can describe the decision strategies being used. If the group changes strategies, try to diagnose why the change was made. You can even turn your observations into a decision game to help others in your organization learn to handle the choices that typically arise.

This exercise will help you recognize decision types and learn more action scripts for handling different types of decisions. By learning to direct your own decision making and that of the group for which you're responsible, you can continue your development as an intuitive decision maker.

How to Spot Problems Before They Get Out of Hand

O ne of the most critical uses of intuition is to alert us that something is wrong, even if we don't know what it is. If your "gut" is sending out signs of fear or apprehension, you should pay more attention—your intuition is sensing the problem way before your conscious mind figures it out.

This ability to detect problems can be critical for success or failure of a plan or a program, or even a career. Let's run through a decision game to provide an example.

> ## DECISION GAME 6.1 MEETING ON THE FLY

Your company is working on a major project, and the key staff members have been constantly in motion, traveling around the country. It's essential that the project leaders meet face-to-face to review what progress has been made and make new plans.

You are a junior member of the team and have drawn the assignment of arranging this meeting. It's impractical to gather everyone together in your headquarters in Atlanta. You've collected everyone's travel plans and schedules, and figured out that there was a half-day window for a meeting in Minneapolis on Wednesday morning. You are going from Atlanta to Salt Lake City, so you will stop on your way west, flying out on Tuesday night. You have to meet with a client Thursday morning, but there is a flight Wednesday night that works for you. Your manager is returning from Seattle, and will fly to Minneapolis Tuesday afternoon. He needs to leave promptly at 3:00 P.M. to return to Atlanta for a major policy review. Two other team members are heading home from Los Angeles, and will fly in Tuesday afternoon. They will catch the same 3:00 P.M. flight to Atlanta as your boss. One of the vice presidents of the company wants to sit in and has to be in Minneapolis all week, but she can get away for this Wednesday session. Another key team member has agreed to fly out from Pittsburgh Tuesday night.

It is Tuesday afternoon, the day before the meeting. The National Weather Service is tracking a large winter storm, but it has already moved past Minneapolis. You conscientiously call the Pittsburgh and Salt Lake City and Minneapolis airports and are given the reassurance that all of their runways are open.

You compile a list of agenda items. There is a lot to cover, but you can just fit it all in during a four-hour meeting, from 8:00 A.M. to 12:00 P.M.

Good work. Now please take out a piece of paper and in three minutes write down any weaknesses you can see in this plan.

Most people have done enough traveling to realize that plans such as this one can run into problems, no matter how skillful the orchestration. So your list probably includes some personal experiences and war stories. Now, put this piece of paper away for a few minutes.

Next, try this exercise another way. Take out another piece of paper and sit back in your chair. Think about the plan for gathering the team members together. How nice that the schedules all fit together. But now we are going to look into a crystal ball to see the future and . . . we see that the plan was a fiasco. The meeting never happened. The project lost direction and acquired a black eye. Unfortunately, the crystal ball doesn't show why the meeting got derailed. Drawing on your experience, spend the next three minutes jotting down all the reasons why you think this plan might have come apart.

When you're finished, compare your two sets of responses. The first critique is a traditional review. The second, using the crystal ball technique, usually frees people up to make more pointed criticisms and identify more weaknesses inherent in a plan. Once you know the meeting has fallen apart, you can easily see how vulnerable this plan was to weather problems, flight delays, competing priorities, illnesses, family emergencies, and so forth. It often reveals the flaws that you couldn't see before, when you were assuming your plan would work. Now you see that maybe you should have prepared for a two-hour agenda, to buy some flexibility in case the early morning flights were delayed. Perhaps you should have arranged for a teleconference in case one of the participants was stranded. Were all the participants essential? Learning to sense trouble is key to intuitive decision making.

I know that I told you that intuition had nothing to do with ESP, but bear with me on this crystal ball approach. It's the basis for the PreMortem exercise.

The PreMortem Exercise

This is a method for helping decision makers anticipate problems. In a postmortem, an autopsy is performed on a patient to try to learn why the patient died. But while it may be helpful to those who perform it and hear about the results, it doesn't help the central figure in the medical drama—the patient.

Instead of waiting for the patient to die, or waiting for a project to fail, start investigating what could be potentially "fatal" to your plans at the very beginning. In my company, where we've been using the PreMortem for many years, we have a kickoff meeting to begin each new project, and the PreMortem is a crucial part of that meeting. There have been days when we are short on time, and have suggested skipping the PreMortem, but the project leader has usually been the one to make the loudest protests. Our project leaders understand that the PreMortem helps to build their intuitions, to build their sensitivities to where the future problems might be.

The exercise takes forty minutes to an hour. It may sound like a long time, but I guarantee you the time invested in this exercise is well spent. We usually perform it in project teams, with about eight to twelve participants, at the end of the kickoff meeting, once the project plan has been described.

The purpose of a PreMortem is to find key vulnerabilities in a plan. In most settings, when people critique their own plans, they are hoping that they won't find any showstoppers, any flaws that can't be fixed. And in a team setting, people are often reluctant to criticize the ideas of others. The PreMortem provides a format that supports a productive critique of a plan.

In a PreMortem, the group tries to anticipate a plan's weaknesses through mental simulation. Once this is done, the group looks for ways to counter the weaknesses they have pinpointed. By the way, just because a plan has weaknesses doesn't mean it's a bad plan. Failing to defend against the weaknesses, however, can be a sign of a bad planner.

As a by-product of using the PreMortem exercise, team members will become better at mentally simulating how a plan or project is likely to play out. They will learn from each other about ways that plans can fail, and thereby increase the patterns they can recognize and their mental models, which in turn strengthens their intuitions. These skills enable people to produce better plans and avoid pitfalls.

Step 1: *Preparation.* Team members take out sheets of paper and get relaxed in their chairs. They should already be familiar with the plan, or else have the plan described to them so they can understand what is supposed to be happening.

Step 2: *Imagine a fiasco.* When I conduct the PreMortem, I say I am looking into a crystal ball and, oh no, I am seeing that the project has failed. It isn't a simple failure either. It is a total, embarrassing, devastating failure. The people on the team are no longer talking to each other. Our company is not talking to the sponsors. Things have gone as wrong as they could. However, we could only afford an inexpensive model of the crystal ball so we cannot make out the reason for the failure. Then I ask, "What could have caused this?"

Step 3: *Generate reasons for failure.* The people on the team spend the next three minutes writing down all the reasons why they believe the failure occurred. Here is where the intuitions of the team members come into play. Each person has a different set of experiences, a different set of scars, and a different mental model to bring to this task. You want to see what the collective knowledge in the room can produce. In the beginning of this chapter, in the decision game "Meeting on the Fly," you worked on the PreMortem by yourself. We find it much more valuable to use the PreMortem method with the team that will be carrying out the project. The activity helps the group share experiences, and calibrate their understanding of the difficulties they are facing.

Step 4: *Consolidate the lists.* When each member of the group is done writing, the facilitator goes around the room, asking each person to state one item from his or her list. Each item is recorded on a whiteboard. This process continues until every member of the group has revealed every item on their list. By the end of this step, you should have a comprehensive list of the group's concerns with the plan at hand.

Step 5: *Revisit the plan.* The team can address the two or three items of greatest concern, and then schedule another meeting to discuss ideas for avoiding or minimizing the other problems.

Step 6: *Periodically review the list.* Some project leaders take out the list every three to four months to keep the specter of failure fresh, and to resensitize the team to problems that may just be emerging.

Some people have criticized the PreMortem exercise as being too depressing. I disagree. I think it's a useful corrective to the overconfidence that usually marks new projects. This way the team gets worried about the right things, and any complacency is cut short.

If this were the least the PreMortem could accomplish, it would be worthwhile. But decision makers can also use the PreMortem to improve their plans, identify where more resources are necessary, and start on problematic tasks earlier. In addition, when you offer the PreMortem to your team, you help to create a climate where people are encouraged to voice their concerns, and this can improve the morale of your team throughout the project.

When I've taught the PreMortem method in management training seminars, I have sometimes heard managers say that their organization already has a method like this in place. They may call it a "murder board," or a "red team," or a "problem analysis." Engineers talk about doing a risk analysis or a failure analysis. So the idea of the PreMortem is not a new one. Nevertheless, the strategy of the PreMortem is different from—and more effective than—these other methods. The idea of the red team is to assemble outsider advisors to review a proposal or a plan, but this eats up resources and is hard to schedule. Consequently, organizations that use red teams usually don't call them together very often. Even when an organization uses a problem analysis, it's often conducted with the subtle message that

INTUITION AT WORK

the leaders hope no showstoppers will be identified. ("Okay, does anyone see any problems? No? Good.") The project team is proud of its plan, and is usually not eager to hear about devastating flaws. The posture may be to deflect criticisms, or to present them in a way that will not challenge anyone. The difficulty here isn't with the problem analysis technique but with the way that some organizations carry it out.

Risk analyses do try to identify potential classes of problems. Sometimes, however, the risk analysts can get caught up in the details of quantifying the likelihood of each risk. Often, risk analyses are designed to figure out how much of a safety margin is needed in order to achieve safe operations. The quantification of a risk analysis may not be useful in scrubbing a plan, and the team may be better served by appreciating the limitations of the plan.

In contrast to a risk analysis, the PreMortem begins with the assumption that the plan has failed. The attitude of complacency and the false sense of security is punctured, at least temporarily, and is replaced by an active search aimed at preventing trouble later on. You get to show off your smarts through the quality of the problems you can find. You might predict problems with the plan's concept, the timetable, the financial resources, or with the makeup of the team itself. In our experience, we have found a much higher level of candor in this exercise than in more passive attempts at self-critiquing.

The PreMortem method is one of the tools you can use in an intuition skills training program, to get your projects off to a good start. However, it doesn't serve as a replacement for your intuitions. Regardless of what technique you use, it's crucial that you develop good intuitions to help you anticipate potential problems.

How Do People Detect Problems?

In 1995, the Japan Atomic Energy Research Institute sponsored my company to perform a research project to investigate how people first spot problems. Rather than trying to study this under laboratory conditions, we worked as naturalists: finding and studying examples in real-world settings. My colleagues Beth Crandall, Rebecca Pliske, and I, working with David Woods at Ohio State University, have reviewed old incidents and examined new ones. We started with fifty-two incidents from our database of over 1,000 records of difficult decision-making cases. These fifty-two incidents primarily came from three groups: neonatal intensive care units, weather forecasters, and Navy antiair defense operations. We added more observations from cases involving space shuttle mission control, process control rooms, anesthetic management during surgery, and aviation. Then we conducted some more interviews with surgeons performing gallbladder surgery and with wildland firefighters.

Thanks to this extensive study, we now have a better idea of how people begin to realize that a problem is brewing. Your success in spotting a problem seems to depend on three things—the problem type, your own level of expertise, and the stance you take toward your work. Each of these factors can run into barriers that will make it harder for you to pick up the early signs of trouble. On top of that, organizations have a way of adding bureaucratic barriers to detecting problems.

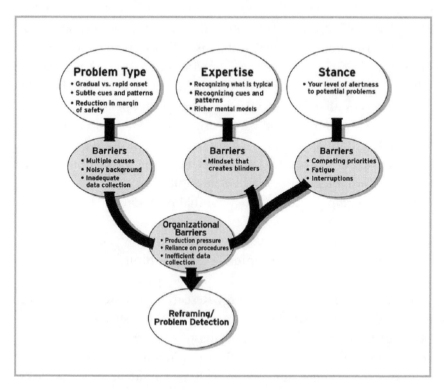

Figure 6.1 The Problem-Detection Process

INTUITION AT WORK

In doing our research, we were struck by the variety of problem types we found. Speed of onset is a key feature of problems. Obviously it is easier to notice problems that have a sudden onset, such as an airplane that dropped 10,000 feet without any warning. We didn't include these types of incidents in our sample because the problem detection was so trivial. We concentrated on the difficult cases of problem detection, like the NICU example in Chapter 1 in which an inexperienced nurse overlooked a baby's symptoms of sepsis. The onset of the sepsis was gradual and that made it harder to detect. Another problem type is where the cues are very subtle—again, contrast the out-of-control airplane to the minimal cues for detecting sepsis. A third reason why problems can be hard to spot is that experience is needed to put the cues together to see the pattern, as with the sepsis example in Chapter 1. A fourth reason why we might not notice a problem is that the margin of safety has gotten too small. For example, surgeons performing a risky procedure might change their tactic if they felt that the chances for an error were too great, even if nothing was going wrong at the time.

In the decision game at the beginning of this chapter, "Meeting on the Fly," some of the potential problems to pulling off the meeting were obvious, such as the chance that a malfunctioning airplane may disrupt the schedule. Other problems were more subtle—if some of the team members were routed through Chicago or St. Louis they could have been affected by a winter storm. Regardless of where they made their connections, the storm may have tied up the airplane they were to take. So experience is needed to put the pieces together to see the pattern. And we can "type" this problem as a case where the margin of safety may be too small. In the decision game, nothing has gone wrong—yet. The skill is in appreciating how little it will take to thwart the plan.

So, some types of problems are harder to notice than others. In addition, we found that there are specific barriers that make it harder to spot problems:

> *a.* If more than one thing goes wrong at the same time, then there is a good chance you'll blame the symptoms on just one of these

causes, perhaps the most obvious or the first one, and miss the others.

b. If there's a noisy background, it's harder to notice a signal. For instance, it is harder to notice a gunshot during the Fourth of July than on other days. You won't notice a masked robber during Halloween as easily as at other times. And, it is harder to spot an unauthorized withdrawal from a checking account if there are many deposits and withdrawals recorded than if the account has been dormant for months.

c. A third reason why you may not pick up the symptoms of a problem is if you're not collecting data effectively. For example, if you audit your books once every five years you may not have enough protection against fraud. But if you do an audit every week you won't get much other work done. You have to find a monitoring rate that gets the job done without degrading your performance.

How can you reduce these barriers to your problem-detecting sensors? First, you can try to resist the temptation to blame everything on the obvious fault, and ask whether it makes sense for that fault to cause the symptoms you are seeing. Second, you can increase your level of alertness depending on the background "noise" levels—if you're facing a barrage of signals you have to pay more attention. Third, you can do a PreMortem on your data sources and try to imagine how an important cue might slip past them.

Expertise

We have discussed how expertise and intuition are based on being able to recognize situations as typical—and that means that skilled decision makers can also recognize anomalies as atypical events that violate their expectancies. This is key for using intuition to spot problems. Expertise also helps you better appreciate cues, and to recognize patterns. As you gain expertise, you also develop mental models to understand how things work—from natural events to organizations to equipment. Because experienced decision makers have such a good idea of what to expect, and such a good sense of what is typical, they're much faster at picking up anomalies. They can rely on their own feeling of surprise as an intuitive, emotional reaction that things are not right.

Remember Darlene and Linda, the two NICU nurses in Chapter 1? Darlene, the supervisor, noticed several cues that indicated a baby had a life-threatening infection. Any one of these cues would have worried her; the convergence of all of them showed clearly that this was a crisis. She wasn't simply reacting to the accumulation of evidence, but to the way the evidence all fit together. Linda, however, was aware of a few of the cues, and could have noticed the others if they were pointed out to her, but she had never appreciated their significance because she had not seen infants go through a cycle of infection.

Experts don't even have to be deliberately looking for possible problems. Their subconscious can do some of the work for them, as in this software engineering example.

> ### EXAMPLE 6.1 THE BUG DETECTORS

Many years ago we had a chance to study quality assurance engineers for Bell Laboratories. We studied a large-scale program that relied on 950,000 lines of code. The quality assurance specialists had to find the bugs before the system was rolled out. The team would divide up the task by subroutines or other convenient boundaries, and examine each line of code, hunting for typographical errors or other types of mistakes that would create a bug. They tried to review up to 5,000 lines of code a day. Overall, this strategy worked well for locating the obvious errors that could show up in this kind of program.

The engineers, however, warned us that there were other kinds of bugs that were more insidious, but the quality-assurance program they were using didn't enable them to check for these directly. Instead, they found that when they were showering in the morning, or driving to the beach on a weekend, the realization would suddenly hit them: "Oh, if this signal arrives when the system is in that configuration, it will be interpreted in that way, and then the program can crash." This was their intuition at work, without warning, without any conscious effort.

Sometimes our subconscious will pop the anomaly into our mind, and other times we just "feel" the problem, an emotional sense that something is not right. Evidence shows that humans engage in a lot of sophisticated thinking of which we are not aware. When we use the emotional signals accompanying these brain activities, we have tapped into our intuition. This conclusion is based on several different lines of research.

Antonio Damasio and his colleagues at the University of Iowa have published a series of experiments showing that our judgments and emotional reactions to a problem can be expressed even before we have any conscious awareness that a problem exists. In one experiment researchers asked subjects to turn over cards from four different decks. All the cards announced monetary rewards and all the decks were rigged. At first, two of the decks, A and B, offered larger rewards and subjects learned to select these decks over the other two, C and D. Then, without warning, the experimenters added penalties to the decks. The monetary penalties were larger for decks A and B, and resulted in an overall monetary loss of money from selecting these decks. The experimenters were interested in seeing what happened when the subjects started to get hit by these penalties.

The study compared the performance of normal subjects to subjects with brain damage in a specific site—the ventromedial sector of the prefrontal cortex. Soon after the penalties were introduced, the ten normal subjects started generating emotional anxiety responses when they sampled cards from decks A and B, even before they were consciously aware that these were the bad decks. Three of these subjects never figured out why decks A and B were the bad ones, but even they had learned to avoid these decks.

None of the subjects with brain damage, however, registered any emotional awareness about the different decks. Three of these brain-damaged subjects did learn to accurately describe which were the good and bad decks, but it didn't matter—they still didn't make good choices by avoiding decks A and B. Without the emotional awareness backing their knowledge, they had no intuitions to translate into action.

Another line of research has suggested that we differ in how sensitive we are to emotional cues—our gut feelings—when we recognize a pattern without consciously realizing it. Edward Katkin and his colleagues first asked subjects to monitor their heart rates while they were resting. A third of the subjects were reasonably accurate at estimating their heart rates. Next, Katkin showed photographs of images such as snakes and spiders to the subjects, but at a rate that was too fast for the subjects to consciously register what they were seeing. He also paired some of the images with shocks. Then he went through the images again, more slowly this time, and asked the subjects to predict when the shocks would occur. Because the subjects could not consciously recognize the images, the only cue they had available was an increase in heart rate resulting from the shock conditioning. The subjects who had earlier shown themselves to be more sensitive to the rate of their heartbeats were also the most accurate in predicting the shocks. They had absorbed the images subconsciously and linked them intuitively to the shock experience. They were able to take advantage of the learning opportunity, even though they weren't conscious of the connections.

I take the idea of emotional cues very seriously because I've seen firsthand how powerful—and on target—they can be, as illustrated by Example 6.2, Selling the Company.

One of the barriers to making good use of expertise is the mindset problem wherein a powerful repertoire of patterns can blind people to unanticipated symptoms. Methods for dealing with the mindset problem are described in Chapter 8.

Stance

You can miss problems if you aren't alert and carefully monitoring what is going on around you. "Stance" refers to your attitudes and approach in carrying out your work—whether you are actively searching for potential difficulties or are focused on your tasks and oblivious to everything else. In a neonatal intensive care unit, part of the nurses' job is to be on alert for problems. In other types of settings, such as assembly lines, the decision makers usually aren't suspicious, or worried, or actively searching for anomalies.

David Garvin, a professor at Harvard Business School, once described to me how he learned to fly. His instructor taught him to assume that the landing was going to run into trouble, and that he

Many years ago, after a frustrating series of business difficulties, I managed to win a large contract to develop an analogical reasoning technique for predicting the effectiveness of training devices. I was pretty burnt out on the risks of having a small business, and I wondered if I might do better folding my operation into a larger company. A friend of mine, who worked for a major corporation with many offices around the country, volunteered to help me make this change. He described how exciting it would be if my colleagues and I could work with his center in Ohio (the headquarters was in Maryland). This triggered a series of discussions with his manager, resulting in an offer to purchase my company and make the acquisition work.

I was very relieved by this outcome. I was happy to be getting a good price, better than my accountant had expected, and to be getting rid of the distractions keeping everything on course had been causing me.

Nevertheless, every time I came back from a negotiation session with my friend's manager, I felt tense and agitated. Sometimes I had to go for a run just to recover from these meetings. When I told people how pleased I was at the prospect of the shift, they commented that I didn't *sound* pleased. Eventually I decided to turn the offer down, even though I couldn't provide any objective explanation as to why.

Weeks later, I met my friend for lunch to try to sort out what had happened. Only then did my friend admit that his manager was creating an icy atmosphere that left everyone in the office on edge. My friend had hoped that when I came over with my co-workers, we might help reduce the tensions. That had been his primary motivation in trying to arrange the transaction.

I could have dragged myself and my employees into an unbearable working situation if I had not followed my hunch that I wouldn't have been happy working for my friend's manager.

What was behind my hunch? I believe it was the strain of the interactions with the manager. Even when he was saying all the right things I was getting a sense of confrontation and punitiveness and pressure. I wasn't labeling these qualities at the time. I was just noticing that our meetings were taking a toll on me.

There is a postscript. The company I almost joined closed down their Ohio office a few years after I ended our negotiations.

would have to do a go-around (that is, abort the landing and increase power and altitude for another attempt). After he got his license, Garvin retained that attitude. On one occasion he was coming in to land and at the last minute an airplane on a runway veered onto the runway he was coming in on. He reacted with annoyance and performed the go-around without any difficulty. That's when he realized how valuable his training had been. Because he was set to do the go-around, the incursion was just an annoyance. However, if he had been thinking only about landing, if his stance had been less poised for an unexpected disturbance, the need for an emergency reaction might have caught him by surprise, and perhaps caused him to freeze or make an error.

It's hard to maintain an active stance. If you have additional tasks and priorities competing for your attention, or if you're very tired or continually being interrupted, you'll be less alert for the early signs of problems.

One strategy that some senior executives use to maintain an active stance for picking up anomalies is to be more sensitive to their emotional reaction of surprise. If an event occurs that takes them aback, that doesn't make sense to them, they respond to their surprise as if it were an alarm, not by trying to dismiss it. Their experience base has primed them to inquire into things that surprise them or make them uncomfortable: "What's behind the personal loan by my vice president of sales that appears on the books?" "Why did the management committee spend over an hour discussing a problem in my organization?"

Organizational Barriers

Many organizations just want you to get your job done rather than be sensitive to potential difficulties. They'll encourage you to press on with your work rather than react to every little unexpected event. An organization may pay lip service to wanting honest criticism, when in fact it ignores or ostracizes critics. The alarmists in our midst are not always treated with respect. They may be seen as hypersensitive, as too nervous, as doubters. They spoil our mood.

One friend of mine described a meeting in which her manager

"What we didn't have but obviously needed was an alarmist."

Figure 6.2 The Alarmist

and group were discussing whether to bid on a new project. My friend argued against it. She pointed out how difficult the project was going to be. She reminded the group that they had done a similar project for this same client a year earlier, and they had lost money. She convinced the group to pass on this project. She probably saved the group $20,000 (based on the previous effort and the scope of this one), but no one expressed any appreciation. In the same meeting, she was congratulated on bringing another project in under budget, and making $12,000 for the company. People can acknowledge the successes, but they often have trouble appreciating the disasters that were avoided.

As a result, organizations can show a lot of inertia about detecting problems, particularly types of problems where the margin of safety is eroding.

What were the barriers to problem detection in Example 6.3? One barrier was that the different danger signals came from different sources. Some geologists raised an alarm about the seismic activity in

INTUITION AT WORK

The Teton Dam was built in 1972, and the engineers had great confidence in its safety. However, during its construction geologists discovered that the eastern Idaho region in which it was being built had recently had earthquakes—five earthquakes within thirty miles of the dam in the preceding five years, two of which were of substantial magnitude. Another concern of theirs was the evidence that dams can cause earthquakes. The geologists sent a memo to officials in the Bureau of Reclamation in Denver, Colorado, and Washington, D.C. But the officials objected to the emotional tone of the memo, and demanded that it be rewritten. Several rewrites were required to tone down the sense of urgency in the document, which was officially received six months after the initial version. Needless to say, the Bureau of Reclamation saw no reason to halt construction.

But there were other serious problems that needed to be addressed. Studies had shown that the rocks in the area were full of fissures. Rather than take this as another sign that building a dam in this area was a bad idea, the engineers' solution was to fill the fissures with grout. When the size of the fissures was discovered to be larger than expected (including some cracks that were actually caves) the amount of grouting was simply increased.

Still another problem had to do with the rate at which the dam was filled. A safe rate was calculated, but a project construction engineer requested permission to double the rate of fill, to handle runoffs from the heavy winter snows. The groundwater in nearby wells was checked for dangerous saturation by monitors. However, a month later it was discovered that the monitoring was faulty, and that three of the seventeen monitors were malfunctioning. Moreover, the monitors that were working showed that the groundwater was flowing at 1,000 times the rate that was expected. Nevertheless, the engineers continued to fill the dam, and even increased the rate to four times the normal rate.

Then three leaks were discovered downstream of the dam. These weren't considered problems because the leaks were running clear, and clear leaks are common in earth dams.

The next day, two more leaks were found, much larger ones, and before noon, the dam was breached, killing eleven people.

the area. Other geologists noted the fissures in the rocks. The engineers and their supervisors were aware of the increased fill rate and the problem with the monitors. But the organization was determined to proceed with the dam—that is, their stance was to remain task-oriented—and no one inside the organization was made responsible for putting together the cautionary data and sounding the alarm if necessary. The company had no procedure in place to sound an alarm.

Many organizations think they have procedures in place to catch problems in time but these procedures are almost never sufficient when people are faced with critical decisions that have to be made quickly.

For example, wildland firefighters have to balance their job of putting out a fire with knowing when to break off their efforts in order to reduce their risk. This is a difficult decision. It may mean abandoning a mission that has cost them many hours of labor. The "sunk cost" effect makes it difficult to just give up on a fire line that has taken all day to construct simply because there is a weather report that the humidity is supposed to drop or wind speeds are supposed to increase. To counter this resistance, the wildland firefighter community has developed a variety of checklists to help them recognize when they are in danger. They are trying to maintain an active stance to spot problems, using these checklists.

But checklists are not going to protect firefighters from freak accidents, so firefighters still have to judge for themselves when the margin of safety has gotten too small. Checklists are not a substitute for intuition and experience.

For example, one of the checklist items is to post lookouts at a forest fire. The lookouts are responsible for scanning the horizon for signs that the fire may be endangering the crew. But who gets assigned the lookout position? Sometimes it's the firefighter who is injured on that day, or one who is too slow, out of shape, or inexperienced to keep up with the rest of the crew. Lookouts don't go through a training program to prepare for their job. The firefighting teams are carrying out their tasks with the false sense of security that the lookouts are going to help protect them. The organization may have satisfied the checklist, but they really haven't increased their teams' chances of spotting danger.

Organizations can impose other barriers to problem detection. They can rely on outmoded or rigid procedures for collecting information. They can give the job of collecting data to the employees with the least experience. The list of organizational impediments can go on and on. It takes a rare and dedicated organization to be proactive in preventing problems rather than in taking the short-term view of pressing to stay on schedule.

Problem Detection: Reframing Our Interpretation of the Situation

When my colleagues and I started to study problem detection, we figured that peoples' suspicion was raised as they noticed cues and patterns and put the evidence together. They would see something that violated their expectations, and that would do it. And in many cases, this was true. But we also found a number of cases where the decision makers could only recognize the anomaly if they were already reframing the situation—interpreting it in a different and more worrisome way.

For example, in the case of the expert and novice NICU nurses, Linda was seeing an infant with a problem maintaining temperature, and was compensating by turning up the temperature in the isolette. But Darlene was seeing an infant in a downward spiral. If Darlene hadn't been so sensitive to the potential for sepsis she wouldn't have been looking at cues such as skin color.

You may reframe the situation after you spot the anomaly, or you may see the anomaly because you are already rethinking the situation, or you may do both simultaneously. Regardless of which happens, the outcome of problem detection is that *you see the situation differently*. This is the primary goal of the problem-detection process.

If you think you are having trouble reframing, call in colleagues to review the evidence with fresh eyes. They will not have spent hours or days becoming tied to any initial interpretation and may be better able to see things in a different light.

Now that we have discussed each aspect of the model of problem detection in Figure 6.1, let's put the model back together again. We can do this by considering Example 6.4.

This incident embodies the problem-detection process at work. A

When it was constructed in 1977, the Citicorp tower in Manhattan was the seventh-tallest building in the world. William J. LeMessurier (pronounced "LeMeasure") was the structural engineer who designed the steel skeleton of the building.

The following year, an engineering student called LeMessurier to ask about the design. The student believed that LeMessurier had put the four columns holding up the building in the wrong place. Instead of locating the columns at the corners of the building, LeMessurier had put them in the center of each side.

LeMessuier explained the reason for this design. Citicorp needed to use the entire block for its building, but a church occupied one of the corners. The church and the bank arranged a compromise whereby Citicorp would replace the old church building with a new one, and Citicorp would gain access to the space above it. The compromise required that the four supports be placed in the center of each side.

LeMessurier had created an unusual system of wind braces to compensate for this design feature. LeMessurier also explained that he had been concerned about quartering winds that could come from a diagonal across two sides of the building at once, increasing the forces on both. The supports were positioned to resist these forces.

After finishing his conversation with the student, LeMessurier realized that the design of the Citicorp skeleton would be a good topic to discuss with his own engineering class. As he mused about his presentation, he thought again about the design of the wind braces. He had established that these braces were sufficiently strong to handle perpendicular winds, the only calculations required by the building code of New York City. But after talking on the phone about quartering winds, LeMessurier wondered how well the wind braces would work against these.

He made the calculations and discovered something unpleasant. The wind braces were arranged into chevron-shaped units, and each tier had eight units. A quartering wind would increase the strain on half of these units by 40 percent. That was much more than LeMessurier had expected.

Ordinarily, this finding wouldn't have been a cause for concern. Buildings are designed to have excess strength, as a margin of safety. However, LeMessurier had made a discovery only a few weeks earlier. He had been called in to review plans for two new skyscrapers in Pittsburgh. These buildings were going to use the same wind brace design as the Citicorp building and, like the Citicorp building, the design was calling for welded joints, rather than joints that are bolted together. (Welded joints are much stronger, but require more labor, and therefore cost more.)

While working on his Pittsburgh project, LeMessurier had asked one of his associates about the process of using welded joints. The associate had explained that this design feature had been changed for the Citicorp building. The welding process was seen as too expensive. The joints had been bolted, not welded. No one had informed LeMessurier because there were many design change details like this. To check each one would have slowed down the building process too much.

The decision to use bolts instead of welded joints had made sense to LeMessurier when he learned about it in Pittsburgh. But now, a few weeks later, he nervously connected these two pieces of information. The wind braces were not as effective as he had imagined against winds coming against the building from a diagonal direction. And the bolted joints were not as strong as the welded joints would have been. Making the link between these two data points marked the instant of problem detection for LeMessurier.

He still hoped that the design team had considered diagonal winds when they designed the bolts. But later, when he checked into this, he found out that they had not. Why? The building code did not require it.

Even worse, he learned that his building team had defined the diagonal wind braces as trusses, not as columns. In doing so, they were able to evade a stringent safety specification regarding the required strength of joints, and could get away with using many fewer bolts holding the joints together. Trusses are exempt from this safety factor.

By now, LeMessurier was not feeling very confident in the design. He wrote up his discoveries in a report he titled "Project SERENE"—Special Engineering Review of Events Nobody Envisioned.

He called in a Canadian expert to review his new data, using wind tunnel analyses from the original design. The results confirmed LeMessurier's fears. Under the right conditions, the winds could set the building vibrating like a tuning fork. LeMessurier next checked the weather data for New York City. The right conditions occurred, on average, every sixteen years. To LeMessurier, that frequency was intolerably low.

His design had included a damping system to reduce sway, but it depended

cont.

Example 6.4 (cont.)

on electrical power, and a major storm might create outages. He could not count on it to work. By this time, it was July of 1978, with the fall hurricane season approaching.

LeMessurier blew the whistle on himself. He contacted the building architect, and the architect's lawyers, and then Citicorp's executive vice president. He explained the problem and described the repairs that would be necessary to strengthen the critical connections that were most vulnerable. His suggestion was to weld two-inch-thick steel plates over each of the vulnerable bolted joints—more than 200 of them. Citicorp went along with the plan. To avoid panic, Citicorp issued a public release about how the work was to strengthen the wind-bracing system through additional welding. A Citicorp representative explained that, "We wear both belts and suspenders here."

The welders went to work, but only after office hours, from 5:00 P.M. until 4:00 A.M., with cleanup crews taking over before the first secretaries arrived. This schedule continued for a month. The Citicorp building itself was wired up with strain gauges that read data to a nearby monitoring center. The building, still in use, looked like a patient in an intensive care unit.

Then, on September 1, Hurricane Ella made its appearance off Cape Hatteras, heading for New York. Most of the critical joints of the building had been repaired by then, but there was no great enthusiasm for testing the braces just yet. Fortunately, Ella changed course and headed out to sea.

By October, the repairs were completed. The building had now been transformed into one of the safest structures in the city.

---

hidden problem was noticed, by accident. It took expertise to fit two pieces of a puzzle together. It took intuition to recognize that something could be very wrong and needed to be investigated.

The type of problem troubling LeMessurier was a reduction in the margin of safety, as opposed to a defect that was actively spreading through the structure. Many barriers made it hard to detect this problem: There were multiple causes, as the design was altered and the cumulative changes were not charted. Further, there were competing priorities—the successive modifications were made in different contexts and by different people. From an organizational viewpoint, there were production pressures and building codes to worry about. Expertise could not easily be brought into play because of the mindset that as long as everyone complied with the building codes, the structure was safe. There were no building codes or procedures, however, for a backtrack review of what had been done once the design was changed.

The building safety became compromised by a series of design decisions, none of which were critical on their own. Only a person who had tracked the entire process and realized the implications would notice the cumulative impact. Only a person who was worried about safety would have gone back to audit the history of the construction.

No one except LeMessurier had taken an active stance looking for problems, because no one expected that there were any. Although the published account of this incident doesn't address this, my speculation is that LeMessurier only spotted the problem because he was able to reframe his perception of the building he had designed. His discovery in Pittsburgh must have shaken him—the building he thought was so strong turned out to have been compromised. So he was viewing it differently. As a result, LeMessurier was more troubled than he might otherwise have been by the idea of the quartering winds that emerged from his telephone conversation with the engineering student. I wonder if LeMessurier would have done the calculations about the effect of quartering winds if he had not made the discovery in Pittsburgh.

We see the effect of LeMessurier's experience and his intuition. Once he had reframed his understanding of the Citicorp building, he knew where to look for more evidence, and how to test his fears. Instead of commissioning a study that might drag out for many months, LeMessurier was able to sort out the problem in a few weeks. He did most of the work himself, because of his desire to maintain secrecy in case his worries were groundless. Yet the fact that he did this investigation himself meant that it was done quickly and—to his mind—competently. He was much like Darlene in Chapter 1. He was looking at the building, his patient, in a skeptical way, terribly aware of the possibility of breakdown.

Steps of a PreMortem

Step 1: Preparation.

Step 2: Imagine a fiasco.

Step 3 Generate reasons for failure.

Step 4: Consolidate the lists.

Step 5: Revisit the plan.

Step 6: Periodically review the list.

How to Manage Uncertainty 7

ome of our most desperate appeals to intuition come when we are wrestling with uncertainty. In facing a decision, we can be uncertain about many things. We can be uncertain about what type of problem we are dealing with. We can be uncertain about what is going to happen in the future. We may be uncertain about what resources we have, and what to do if there aren't enough. Even if we fully understand our dilemma and our available options, we may be uncertain about which option to choose.

In business, these types of uncertainty are pervasive. We struggle with how much to pay for supplies, and how much to charge for services. We speculate about whether demand for our services and/or products will be going up or down.

> ### DECISION GAME 7.1 THE CELLMET

You are the CEO of a manufacturing company that produces bicycle accessories such as odometers, storage racks, and helmets. Your newest line is the Cellmet, a bicycle helmet with a built-in cell phone that is powered by the bicycle itself and does not need batteries. This enables busy people to exercise while also catching up on telephone calls. Your company has been in business for fourteen years, and last year the revenues hit $12M. The Cellmet seems to have caught on with customers. Sales have increased dramatically each quarter for the past year and a half. You introduced the Cellmet over a year ago, in June, and the latest figures are from December.

At first, you made the Cellmet using machinery at one of your plants. Then you devoted that entire plant to the product. Later you added a third shift. You increased capacity by converting a second plant to manufacture the items. Even that isn't enough to keep up with demand. Your marketing director is forecasting a sales increase of 50 percent for the first quarter of the next calendar year, compared to the first quarter of this year. That means a monthly average of about 2,200 Cellmets. She is also warning that if you don't act quickly to meet demand, your competitors will move in and take over this market.

Your vice president of operations has provided you with a plan to build a large new factory. He has scouted out the space, figured out the construction, and believes it can be up and running in ten months. The cost will be high, around $8M, but it will double your production. Currently, you are manufacturing 1,500 per month at $130. By doubling capacity, you will recover your costs in less than two years.

This is your moment. You have worked hard to design and advertise this product. You were hoping for a favorable consumer response. You got it. What are you waiting for? Do you give the thumbs up for the new factory?

Take five minutes and write down all the sources of uncertainty, all the things you don't know enough about to confidently make this decision.

What don't you know? You don't know if the sales will hold up. You don't know about potential competitors. You don't know the point at which you will saturate the market. You don't know about market demands in different countries. You don't know if accidents will be blamed on this device, causing negative publicity. You don't know if the devices might have additional uses. You don't know how the United States economy will be doing in ten months. You don't know how distracting the factory construction will be.

You might recognize this type of expansion as a classic "sucker hole," in which a business calculates a simple continuing trend, overexpands to meet the forecasted demand, and winds up with excess capacity as a business cycle asserts itself. There are many historical precedents for building excessive capacity as a result of mistakenly overestimating demand. But maybe this time you will be the exception.

Managers and executives are continually pressed to make decisions in the face of uncertainty. Secretary of State Colin Powell has claimed that if he ever was less than 40 percent confident, he needed to gather more information. But we can't wait for all the data before taking action. Colin Powell also said that if he was more than 70 percent confident, he had probably gathered too much information.

Some researchers have tried to tame the concept of uncertainty. They have tried to treat it as a commodity that could be scaled. In performing decision analyses, clients might be asked to estimate the likelihood for different outcomes in a diagram known as a "decision tree." They might be asked to estimate the satisfaction they would derive for each of the outcomes as the decision tree unfolds. Then, through simple calculation, the analyst could calculate which outcome was preferred—the one with the greatest anticipated satisfaction coupled with the highest likelihood of occurring. This only addresses one type of uncertainty, though, the uncertainty about which outcomes will occur. This approach keeps the emphasis on which action to choose, as opposed to understanding the situation. But once the decision makers have a good sense of the problem, they usually don't have difficulty selecting a course of action.

I have had the good fortune to conduct several research projects that were sponsored by the U.S. Marine Corps to make sense of the types of uncertainty that Marines frequently face. Three primary factors repeatedly come into play, and these seem to generalize to most settings:

    a. The source of the uncertainty. There are more different sources than you might think.

    b. The type of tactics available for handling the uncertainty. Most people don't appreciate the large repertoire of tactics available to them.

    c. The decision maker's personal tolerance for ambiguity. People have different personal styles and are sometimes surprised that others don't share their feelings about uncertainty.

To become more effective at managing uncertainty, you can strengthen your intuitions about all three of these factors.

Before we discuss these three topics further, think about the current projects or decisions you are facing. Now, select one where your uncertainty is keeping you from moving forward. Hopefully, by the end of this chapter you'll have a better sense of what's troubling you with the project and what to do about it.

Five Sources of Uncertainty

The five sources of uncertainty are missing information, unreliable information, conflicting information, noisy information, and confusing information. Just because they are all called by the same term, "uncertainty," we should not treat them as equivalent.

We can be uncertain because we are *missing* important information. We may not have it, or we may not be able to locate it if it is buried in an information overload. Either way, we cannot access the information when we need it.

We can be uncertain because we aren't able to *trust* the information, even if we have it. We may suspect it is erroneous, or outdated, or that we are receiving the same report from several different sources. Even if the information is perfectly accurate, our doubt about it will create uncertainty that will affect our decision making.

We may have the information and trust it, but it might be *inconsistent* with other information we have and trust. If this is the case, we are facing an anomaly.

We may have to sift through a lot of irrelevant information—*noise*—but if we can't be sure if it really is noise, we have to take it seriously and that adds to our uncertainty. We are often being bombarded with data and we don't have an easy way to recognize the noise so we can be confident that it's okay to ignore it.

We may have all the information we need, trust all of it, find that it is all consistent, find that it is all relevant, but we could still be uncertain if we cannot *interpret* it. This would happen if the data were so complex that we couldn't build a coherent story for purposes of explanation. Or else the data allow more than one reasonable interpretation.

The reason to ask yourself these various questions is that the way you would respond to missing information about a problem could be different from the way you would respond to doubts about the quality of data regarding future trends. If the CEO in the decision game realizes that it's important to know why customers are buying the Cellmet, how they are using it, what they like about it, and what is frustrating them, then it's necessary to allocate money for market research to get inside the heads of the customers. Or, the CEO may worry that the appeal of novelty technology may be diminishing, so now the research to be ordered would be geared toward general forecasts for the economy and for electronic gizmos in general.

For the work project that's important to you, list the things you are uncertain about. Once you have compiled your list, try to map the items onto the set of five uncertainty sources. Are you struggling with missing data or with making sense of the data you have? Sometimes we keep trying to get more data to avoid admitting our inability to interpret the information at hand.

Tactics for Managing Uncertainty

There are many ways to handle uncertainty, and the larger your repertoire of tactics the more flexible and efficient you can be. Over the years I have compiled a wide variety of tactics used by skilled decision makers.

Delaying

You don't always have to make a decision right when a problem presents itself. In many cases, the crisis that got everyone worked up yesterday turns out not to have been a big deal today. Skilled decision makers have a good intuition about what is a real crisis, and so they can safely delay making a move in the hope that, as time passes, they will learn more. However, some people make the mistake of delaying because they're afraid of making a tough decision under uncertainty. You don't want to lose an opportunity while waiting to get perfect information. This is where your intuition is needed, to help you gauge when the delay makes sense because the situation is likely to resolve itself or because more information is likely to come in.

Seeking More Information

Demanding more information is the classical reaction to uncertainty. Sometimes it makes sense, but people often use information-seeking as a way to buy more time. This strategy looks better than merely delaying because at least you are doing something. But really, all you're doing is wasting energy. There's no point in trying to turn a good plan into a perfect one.

If you do need to gather more data, you will need intuitions about how to do this. Skilled decision makers know when to seek more information, and can gauge whether the information is sufficiently valuable and is likely to arrive in time to make a difference.

Increasing Attention

If you're faced with a major decision and your uncertainty is very high, you may want to change your stance to become more active in monitoring the situation—perhaps calling for more frequent updates on how the problem is playing out. This is different from seeking information because you're not trying to obtain any specific data. Rather, you're monitoring an ongoing situation so you can make your move at just the right moment. However, don't overdo it. For instance, at LexisNexis, top management adopted a strategy to review every project quarterly. The motivation was a good one—to more closely track the ongoing projects. However the result was that the project managers believed *they* were being evaluated every three months, and that no project had full management commitment. The policy of quarterly project reviews resulted in a constant level of panic within the company.

Filling the Gaps with Assumptions

Instead of gathering more data you can reduce uncertainty by making assumptions about what the missing data are likely to be. This is obviously a little risky, but we all need to make assumptions or we couldn't proceed very far. In some settings people are cautioned to track all their assumptions so that they can double back later and check them. This advice sounds good, but we commonly make so many assumptions that it's an impractical exercise. The CEO of the Cellmet manufacturing plant assumes that there will not be shortages of the basic materials needed to make the Cellmets, local regulations requiring cyclists to wear helmets will be upheld, and so forth. Instead of trying to track all the assumptions, you can rely on your intuition to flag the assumptions that strike you as tenuous.

Building an Interpretation

Once you've collected all of your data you can try to paint a picture of the decision at hand. This strategy goes beyond merely filling in gaps. It is about making sense of a situation—constructing explanations, categorizing situations, correcting interpretations. The process of sensemaking is very important for intuitive decision making and I'll cover it more in Chapter 8.

Pressing On

Despite our preference to have all the information we need before making a tough decision, there are times when we have to realize this isn't going to happen. Colin Powell's comment about not needing more than 70 percent confidence shows his readiness to live with uncertainty.

Shaking the Tree

Sometimes the best way to handle uncertainty is to conduct a preemptive strike against it, to actively shape your environment. Instead of worrying about whether a competitor is preparing to cut costs, you can preemptively cut costs and make your competitor react to you. You may not be sure if your organization can deliver a new product on time, but you can challenge your staff to meet the aggressive timetable you set up. Consider Sony's strategy of rapidly introducing new products. That way, Sony doesn't have to worry about imitators. Sony's products are long gone by the time another company tries to imitate them.

One research study found that senior executives often initiated a course of action simply to learn more about an issue: "We bought that company because we wanted to learn about that business," one person explained. The managers were not comfortable in the passive role as analysts. They needed hands-on experience.

Designing Decision Scenarios

In his book *The Art of the Long View*, Peter Schwartz describes how managers can build decision scenarios to try to make sense of a situation, and to communicate to others the dynamics of the problem and the assumptions the decision makers were counting on. The decision scenarios illustrate possible ways the current situation could play out in the future. Schwartz suggests only using a few scenarios, because people become confused if they have to track too many hypothetical situations. You aren't trying to make predictions with a decision scenario; rather, you are trying to build a richer mental model. In some ways, decision scenarios resemble decision games—both are ways to learn through exploring dilemmas and tradeoffs.

Simplifying the Plan

Another way to reduce uncertainty is to reduce the complexity of the plan you are formulating. For example, you can make your plan more modular so the tasks can stand on their own. (The contrast is to a very interactive plan where every task influences the others.) A modular plan lets you gain flexibility. The failure of one part may not endanger the others. We can make changes in one part of a modular plan without worrying about how the changes will affect the other parts. Interactive plans usually are more efficient but they are more brittle and riskier than modular plans. As our uncertainty increases, we want to give ourselves the capability of altering parts of the plan when we later carry it out and learn more about the situation.

Preparing for the Worst

Besides simplifying your plan of action you also want to plan for the worst, to make sure that you haven't left yourself vulnerable. Adding more resources—more funding, more team members—is one way to make a plan more robust. There are other things you can do to harden the plan and reduce risks. For example, when preparing to take on a new product a company might budget for a year of flat revenues so that it doesn't get caught short.

Using Incremental Decisions

One of the most common tactics for handling uncertainty is to take an incremental approach. Instead of deciding all the issues at once, you can make a small investment and see if it works. You don't always have to commit to a new product. You can authorize the design team to try a few ideas out. You can authorize the engineering studies to prepare for manufacturing the item. Through these small steps you allow yourself the opportunity to learn, to get feedback, to make improvements. This approach has severe drawbacks. It signals that you are not fully committed, and this can reduce the enthusiasm of the team. If you use this tactic, you need to be careful not to be trapped by "sunk cost" arguments. Proponents for a program may argue that it's a shame to waste the initial investment by discontinuing the effort. Your job is to treat this initial investment as a cost of doing business, not a stake that has to be recouped.

Embracing the Uncertainty

If you think your organization is more adaptive than your competitors' organization, then uncertainty is on your side, and the more uncertainty the better. The idea of embracing uncertainty goes beyond simply accepting it—here we are talking about valuing uncertainty for what it adds.

Some senior managers make a virtue of uncertainty. In Dan Isenberg's research, one manager explained that ambiguities "yield a certain freedom you need as a chief executive officer not to be nailed down on everything. Also, certain people thrive on ambiguity, so I leave certain things ambiguous. The fact is we tie ourselves too much to linear plans, to clear time scales. I like to fuzz up time scales completely." Isenberg notes that ambiguity can be particularly helpful in dealing with competing stakeholders. If managers are too clear about their opinions, there is a good chance of antagonizing one side or another. Ambiguity is a smokescreen that preserves harmony while an organization works its problems out.

We can embrace uncertainty when we treat our plans as platforms for change. If you fall in love with your plans, if you get frustrated when you have to deviate from your plans, you will find it difficult to adopt a flexible attitude.

Putting the Tactics to Work for You

P lease take out the sheet listing the sources of uncertainty with which you are currently wrestling. For each of the sources of uncertainty you have listed, review the tactics in this section to see which ones you currently are using, and which ones you could be using. By taking stock of the tactics available, you might get some ideas about how to get what you want.

Tolerance for Ambiguity

T he easiest assumption to make about others is that they are basically like us. This is a good starting point, but it's not necessarily accurate. Research has shown that decision makers can be very different in their reactions to uncertainty. Some of us become uncomfortable when we have to make a choice amidst a great deal of ambiguity. Others don't seem to mind—it's almost as if they like the risk.

Do you know your profile? Do you have a greater tolerance for ambiguity than the average person, or a lower tolerance?

There is an easy way to find out. Stanley Budner developed a scale to help you identify your own style. It is used both in psychological research and in business applications such as personnel selection.

To measure your tolerance for ambiguity, indicate the extent to which you agree or disagree with the following statements. Fill in the blanks with the number from the rating scale that best represents your evaluation of the item.

RATING SCALE

1 Strongly Disagree	5 Slightly Agree
2 Moderately Disagree	6 Moderately Agree
3 Slightly Disagree	7 Strongly Agree
4 Neither Agree nor Disagree	

_____ *1.* An expert who doesn't come up with a definite answer probably doesn't know too much.

_____ *2.* I would like to live in a foreign country for a while.

_____ *3.* There is really no such thing as a problem that can't be solved.

_____ *4.* People who fit their lives to a schedule probably miss most of the joy of living.

_____ *5.* A good job is one where what is to be done and how it is to be done are always clear.

_____ *6.* It is more fun to tackle a complicated problem than to solve a simple one.

_____ *7.* In the long run it is possible to get more done by tackling small, simple problems rather than large and complicated ones.

_____ *8.* Often the most interesting and stimulating people are those who don't mind being different and original.

_____ *9.* What we are used to is always preferable to what is unfamiliar.

_____ *10.* People who insist upon a yes or no answer just don't know how complicated things really are.

_____ *11.* A person who leads an even, regular life in which few surprises or unexpected happenings arise really has a lot to be grateful for.

_____ 12. Many of our most important decisions are based upon insufficient information.

_____ 13. I like parties where I know most of the people more than ones where all or most of the people are complete strangers.

_____ 14. Teachers or supervisors who hand out vague assignments give one a chance to show initiative and originality.

_____ 15. The sooner we all acquire similar values and ideals the better.

_____ 16. A good teacher is one who makes you wonder about your way of looking at things.

To score this scale, add up all the ratings you made for the odd-numbered items. Next, reverse-score the even-numbered items. For example, if you filled out a "1" for an even-numbered question, score it as a "7," if you answered "2," it becomes a "6" and so on. The reason is that the test was designed so that your answers wouldn't all cluster on one end (all 6s and 7s) or the other (all 1s and 2s).

The average range of tolerance for most people is 44–48. If you score higher than 48, this suggests you have a lower tolerance for ambiguity than most people. And if your score is less than 44, your tolerance is higher than average.

Some of the tactics for dealing with uncertainty that were listed in this chapter must seem more reasonable to you than others. Does this fit with what you've learned about your tolerance for ambiguity?

Developing Your Intuitions About Uncertainty

As you practice figuring out the uncertainty in decision-making situations, it should become easier for you to see what you're up against. When you use the decision-making critique, described in Chapter 3, you can add questions about the types of uncertainty you face and the tactics you've used to manage uncertainty.

You can actively pay attention in meetings to the types of uncertainty that are hanging the group up, the types of tactics people are suggesting, and any relevant uncertainty management tactics that are being ignored. You can try to pick up personality differences in tolerance for ambiguity, and see if these are creating conflicts. As your eye gets keener, you will be building up intuitions about managing uncertainty more effectively.

The PreMortem can also help you identify areas of uncertainty, in order to prepare plans to handle the uncertainty.

It makes little sense for you to force yourself to use tactics that don't fit your personal style. These tactics will not be natural for you, and you won't have the intuitive moves to make them work and to adjust them readily. Instead, you might consider working differently with others on your team. Maybe their styles can complement yours.

In preparing to manage uncertainty for future projects you may find it helpful to use this uncertainty management worksheet.

1. Identify a current project, program, or initiative in your life that is struggling somewhat because of uncertainty.

2. List the things you don't know or are confused about—the sources of your uncertainty.

3. For each one, write down the type of uncertainty you're facing.

Table 7.1	Uncertainty Management Worksheet

1. Name of Project: _____

2. List the <u>things</u> you are uncertain about:	3. Type of uncertainty for each:	4. Relevant tactics you could be using:

- You can be uncertain because you are *missing* important information.

- You can be uncertain because you *distrust* the information, even if you have it.

- You may have the information and trust it, but it might be *inconsistent* with other information you have and trust.

- You may have to sift through a lot of irrelevant information—*noise*.

- You may have all the information you need, trust all of it, find that it is all consistent, find that it is all relevant, but you could still be uncertain if it *is too complex for you to interpret*.

4. For each area of uncertainty, look at the list of uncertainty management tactics and select all the relevant ones.

5. Identify all the *relevant* tactics you could be using but aren't.

6. How do your tactics line up with your tolerance for ambiguity?

7. Now, do you have any ideas for how to proceed more effectively?

UNCERTAINTY MANAGEMENT TACTICS

- Delaying
- Seeking more Information
- Increasing attention
- Filling gaps with assumptions
- Building an interpretation
- Pressing on
- Shaking the tree
- Designing decision scenarios
- Simplifying the plan
- Preparing for the worst
- Using incremental decisions
- Embracing the uncertainty

I hope this exercise is useful for you. But remember that the exercise is only a tool. From the standpoint of intuition skills training, it is more important that you learn to intuitively respond to uncertainty with the appropriate tactics than to do a compulsive job of filling out the worksheet.

How to Size Up Situations   8

A s you've learned, our intuitions alert us to the facts of any given situation, and they help us recognize what to do. This process is central to the recognition-primed decision model discussed in Chapter 2—you see the cues, you recognize the patterns, and you recognize how to react. But it isn't always this simple. What if you don't see any patterns? What if you see more than one pattern? We have to look more deeply into this process of making meaningful interpretations of events.

Karl Weick, a researcher at the University of Michigan, has introduced the term "sensemaking" to describe what happens when we size up situations. For example, we may be performing a task and detect an anomaly. The surprise we feel signals us that we need to reinterpret the way we understand the situation. Because of this, we will search for more discrepant cues that might have been missed earlier, but are now seen as relevant. We generate stories and explanations to account for the discrepancies.

We need to make sense of situations in order to figure out "the problem of the day" (as weather forecasters call it)—the potential trouble spots we have to track closely. We need to make sense of situations in order to anticipate how a proposed change in a plan is going to play out and what kinds of difficulties might result. We need to make sense of situations in order to appreciate what we can realistically accomplish.

Let's begin our examination of how to size up situations with a decision game. The objective of this game is for you to make sense of a situation as you receive more information, and to understand how the changes in the situation affect your ability to perform a project.

Background: You are a mid-level employee at an information technology company. You work in a group that develops, adapts, and customizes databases for clients. Your company once had 600 employees, but a recent economic downturn has affected revenues, and the company is down to 450 employees.

Because the workload has gotten light, the company president has decided to turn this to an advantage by proceeding with some internal research and development projects. You submitted an idea for a project to develop a new type of interactive database that can be used through cell phones. The concept was given high ratings, and you were told to start work and lead the effort. The president expects the lull in work to be temporary, so you have to stay within your schedule of building a prototype in eight months. You will be evaluated on the basis of meeting that schedule and turning out an impressive demo. This is a chance for important visibility, and you're enthusiastic about the opportunity.

You have the full-time services of a staff of twelve people, including yourself as leader. You have six others from your department, plus another two human factors specialists on loan, plus another three communications specialists, also on loan. In addition, you also have arranged for a key piece of software to be developed by your company's software team.

Task: What follows is a series of announcements. Cover them up and then move the cover down, showing each announcement in turn. *If you see an announcement that seems significant, write down your interpretation of how the announcement affects your project.* You should determine if you can still meet your goals of schedule and performance in light of the announcements you feel are worth paying attention to. Most of the announcements will have no effect at all, so do not feel you have to write something for each item.

1. A competitor has announced the near completion of a product that in some ways is similar to yours.

2. An additional twenty layoffs are announced for your company, but none of these is from your team or your group.

3. The president of your company announces a hiring freeze that is absolute and (hopefully) temporary.

4. An experienced marketing executive tells you that she is dubious about the competitor's announcement. They have made similar claims about vaporware in the past, and her inside sources are hinting that they're just trying to discourage others from moving into this area.

5. Good news! Your company wins a large contract with an insurance company to increase the usability of links from the Web to customer service.

6. Your project is now starting its third month and is on schedule.

7. Good news! Your company announces that a new contract has been signed for a project to develop software for a major bank.

8. A different competitor has just hired some of the former employees of your company who had been laid off a few months earlier.

9. The company's financials show a lot of red ink. Your company lost a fair amount of money in the preceding quarter.

10. Rumors are circulating that your parent company is unhappy with the revenue picture. Some are speculating that your president may be replaced soon.

11. Good news! Another large new contract is signed, with work set to begin in the next month. Many are hoping that this is signaling a turnaround for your company.

12. You hear that the management information systems department requested a waiver of the hiring freeze, but this was denied.

13. Two people from your database group announce their resignations. They each describe different reasons, but some are suspecting that the revenue uncertainty is taking its toll on morale. Neither of the people is from your project team.

14. A company email announces that there will be a move in the next three months to a new office complex, as a way to cut costs.

15. You receive reassurances from upper management about the long-term importance of your project.

16. Your project is now starting its fourth month and is on schedule.

17. You are informed that the software group may be unable to

deliver the programs that you need. The task is more difficult than they had anticipated.

18. The communications systems specialists complain to you that they are getting pressure to work on the new contracts that have just come through, because those will generate revenue.

19. You hear from a secretary that the problem with the software program was that the developers were being pulled into the bank software effort, and that is why they are lagging in delivering what they promised.

20. You overhear a lunchroom discussion about how senior management may be getting ready to rescind the hiring freeze, or at least make it less inclusive.

21. You have a productive meeting with the software group. You are able to redesign the program to cut down on the number of its features so you can keep on schedule.

22. Your project is now starting its fifth month, and seems to be falling behind schedule, although the changes you made to reduce the system features makes your progress difficult to estimate.

23. The human factors specialists on your team have missed the last two scheduled meetings. Their excuse is that they have to start ramping up for the insurance company usability project.

24. A senior vice president announces that she is taking early retirement.

25. The financial department has started issuing daily graphics showing that the revenue curves are heading up again.

26. Your manager tells you that over half of your team is being reassigned to projects for clients, to increase the revenue stream. You are losing both human factors specialists, all three of the communications specialists, and two of the database specialists. You are asked to wrap up your effort by using the remaining personnel to document progress thus far, so that the effort can be mothballed until the financial picture improves.

This sequence of events is unfortunately not atypical. The moves made by upper management in this scenario are frustrating, and would certainly sap your morale, but you know they make good sense. It is the final move that crushes you—the loss of more than half your team. Look back over your notes. When did you see this coming? Did it hit you by surprise when you read item 26, or were you picking up the signals earlier?

In some ways, this is like a vision test. Anyone can see what's wrong after reading item 26. In running this game with a variety of people, however, I have found many who see trouble earlier, by item 23 or item 19. One person wrote next to item 17 "This is the first major hitch" and then added "Things are now unraveling" next to 18, and "Major problems" next to 19.

But if you're looking carefully at patterns that emerge, the situation can come into focus even earlier than that. Some experienced intuitive decision makers are nervous almost from the beginning, from items 5 and 7. They see the contradiction between starting a project to use surplus labor while preparing to downsize to reduce the labor surplus, and needing to get the surplus labor tied into funded work. The hiring freeze (3), too, could turn out to have some important implications if demand for services picks up. The new contracts (5, 7 and 11) also pose risks because skilled employees are going to be diverted into revenue-generating work. The loss of two people from the database group (14) reduces the surplus capacity while workload is picking up. How many of these connections did you make?

If you're a manager you might want to ask people on your team to go through the same game. Don't just track how quickly they saw that the project was going to lose its staff. See how colleagues with less experience read the situation, and compare their answers to yours. Or try this with a veteran to see that person's thought processes. You'll learn a lot from observing the different way the veteran interprets the messages and the situation.

This decision game shows how sensemaking is related to the other processes we have been discussing. The faster you put together the pieces of a potential problem, the faster you can make decisions about accelerating your schedule to generate at least some products before you lose your team. Picking up the picture faster means that you have spotted the problem earlier, and have reduced uncertainty—you are alert to a possible outcome and can start preparing for it.

The lance corporal in Example 8.1 didn't see any of this. Like Linda, the NICU nurse in Chapter 1, he could register the events but he couldn't go beyond the events. It's this ability that makes it seem that experts can "see the invisible."

> *EXAMPLE 8.1 THE INVISIBLE ADVERSARY*

John Schmitt is a former Marine who is highly skilled at making sense of tactical situations. In one exercise, John shadowed a squad of relatively inexperienced corporals and sergeants as they moved through open terrain in southern California, at Camp Pendleton. The instructors controlling the exercise—and acting as "the enemy"—called in mortar attacks, sniper fire, and mine explosions to decimate the team. After this had gone on for a while, John asked a young lance corporal what kind of adversary they were up against. "Dunno," was the response. "The enemy is just clobbering us." Further questions to probe more deeply went nowhere. To the lance corporal, it was undifferentiated mayhem.

To John, though, it was obvious that the squad (typically around 20 Marines) was facing at least a platoon (about 40 soldiers), or more, probably even a company (about 150–200 soldiers). He knew this because of the mortar rounds—there had to be forward observers to call them in. And mortars are weapons that usually belong to companies or battalions, not to platoons. John was keeping track of the number of enemy contacts that had been reported—but if he could account for a platoon based on the actual contacts, there were probably many more soldiers they hadn't yet encountered. Therefore, they were almost certainly facing a larger force than a platoon. And the area covered by these different contacts suggested that they were facing a company. Further, the mining of the team's path showed how their adversary planned a defensive operation and a commitment of effort. This implied a force that was certainly larger than a squad. The mortars and mines and snipers all seemed to be trying to channel them off of the paths and into a nearby field that was probably the intended killing zone.

In industry, effective managers and executives have developed their intuition to see patterns that are invisible to people without a solid base of experience.

An expert like Baker in Example 8.2 had little trouble categorizing the type of business in which this company was engaged. In contrast, the owner-manager didn't realize there were any other ways to operate the company. Why? Because the owner didn't have the experience base to recognize different patterns. He was powerless to fix his problem because he didn't understand what it was.

Bob Baker is a business advisor who's worked with start-up and closely held companies for thirty years. On one occasion Baker was brought in to assist a company that was configuring and selling computers to businesses. The company was hitting its revenue and sales goals, but it wasn't making much money and the profits were declining, not increasing. The CEO couldn't understand it.

Baker spent a little time getting the CEO to describe his business model, and then quickly recognized the problem. "You're killing the customer," Baker explained.

The business model was to sell a customer—usually a business client, but sometimes a school—a new and expensive computer system. Once the sale was made, though, the customer disappeared. The company had to start from zero each month and find a whole new batch of customers. The costs of this zero start-up were grinding the company down. The CEO hadn't realized this dynamic, but Baker had seen it so often that it had formed a distinct category in his mental model of businesses—he called it the "killing the customer" model.

The company had started in 1989 and had $11M in sales by 1997. Its gross profit was 19 percent. But it was using all of its $1.5M line of credit, plus spending a great deal to attract new customers. So, as a result, it was just above the break-even point. After more than a decade of hard work, frustration was setting in for the employees and the CEO.

Baker helped the company change its model. He explained that the business clients just wanted to get customized hardware and had their own specialists to support the systems. So there wasn't much gain in pursuing a continuing relationship with them. In contrast, schools didn't have much need to customize the hardware they purchased, but schools were also generally too small to have their own information technology specialists, so they needed continuing service and project support. Therefore, it made sense to refocus the business to provide services to schools through long-term contracts. By making schools the primary client, the company could get out of the "kill the customer" category.

Previously 80 percent of the company's sales were to businesses and 20 percent were to schools. After the transition, 20 percent of its sales were to businesses and 80 percent to schools. The company stayed profitable all through the transition. Its sales decreased to $6M, but its gross margins went from 19 percent up to 41 percent. And it wasn't using any of its line of credit. In this way, the company's cash flow reversed from perpetually negative to reliably positive.

Sensemaking is hard for novices who lack the experience to notice patterns. It gets even harder if the situation is "noisy." Let's explore the nature of noise, to see what we are up against.

Noise

Making sense of a situation is not merely putting the pieces together, recognizing a pattern, or building a story. Often we may struggle to figure out what the pieces are in the first place. This is particularly hard if the background has a lot of noise. For instance, it's easy to follow a news broadcast coming from a radio in a quiet room. But turn on more than one radio and set them to different stations and it gets difficult.

Try this: Sign your name twice on a piece of paper. Draw a single line through the first signature. That doesn't make much of a difference in its readability, does it? Draw another line, and another. You can still probably read your signature. Now take the second signature and simply write a different name over it, perhaps that of a high school teacher. Compare how much harder it is to read this signature because of the way you added noise. I am defining noise as irrelevant data that overlaps the relevant data you need to "read" when making a decision. It is one of the sources of uncertainty that we considered in Chapter 7.

A noisy background contains its own cues and patterns that intersect with the ones that are relevant to you. The variety of connections opens up more and more possible ways to interpret the problem you face. When you crossed out your signature, the straight line didn't add much noise because it didn't contain any interesting features or patterns that had to be taken into account. But the features of the second, overlapping signature added a lot more noise, and it became hard to tell where one signature began and the other one ended.

Mystery writers delight in misleading us about the identity of the criminals. The good writers are honor bound to make the relevant clues and motivations clear but they know how to use their skill to provide the right type of noise to mask these signals. They plant red herrings, they cast doubt on the accuracy of the signals, and they prevent us from building an accurate story. By the time they're done we can't tell which are the important clues and which are the distractions.

In the "Good News" decision game, many of the messages were irrelevant to the real issues. It wasn't until you knew the end result that you could accurately judge how much attention to give each announcement, how much you needed to remember it.

The Japanese attack at Pearl Harbor provides an example of how noise can obscure perfectly good signals; see Example 8.3.

If these had been the only data presented to the decision makers, the pattern would have been clear. However, there was other information circulating in the mix—a stream of thousands of messages. Some of these pointed to the U.S.S.R. as the target of attack. Some pointed to a push through Southeast Asia. Further, some signals were scattered, some received by different agencies. Some signals never reached a decision maker. Thus, the increased Japanese message traffic to Pearl Harbor and Manila was never noticed, because no one was monitoring the worldwide picture to see this increase against the steady state at other sites.

Some of the cues were explained away. The Japanese had differentiated sectors of Pearl Harbor to fix ship positions according to which sector the ship was in. The American analysts who discovered this saw it as a laughable passion for thoroughness as well as a way for the Japanese to shorten messages, so no one told Admiral Kimmel, the head of the Pearl Harbor fleet. Also, the burning of codebooks might mean the Japanese were preparing for an American attack, not the other way around.

Even at the very last moment, critical information was explained away. At around 4:00 A.M. on December 7, an American radar station picked up the Japanese fleet. Or, at least, the radar station reported unknown contacts. The report went to a junior watch officer, who interpreted it as American bombers being flown in to Pearl Harbor.

The signals seem clear in retrospect. But they were surrounded by noise, and so they became obscured.

Noise is a pervasive barrier to accurate sensemaking. Consider the task of monitoring a nuclear power plant. It might seem that the operational task would simply be to look for anomalies in the regular functioning of the plant. But there is no "regular" functioning of the plant—the status of the plant is continually changing and therefore the anomalies are very difficult to track.

A nuclear power plant consists of thousands of components and

> *EXAMPLE 8.3* DETECTING THE JAPANESE INTENTION TO ATTACK
> PEARL HARBOR

There were strong and clear signals that an attack was imminent on December 7, 1941:

- A well-documented gathering momentum of Japanese troop and ship movements.
- Two changes in the Japanese naval call signs (highly unusual, and typically interpreted as preparation for an offensive).
- Loss of contact with the Japanese aircraft carriers.
- A new military cabinet in Tokyo, with a more aggressive intent and a deadline for success in negotiations with the Americans. (This piece of information came via code-breaking successes.)
- D-Day was identified by the U.S. Army and Navy as the weekend of December 7.
- Evidence that the Japanese were compiling a list of British, American, and Dutch targets. The Japanese were particularly diligent in sectoring Pearl Harbor into zones and identifying which zone each ship was in.
- Instructions sent to Japanese embassy officials to burn their codebooks.
- Observations of Japanese diplomats burning documents that appeared to be codebooks.
- An increase in message traffic to Manila and Pearl Harbor in the weeks before December 7, but not in any other site around the world. (The Japanese attacked the Philippines right after Pearl Harbor.)
- A reported rumor from the Peruvian embassy in Tokyo about a planned strike at Pearl Harbor.
- Radar signals on the morning of December 7 that showed a large number of approaching tracks.

instruments. The reliability of the components and sensors is high, but with so many components some equipment failures inevitably occur on a regular basis. If a failure doesn't affect the safe operation of the plant and can only be repaired when a unit is shut down, it may persist for a long time before being repaired. Therefore, a plant *always* has some components that are missing, broken, working imperfectly, or being worked on. (Plants can function safely under these conditions because of redundancy.)

Of course, these small failures affect the operators who are monitoring the plant. They have to know at all times which components are broken, being repaired, or working imperfectly, and they have to know the status of the entire plant, in order to interpret the displays. Otherwise, they can draw the wrong conclusions from the displays, and possibly take the wrong actions.

To make things harder, the components heavily interact with each other. A plant operator has to know about all of them in order to interpret any of them.

The difficulty of monitoring a nuclear power plant is a useful metaphor for trying to size up a situation. In any type of business activity, it is possible to have background noise that consists of faulty or erroneous signals, missing data, or irrelevant information. Managers receive official reports documenting expenditure rates, work hours spent per task, and so forth. But managers have to understand their programs in order to know how to interpret these reports. They can't simply take the data at face value. They have to construct stories in the face of different types of uncertainty.

Using Stories to Make Sense of a Situation

There are many reasons why it can be hard to make sense of a situation. The time pressure may be too high; you may not have all the information you need; you may not be sufficiently prepared; the situation may be very complex; the critical cues may be very subtle. Lots of things can get in the way.

The process of assessing situations can require more than the pattern-matching process discussed in Chapter 2. What happens if several patterns seem to match? What happens if you don't recognize any patterns? In one study of Navy commanders facing real-world crises, we found that about 90 percent of the time they were sizing up the situation by pattern recognition—but the other 10 percent of the time they needed to consciously build stories to account for events. Accordingly, we expanded the recognition-primed decision (RPD) model to include this use of storybuilding.

Storybuilding is needed in cases where we might identify several different patterns, or where we are having trouble finding any patterns. In constructing a story, a decision maker tries to connect the observed events to explain how they might have come about. For example, when diagnosing a patient, a physician wants to know where the patient has been visiting, what the patient has been eating, and any other background facts, in order to construct a story of how the symptoms could have arisen.

When John Schmitt shadowed the Marine squad at Camp Pendleton, he was picking up patterns and folding these together to build a story about the type of adversary they were facing. Once the story is constructed, it becomes a very powerful means of organizing the data and explaining them. It becomes a means for making sense of the situation.

The story you construct to link events together works like the picture on the puzzle box that tells us what the scene is supposed to look like. Without the picture it is much more difficult to interpret the pieces and figure out how they fit together. Likewise, to construct an explanation we have to use a story to tell us what is an important cue and what is noise. At the same time, we use the cues to build the story.

But the pieces of a puzzle have a stable shape, whereas in many settings the pieces of a story can change shape. That's what makes it difficult sometimes to construct an explanation that makes sense of a situation.

Correcting a Story—Breaking a Mindset

Sensemaking can go wrong, particularly as a result of the mindset problem—the risk of being blinded to other explanations when we rely on our intuition and expertise. The use of pattern recognition and storybuilding to size up situations can render us insensitive to unexpected or novel events that haven't yet been captured by our patterns or stories. This type of limitation is the flip side of the strength of expertise.

This breakdown—the mindset problem—takes a few different but related forms. Sometimes it causes us to fixate. That is, we construct a story, decide upon an interpretation, and lock into that, resisting the signals that tell us that our story is inaccurate. Charles Perrow, in his book *Normal Accidents*, goes further and describes a process in which people actively explain away the inconvenient data. A gauge gives an odd reading? Well, perhaps the gauge isn't reliable. A worker reports that a valve is open whereas the story you've created in your mind—the plot that you've written and expect to see played out—requires that it be shut? The worker was probably confused and was checking on the wrong valve. And so on.

You can watch this process in action the next time you get lost while navigating your way around an unfamiliar city, following directions that aren't very thorough. If you make one mistake in building your mental map of where you are, it can quickly compound as you explain away other anomalies to make them consistent with your original and erroneous belief. Hikers refer to this process as "bending the map." Once you have bent the map too far, you'll have trouble recovering.

How can we avoid this problem? A common suggestion is that we need to keep an open mind, particularly when we are gathering evidence. Instead of jumping to conclusions, formulating hypotheses, or trying to make sense of the data, we should deliberately inhibit ourselves from building an explanation until we have gathered all the evidence. This is the rational way to approach things. It is the scientific way. If you interpret a situation too quickly, if you build a story too early, then all of the data are going to be colored by that story. Once you see the data in one way, it is going to be hard to see them from another perspective.

Unfortunately, this advice does not seem to be very realistic. Attempts to encourage, or even force, people to conform to this "open mind" stance have been unsuccessful. We are sensemaking creatures. Expecting us to stifle our sensemaking tendencies would make us more like computers than humans.

If we try to keep an open mind, the likely result is that we will become confused and overloaded with data. Only by actively trying to make sense of a situation can we package the data into meaningful stories.

Yet if this mindset problem is built into our tendency to rely on pattern recognition, and if we can't easily keep an open mind as we sift through evidence, what can we do?

The practical way out is to accept the limitations of our sensemaking strategies by being prepared to find flaws in our interpretations and change them. Most of us appreciate our own fallibility. Most of us acknowledge that we can be wrong. Therefore, the next step is that we have to be ready to correct our explanations—to look for anomalies and be prepared to reinterpret the situation.

That's not always easy to do. How do we know when we're becoming fixated on the wrong explanation? How can we tell when we've been bending the map? Here are some suggestions:

• *Test for Fixation* The strategy here is to challenge yourself. You can ask: "What evidence would it take to convince myself that my interpretation is wrong? What information might make me change my mind? What data would it take to make me give up my opinion?" If you cannot answer, then it's likely that you are gripped by a fixation.

If you want to take this a step further, you can seek outside help in questioning your mindset. For example, some organizations staff their executive boards with friends, admirers, and networkers, but others make sure that the board includes at least some members who will ask the tough questions and make sure they have done their homework. If someone with whom you are working is showing signs of fixation, you can try the same questions stated above about what evidence it would take for the person to change their interpretation.

One senior executive, who is African-American, described to me an incident early in his career when he was a manager. A higher-level position had opened up, and because of his accomplishments in the company, he assumed he would be tapped to fill the position. He went in to talk to his supervisor. Trying to be modest, he asked if he would be invited to interview for the position. To his surprise, the supervisor told him, "Just because we don't have any black vice presidents, don't expect this is a shoo-in for you." This statement was accompanied by nonverbal signs of anger and resistance. The reaction was out of keeping with the question, and the manager realized there was a basic disconnect. He remembered that his supervisor had previously worked for an organization that had been plagued with equal employment opportunity (EEO) problems and pressures. He suspected that the supervisor was seeing him through those glasses, as if he had just threatened an EEO action. "What are your assumptions about where I'm coming from?" the manager asked. That snapped his supervisor back into reality and he immediately apologized. He realized that he was talking to an effective problem solver, not a whistle-blower.

◆ *Assess How Far You've Bent the Map* If you are misinterpreting a situation, then there will be a lot of data that are inconsistent with what you believe to be true. You may try to explain them away. Some bending of the map is inevitable because the signals are sometimes faulty and deserve to be explained away. If you can step back and take note of how many inconsistencies you've explained away, you might start to see there's a reason to question your judgment.

However, in the midst of working on a task, it's easy to lose track of all the explaining away you've done. What you can do is monitor all the discrepancies you've explained away, perhaps even listing them, in order to track the effort you are expending in holding on to your fixation.

And if you are facing two or more rival stories, you can consider the discrepancies in each one. By seeing how much you have to explain away, you'll gauge which one is more plausible than the other.

◆ *Set Tripwires* One way to recognize how much effort and map-bending it's taking you to hold on to your fixation is to establish tripwires—events that should not be happening or levels that are not supposed to be exceeded—that would indicate that your interpretation of the situation may be inaccurate. For example, one physician described to us how he performs a risky type of surgery. He estimates how long the procedure is supposed to take and if the operation exceeds this time he takes that as an indicator to reexamine whether to proceed or to convert to a more traditional technique. The tripwire is the fact that he has exceeded the typical amount of time for the procedure. Much of project management consists of using tripwires—called milestones—to let the supervisors see where they need to update their understanding of how the project is progressing.

◆ *Write Several Stories/Scenarios for the Future* This approach is to formulate a range of stories—two or three is plenty—rather than trying to converge on a single story. These stories are termed "decision scenarios" by Peter Schwartz and his colleagues at the Global Business Network. We mentioned this work in Chapter 7. Their approach is to help decision makers deepen their understanding of the dynamics of a situation by formulating different possible scenarios that could explain what is going on. The function of these scenarios is not to be accurate, but to help decision makers understand more fully their beliefs and key assumptions.

• *Replace Your Interpretation* When you have fixated on an explanation, it's hard to imagine the world from any other perspective. One way to pry a person loose from a fixation is to help the person imagine that there are other ways to account for the same data. Marvin Cohen, the president of Cognitive Technologies, uses a crystal ball method to achieve this. After people describe their interpretation of events, Cohen might say, "I am looking into an infallible crystal ball and it shows that your interpretation is wrong—now account for the same data in a different way." For example, a product manager may be explaining that a slump in sales is due to the poor economy. If the infallible crystal ball rules this out, can the product manager offer another plausible reason? The exercise continues with the crystal ball invalidating the easy attempts to explain away data. The point of the exercise is to free decision makers from their fixations and get them to engage in alternative speculations using the same data.

This use of a crystal ball is different from the way it was used in the PreMortem exercise. Here, the goal is to spot weaknesses in the way a person is *interpreting* the situation. In the PreMortem exercise, the goal is to spot weaknesses in the planned *course of action*.

• *Compare and Contrast Your Options* Decision analysts have admitted to me that the formal option comparison approach isn't very helpful in choosing one option over another. The real value is that it helps their clients learn about situations. So, you might try to consider several options, and evaluate what is good and poor about each as a way of identifying important features of the situation. In Chapter 4, I was critical of using decision analysis to compare options as a way to select the best one. The strategy I am suggesting here is different—to compare options as a way to better understand what you really want.

• *Learn from Breakdowns in Sensemaking* When we discover that our interpretation of a situation doesn't make sense anymore, we have the opportunity to make radical improvements in our mental models. We keep on patching and repairing our models of the world as long as we can get away with it. Failures force us to discard outdated systems of thought, to become more sophisticated, and to develop stronger intuitions.

To learn more from failures or struggles, you can conduct debriefings after projects in a way that records the new patterns and cues you've discovered. The decision-making critique, discussed in Chapter 3, should be helpful here.

Don't underestimate the difficulty of escaping from your fixations and mindset. It's hard, but it's a crucial talent in building up your expertise and increasing the accuracy of your intuitions about what is happening in a situation. You'll be more comfortable using your intuitions if you don't have to worry that you'll get trapped by them. You particularly need to escape from fixations when you have to come up with creative solutions to problems, the topic of the next chapter.

Getting Creative—How to Go Beyond Brainstorming

Flashes of inspiration often emerge from our intuitions, leading us to discover a new way to achieve a task or design a product or express an idea. By understanding how these flashes happen you can achieve more breakthroughs—and you'll see why some of the usual approaches to creativity don't work as well as you've been led to believe. This chapter is about building creativity in groups, and about ways to improve on the traditional group exercises such as brainstorming.

First, though, we need to reconcile a potential contradiction. Creativity, by definition, isn't tied to our past experiences. Yet intuition is a product of the patterns we experienced in the past. Therefore, an intuitive approach to creativity relies on previous experience, yet also transcends that experience.

To ground this discussion, let's take on the following decision game.

> ### ➤ Decision Game 9.1 "Bad News"

You are the same mid-level employee at an information technology company that you were in Chapter 8, in the "Good News" decision game. Your group still develops, adapts, and customizes databases for clients. This has been a roller-coaster ride recently—your company once had 600 employees, shrank to 450, bounced back to 500, but in the last ten months has cut back to 350 employees because business was very slow. Revenues are expected to continue their slide for another half-year, but then to improve.

Your company president once again calls you in to ask you to take on an internal research and development project. You did a good job last time, although that product was ultimately killed. Now he has an idea he likes even better—the idea came up during an executive board meeting and the president agreed that it was worth trying. He thinks this one could really appeal to some of the company's best customers. The president wants you to build an impressive working prototype in six months because he expects the current lull to be temporary. "You know how these things go, feast or famine," he jokes.

This time you don't laugh at his joke. You have bitter memories of the last time: Just as you were building momentum, your staff got called away to work on new projects that had just been funded. You realized how little priority your internal project had, compared to ones that generated revenues.

Just as before, you'll have the full-time services of a staff of twelve people, including yourself as leader. You have six others from your department, plus two human factors specialists on loan, plus three more slots that you can fill as you wish. The product centers around an important software program with additional functions to be added for different types of applications.

In short, this is the same setup you faced in Decision Game 8.1. The only difference is that you're less idealistic now, more seasoned and cynical. You ask the president to commit to keeping the team intact for six months, but he declines. You didn't expect him to give you the commitment—you were softening him up for your next request, to commit that you and your team will still be employed by the company in six months. You don't want people worrying that they are putting themselves at risk by working on soft money. He agrees to this. Your next request is to talk to the various managers and pick your own staff in the different departments. You want the best talent available. The president assures you that he will send a message of the importance of this project to the relevant departments, stating that it is worthy of their best people. With a shrug, you tell him you accept the assignment. He starts to chuckle, but you can't figure out if he's laughing with you or at you.

You run into the head of the software programming department as you leave the president's office and explain your assignment. He sympathizes with you. You ask him if he can spare some of his really talented programmers—if not for six months, then at least for one to two months. He agrees, explaining that even during busy periods, some of his best people are idled for a few days, sometimes a week, when there is a gap in a schedule. Next, you check with the system design group; they also agree to give you two of their most skilled human factors specialists.

Question 1: In two minutes, write down the key leverage points you have to work with in carrying out the assignment. These are the basic building blocks.

Question 2: In three minutes, write down your project plan. What are you going to be able to do this time to prevent the debacle you experienced last time? As you prepare your plan you will probably add to the list of leverage points.

To build a creative solution, you need to take stock of the leverage points—the opportunities—that you have to work with. There aren't many here, but some of the ones I see are

a. the opportunity to surge right now, for the next one to two months;

b. the possibility of designing a central software program along with modules rather than trying to work on everything from the outset;

c. the fact that skilled programmers are sometimes idled during normal work periods;

d. the president's assessment that this product will appeal to important customers; and

e. your expectation that these dramatic business swings are going to be a part of the landscape for your company, rather than exceptions.

I expect many readers have identified additional leverage points beyond these five. The leverage points help us construct effective and creative courses of action—it's more important to have a good set of leverage points than a lengthy list that includes a lot of useless ones.

Now, looking at the task of generating a plan, and reviewing your leverage points, there are a number of ways to proceed.

Some people would direct the skilled programmers to spend four to six weeks just coming up with a really powerful design for the key portion of the software program, and specifying that in sufficient detail so that others can do the coding. Then, the coding can proceed, followed by the various modules, even after the skilled programmers disappear from your team. These modules would be developed in order of their value, their excitement factor, and the estimated speed of completion. In this way, you are trying to ensure that you will have a good return on the investment of time and energy even if the project gets cut short along the way.

Another suggestion is to take advantage of rapid prototyping techniques in order to have something to show management very quickly. The disadvantage is that time pressure may force you to hold on to your rapid prototype rather than replacing it if necessary.

On a political front, one recommendation I have heard is to line up political support from the beginning. Rather than waiting for a grand unveiling before you talk to higher-ups, you can lobby almost from the start, talking to the marketing department to get their support.

An additional suggestion was for you to use one of your slots to pick up a person from the marketing department to make the links to the sales staff and perhaps talk to key customers, to confirm their need and to turn them into advocates.

You have two more open slots on your team. Perhaps these should go to documentation specialists. You can expect a lot of staff reshuffling, so why not make sure the documentation is in place to get new team members plugged in with minimal delay.

In fact, if these business cycles are going to be a fact of life, you could try to line up support from the chief information officer to use your project as a test bed for methods of low-effort documentation that can become part of the company's operating strategy.

Going further, maybe you can pitch your project as a new concept of "just-in-time project management." If your company is going to use the temporary business slumps as a means of doing internal R&D projects, you can demonstrate how to make that work. You can show how to use these slumps to get the projects started with a surge. Then the company can take advantage of the idle capacity of its program-mers during normal operations, plus the improved documentation, to continue and complete the projects downstream. Your chief oper-ating officer might be interested in a way of improving productivity by filling the gaps in software programming projects, and your director of R&D might like to find a way to make research and development activities less sporadic.

By looking at the various ways to build from the leverage points, the ones I have covered above and the ones you have generated your-self, you can see that a dreaded assignment could offer a lot of room for creativity.

Now that we have completed this decision game, let's examine the use of brainstorming as a means of providing creative solutions to problems.

Brainstorming

There are a number of methods for generating creative solutions to a problem, but brainstorming is the best known and most com-monly used.

The idea of brainstorming is simple: Group members are asked to generate as many ideas as possible without critically evaluating them. And instead of critically evaluating the ideas of others, the group members are asked to try to improve these ideas. The goal is for the group to build on an idea until the creative streak runs its course. Then the group builds on another promising idea. Brainstorming ses-sions are often very exciting and satisfying.

The research findings, however, are less encouraging. Several stud-ies have been performed to evaluate the quantity and quality of the ideas generated in brainstorming sessions. These sessions were com-pared to control groups in which the participants worked individually for the same amount of time as the brainstorming group. The results were clear: The individuals outperformed the brainstorming groups, both in number of ideas and in their quality. Granted, they probably had less fun. They probably didn't feel they had bonded in the same way. But the creative output was higher.

One research team reviewed a broad range of experiments that evaluated brainstorming. They concluded that "productivity loss in brainstorming groups is highly significant and of strong magnitude . . . It appears to be particularly difficult to justify brainstorming techniques in terms of any performance outcomes, and the long-lived popularity of brainstorming techniques is unequivocally and substantially misguided."

What about all the success stories claimed for brainstorming? I assume they are real. But I also assume no one is cataloging all the useless sessions, the hours of group time that went nowhere.

Why doesn't brainstorming work? One possibility is social loafing—people don't work as hard when they see others carrying part of the burden. Another possibility is procedural—the interruptions in a group setting interfere with efficient transmission of new ideas.

The major barrier, however, seems to be the dynamic of working in a group. Being in a group setting makes us self-conscious. We pay a lot of attention to how we look to our colleagues as well as to the problem we're trying to solve. Asking us not to evaluate ideas or engage in competition isn't enough to inhibit our tendency to compare ourselves to others. The larger the group, the less effective the brainstorming performance.

Consider an explosion set off in a deserted area. The explosion may result in a loud noise, and a colorful display, but it only lasts for a second or two. Then the energy dissipates.

Contrast this with a shaped charge, as in a booster rocket. The fuel is ignited, but in a controlled way, to perform work. As a result, we can take the same amount of fuel and energy as in the explosion, and use it to send a spacecraft into orbit. We don't want undifferentiated explosions of ideas—we want to channel the energy, and shape the generation of ideas so that it actually gets work done. We want that creative energy to result in movement and progress. It's a process I call "directed creativity."

Directed Creativity

The central premise of directed creativity is that we have to discover what we need at the same time we are searching for a solution. That means defining the goal while figuring out how to achieve it.

This premise runs counter to the sequential strategy of problem solving that usually guides creativity sessions:

_____ *1.* Define your goal.
_____ *2.* Brainstorm to consider alternative ways of reaching the goal.
_____ *3.* Evaluate the alternatives.
_____ *4.* Select the top alternative.

In some ways this strategy is appealing. It breaks the process down into steps we can understand and carry out. Brainstorming is plugged into the sequence as step 2 to generate a wide variety of alternatives. Chapter 4 explained why it might not always be helpful to follow steps 2–4, generating and evaluating different courses of action. But that discussion was about decision making. For discovering new courses of action, you *will* want to explore different possibilities.

The trouble with this process is the first step—defining the goal. Obviously that's the place to start. However in most cases we can't complete this step because the types of goals we usually pursue are vague. That's why we need to learn about our goals *while* we pursue them. If we waited for the goal to become crystal clear, we'd never get started.

Now we can see what's wrong with creativity exercises. They permit a wild and often irrelevant search for unusual options but they work from a fixed goal. I think we need to reverse that dynamic. We have to make goal exploration part of the process. That's the basis of the directed creativity approach.

The idea of directed creativity is based on three components: (a) the *goals,* and what we can learn about them; (b) the *leverage points* that can be used to devise a means of achieving the goals; (c) the *connection* between the goals and the leverage points.

These three components are not in sequence. Sometimes the goals initiate the search for solutions. Sometimes we examine a new technology or other type of opportunity—leverage points—and discover that we can use it to solve a problem. Creativity can proceed from either of these directions.

Executives may like to think that they can set goals and expect their subordinates to discover ways to achieve them. However, useful discoveries can come from the opposite direction—from people who spotted opportunities and worked upstream to figure out goals. Post-it notes are one of the best-known examples of this bottom-up sequence. No one set out to invent Post-it notes—their value as reminders and tags was discovered after the technology was worked out to create minimally sticky adhesives.

a. *Goals* The first component of directed creativity is the set of goals that motivated the search for a different type of approach than the one you've been using. You may need a new way to manufacture a part, or a better system for conducting employee performance evaluations, or a strategy for reducing turnover, or a way to attract more customers to commercial websites. We rarely look for a creative answer just because we value creativity. Rather, we seek creative solutions because the conventional answers aren't helping. We usually just want something that works, creative or not.

Often we cannot describe our goal in much detail. We're usually struggling with outcomes we can't picture very well. In the lab, researchers who study problem-solving work with well-structured problems attached to clear goals. That way, it's easy to tell if a solution is good or not. In natural settings, though, the goals are mostly fuzzy. The Decision Game 3.1, "Care Package from the Board," illustrated a case of fuzzy goals. The stated goal of evaluating software packages turned out to depend on the fuzzy goal of what it would take to convince the executive board member that the company was responsive to his concerns. The Decision Game 9.1, "Bad News," showed another example of fuzzy goals. In attempting to devise a project plan for designing a new software system, we discovered additional goals involving better methods of documentation and for time-sharing.

Many important problems are poorly defined, and will never become clearly defined purely by thinking hard about the issues. The only way we can make progress in these cases is to take action, to start thinking about solutions, and to learn more about the goals in the process of trying to reach them. Of course, our initial problem-solving efforts will fail because we don't clearly understand our goal. That's okay. These failures become very instructive because the reasons for the failure help us to discover more about the nature of the goal.

Dan Isenberg has made the same observation:

Managers also often acted in the absence of clearly specified goals, allowing these to emerge from the process of clarifying the nature of the problem . . . Yet how often do managers push their subordinates to spell out their goals clearly and specify their objectives? A creative subordinate will always be able to present a plausible and achievable goal when pressed, but in the early stages of a tough problem it is more helpful for managers to provide a receptive forum in which their people can play around with an issue, "noodle" it through, and experiment. Sometimes it will be necessary for managers to allow subordinates to act in the absence of goals to achieve a clearer comprehension . . . even . . . to discover rather than achieve the organization's true goals.

Creativity depends on the way we reframe our goals while trying to build a new solution to a problem. If we remain stuck with the wrong goals, we're not going to make much progress no matter how creative we are.

b. *Leverage points* The second component of directed creativity is the opportunity—the leverage points we can use. The leverage points may involve a new technology, or a political change, or some other recent development that opens the way for us to achieve things that

---

> *EXAMPLE 9.1* CREATING A MICROCLIMATE

While I am at home writing this chapter, my wife asks me if I can help her out with tonight's dinner. She's getting ready to go to work, and she needs to have the frozen chicken taken out of the refrigerator at 1:00 P.M. That will give it enough time to defrost. Can I handle this simple task?

I mumble my willingness to help, barely turning to her. She knows how risky it will be to trust me in my current preoccupied state of mind. What can she do to remind me? How can she break through the writer's shield I have drawn around myself?

She doesn't bother trying. When I wander downstairs mid-afternoon, I spy the package of chicken on the kitchen counter. My wife has inverted a glass bowl over the package. She has created a microclimate to keep the chicken from defrosting too quickly. She redefined the goal from "making sure husband remembers" to "getting chicken defrosted at the right time" and found a solution to that much more tractable problem.

---

were previously impossible. The Internet has created many opportunities that were previously undreamt of. Air travel has done the same. So has the Global Positioning System. Democracy opens up potentials in countries that were previously governed by dictators. The establishment of a reliable system of law enforcement can make a big difference in a lawless and corrupt society.

We use our experience to recognize the potential significance of leverage points, then we assemble the leverage points in different configurations to see if we can make them work.

The metaphor of rock climbers can illustrate the concept of leverage points. Rock climbers don't chart out in advance exactly how they're going to master a new route. Instead, they carefully scan the rock wall for holds, for opportunities to gain traction. When they find a sufficiently promising sequence of holds, they are ready to give it a try. There is no way to calculate what counts as a hold. It depends on the climber's skills and level of fatigue and experience. Climbers have to be able to intuitively recognize the holds, and how much traction each one will afford.

Often, the key to a creative solution is noticing a leverage point that others have overlooked.

c. *Connection* The third component of directed creativity is making the connection between your goals and your leverage points by realizing that there is now an opportunity that can satisfy the goal. The recognition of a possible connection is what we usually experience as a flash of insight, and it's that connection that's a starting point for the creative solution. It directs our attention to the high-payoff leverage points and motivates us to work on a difficult problem.

Where is the creativity? In part, it is in being able to specify the goal well enough so that it can be pursued. In part, it is in exploring the new opportunity—the leverage point—and appreciating its implications. In part, it is the discovery of the connection. If someone gives you a task but you can't see any obvious ways to approach the goal, you are likely to fail. Working on a project where you see the wonders of the opportunity but don't have a clue about whose need it is going to address is also likely to end in failure. Only where there is a sense of a connection—an intuition that the opportunity can be made to work for a need that isn't well understood—is there a reasonable chance for success.

What do we consider as a creative achievement? Sometimes it is figuring out a way to break through a barrier. Sometimes it is the discovery of a new combination of elements, the type of discovery addressed by methods such as brainstorming. Sometimes it's the realization that an approach used in one setting could be just what is needed in another. Sometimes it is the identification of a critical leverage point, or the expansion of a leverage point into a promising solution, or even the realization of what are the actual goals. These types of discoveries can be supported by directed creativity methods. Creativity can take many forms, and we need a variety of methods to give ourselves a better chance of experiencing it.

Tactics for Directed Creativity

The concepts behind directed creativity explain why techniques such as brainstorming may not be so effective. But we have to turn these concepts into practice. That means outlining a strategy you can use with your teams at work to promote more creative collaboration, and to strengthen the intuitions of your team about what can serve as a leverage point and how to see connections between goals and leverage points.

1. *Present the dilemma.* Bring the team or group together to describe what is known or believed about the goal, any conflicts between aspects of the goal or trade-offs needed, what has been tried to date, why it hasn't worked, and speculations about the barriers to finding a solution. Let people ask questions to clarify what is needed.

2. *Send the team members off to work alone.* Have the team members work individually—preferably in different offices—to generate ideas, possible solutions, and leverage points to be explored further. There are different ways to organize this activity. You might give people a fixed time for this, say twenty minutes to work in their offices, with the door closed, the computer turned off, and the answering machine turned on. You don't want them working side by side in the same room because this does more to inhibit and distract them than to encourage them. You also don't want them working alone for too long, because you are going to be periodically clarifying the goals as you

continue, with cycles of generating options, learning from the options, going back to generate more options, and so forth. Ideally you would schedule this thinking time in the afternoon and then adjourn until the next day. This gives the group members more time to mull over the problem consciously and subconsciously.

3. *Present the ideas.* Next, bring the group together. One person, either the manager or the person needing the solution, or a person with good facilitation skills, should be the leader. One person should record the ideas as they are described by the team members. One person should listen for and record goal refinements as they are made. The team leader should have the members describe the ideas and suggestions they produced while they were working alone. You can go around the room, taking turns so that each member starts with the top item on his/her list. Some people may have information that others need, so this is also an opportunity for everyone to learn more about the problem. Remember: The benefit of the team discussion is to bring together different types of expertise and knowledge.

4. *Critique the ideas.* If people want to build on the ideas of others, that's fine, but you should ask the group to *critique* the ideas as they are generated. Even if the group likes an idea, they should critique it. The purpose of the critique is to learn more about the goal. The reasons why an option won't work will tell you more about what will. The critique can capture what is wrong about the idea, or how the idea suggests new goals. Thus, the critique session is being done to expand a list of goal properties, not to shoot down bad suggestions. An impractical idea that results in a useful discovery about the goal can be more valuable than an idea that is new in a trivial way and doesn't teach you anything.

5. *Integrate the ideas.* The team leader (or facilitator) should examine how the ideas now fit together, and the person recording the group's goal clarification should help the team reframe the problem by describing what has been learned about the nature of the goal and how the original account of the goal has been changed.

6. *Conduct additional rounds.* If time permits, you might want a second round of idea generation, repeating steps 2–5. Each time the team critiques possible solutions, it learns more about the goal, and this improved description of the goal should help the team make more progress working individually to generate new options.

7. *Converge on a solution.* At some point you'll shift from generating ideas to converging on a solution. You can do this as a group or else the project leader can collect the ideas and work on them alone.

In one workshop I conducted with a software management company, several people in the group were vocal supporters of the brainstorming process. Everyone ultimately found the directed creativity session to be very effective but the success of the session didn't change the attitudes of the brainstorming advocates. They still claimed that they would have gotten to the same place had we used brainstorming procedures. But others in the group disagreed strenuously. They felt that if they had used brainstorming they would still be spinning off into hyperspace rather than in possession of a firm action plan. Regardless, even the brainstorming advocates were happy to learn about an alternative method. Some of the people in the group indicated that they planned to have periodic sessions to work together in the future, using directed creativity to provide effective and efficient creativity sessions to help each other with thorny problems and projects. They even speculated that the method could help them collaborate over the Web with offices in other cities and countries.

This type of anecdotal evidence is not the same thing as running a controlled study of the effectiveness of the method. I started the chapter with a criticism of brainstorming, based on careful research, but we have not tested the directed creativity approach using comparable standards.

Another way to understand the process behind directed creativity is to study some projects that required innovation.

Case Studies of Innovators

In 1995 my colleague Rob Hutton and I had a chance to conduct in-depth interviews with almost a dozen highly creative Air Force scientists and engineers.

Our strategy was not to ask them the secrets of their success. Instead, we asked them to tell us the stories of their most successful research projects. They told us about ways they designed displays, and how they designed cockpits for high acceleration jets (to counteract the G-forces that could result in loss of consciousness). They told us about insights they had gained in evaluating distortions in windscreens, and about making more useable night-vision goggles. They told us of flying over the North Pole to understand the effects of magnetic fields on compasses. All of them were passionate and impressive. All of them had made a mark in the Air Force.

As the interviews continued, we found ourselves returning again and again to one common question: How had they selected the research topic in the first place? We found that the success of these researchers depended on their intuitions about where they might effectively direct their attention and effort. The innovative scientists and engineers we studied only began work on a project after they felt an intuitive connection between important goals and new leverage points.

They would not waste their time on pushing an opportunity or technology if they didn't see how it could connect with a real *need* or *goal* in the Air Force. That meant that they had a good idea of where the Air Force was heading, and what problems it was likely to experience. Thus, one engineer looked at the (then) new generation of high-performance fighters, the F-15 and F-16, and realized that the old equations and strategies for slower airplanes were not going to apply anymore. These new fighters were going to create different challenges for managing dogfights and lining up shots on targets, and for resisting the high G-forces in trying to outmaneuver the adversary.

The scientists and engineers we interviewed wouldn't waste their time pursuing a stated need unless they saw some potential, some *leverage point* that they could exploit. Merely having a supervisor throw out a challenge was not enough. Careers have been wasted pursuing important but intractable problems. These innovators had stored up the problems that had stumped everyone else, and when they saw an opportunity to solve a problem, they pounced. Often, the opportunity was a technology that had become available only within the past few years.

When the innovators saw a *connection*—a way of applying a leverage point to a problem or need or goal—they got interested. The sense of a connection was their intuition telling them that the problem was now worth studying.

For example, Lee Task, a specialist in optics, had developed a method for landing airplanes in the dark on landing strips that had to be kept hidden. While demonstrating the system, Task heard the co-pilot and navigator talking a lot to the pilot, offering information about altitude, sink rate, and air speed. Lee Task realized that the pilot, wearing night-vision goggles, could not see his own cockpit displays. This seemed like a simple thing to fix, and Task returned to Wright-Patterson Air Force Base and worked out a design to put flight information on the night vision goggles. In about four months, the Air Force had a solution to a vexing problem. The key was intuitively recognizing the connection—that a solution was readily at hand to solve a real problem.

Our project with the Air Force scientists and engineers helped confirm our speculations about how people invent new options. Creativity depends on selecting the right problems and recognizing better ways to think about the problems as much as finding new types of solutions.

The fluid mixture of goals, leverage points, and connections is further illustrated by the story behind the discovery of a common retirement plan. In this case the connection was the starting point, rather than the need or the leverage point. Only after the connection was made did the inventor get to work.

What were the ingredients for Benna's 401(k) discovery? Most important was the opportunity created by Congress. But almost as important was Benna himself. His knowledgeability about retirement benefits plans was critical, and also critical was his personal stance, his interest in helping lower-paid workers.

The connection was mostly by accident. He had worked on a retirement benefits plan for a different bank a few years before Congress passed the 401(k) provision so he was able to contrast that incident with the situation at Cheltenham National. Further, his discovery was not driven by an explicit need or goal. No sponsor was waiting for Benna to make his discovery—Cheltenham National Bank didn't want to take the risk of pioneering Benna's plan.

Benna was essentially the *vehicle* for the discovery, rather than a goal-directed discoverer. He does not fit the image of the heroic inventor, pressing on despite all odds (although once Benna had made his discovery he became an advocate). He was the agent in which the several forces (contrast between the retirement plans of the two banks, awareness of the 401[k] provision, interest in helping low-paid employees) converged. He was the connection between those forces.

Ted Benna invented the 401(k) retirement plan in 1980. Here's how.

Banks had realized they could save everyone money by putting half of the incentive bonus they paid an employee into a retirement plan, thereby shielding the bonus from taxes. Banks also gave the employee the option of putting the other half of the incentive bonus into the retirement plan, so the employee wouldn't have to pay any taxes on the bonus.

However, the Treasury Department didn't like this system because too much of the money was going to the higher-paid employees—they were the ones getting most of the incentive bonuses. Therefore, in 1972, the Treasury banned these types of plans.

Congress wanted to encourage citizens to save more for retirement, and tried to sort out this situation when it passed the Tax Reform Act of 1978. Section 401 covered tax-qualified retirement plans—the ones that the banks had tried to use. Paragraph (k) was a compromise between the banks and the Treasury Department. Banks could shield retirement plans from taxes but had to limit the amount that could go to the higher-salaried bank officers. The law said that the higher the percentage that the lower-salaried employees put into their retirement plans, the more the top managers could put in. If the low-salaried employees didn't put very much into retirement plans, the higher-salaried employees couldn't shield very much either. This provision closed the loophole, but in a way that seemed to set a low ceiling for such plans. No one expected the lower-salaried employees to shield much of their potential income. They just didn't make enough money to set up retirement plans.

At that time, Ted Benna was an employee-benefits consultant who was becoming frustrated with his work. Most of his effort involved setting up retirement plans to help business owners and top management, rather than the average employees. This inequity bothered Benna. He was getting ready to leave the field and become a minister.

In 1980, Benna was working on a project to help Cheltenham National Bank redesign its pension plan in order to motivate its employees. Benna wondered if he could use paragraph (k) of the recently passed law to benefit all the employees. The wording of the new law might let employees shelter their *regular income* from taxes, and not just their bonuses.

Benna's plan was to create a further incentive for retirement savings by having the company match the employees' contribution. The employees and the company could contribute money into the retirement savings plans from pre-tax rather than after-tax income.

This idea excited Benna because it would particularly help out the middle-class workers earning between $20,000 and $100,000.

The new tax code—which was about incentive bonuses—did not address this type of arrangement, but it didn't prohibit it either. An independent attorney confirmed that the strategy was feasible.

Benna's company was too small to set up this strategy itself, so he approached two large insurance companies and offered to sell the concept for $1,000,000. Both companies turned him down.

Then, Benna's own company took up the challenge and imposed the plan on itself. In doing so, the company discovered that the lowest-paid employees were very enthusiastic about the plan. In fact, the average participation of the low-salaried workers was slightly *higher* than the amount contributed by the top management. Many of the junior employees were women in two-income households, eager to put away money for retirement. In contrast, many of the higher-paid employees were men who were the sole wage-earners in their families, facing mortgage and tuition costs.

Benna tried to get some media interest in his idea, and again struggled. Even though the IRS sanctioned the plan, neither the *New York Times* nor the *Wall Street Journal* were interested. Only when the *Philadelphia Inquirer* covered it did the *Times* agree to write a story. And then the 401(k) plan became important news.

Within a few years, millions of employees had 401(k) retirement plans, and the growth of these plans helped to fuel the stock market gains through the end of the twentieth century.

Consultative Selling

The principles of directed creativity apply to the process of consultative selling. The idea of consultative selling is to form a problem-solving relationship between vendor and customer. Instead just like bicycle riders and birds. This was the major discovery of the Wright brothers. They selected the right problem—how to achieve tighter control—and connected it to the right leverage point—changing the shape of the wings.

For the Wright brothers, the warping of canvas stretched over a wooden frame was the leverage point they exploited. They recognized that by warping the two wings differently, they could directly control the steepness of the bank. They could therefore steer the airplane in any direction they wanted.

Despite their successful flight in 1903, the Wright brothers avoided publicity because they wanted to patent some of their important techniques. As years passed, doubts began to appear about whether they actually did have a controllable heavier-than-air device. In France, a 50,000-franc prize had been announced for the first airplane that could complete a circular flight of one kilometer. Why hadn't the Wright brothers claimed this prize? The Paris edition of the *Herald Tribune* published an article entitled "Fliers or Liars?" Someone else, Henri Farman, built a flying machine and claimed the 50,000-franc prize. His machine used the rudder for directional control, and made only flat turns, laboriously changing course while the body of the airplane remained parallel to the ground. Orville Wright watched this aircraft in flight, and hid his amusement.

Finally, in 1908, the Wright brothers had the patents they needed, and signed the contracts to get commercial support for their work. They were ready to demonstrate their technology. They shipped an airplane to France and on August 4, Wilbur flew two rounds at a racecourse 100 miles from Paris. The spectators in the grandstand watched him bank deeply into the turns, flying tight figure-eights with just some minor adjustments of his hand and wrist, controlling the airplane in a way they had never imagined.

The members of the French aviation community in the audience, used to watching airplanes struggle through flat turns, realized that they were seeing true flying for the first time.

of the vendor trying to sell a product, trying to strip the customer of all possible reasons for not buying, the vendor becomes more of a consultant, trying to help the customer fulfill needs (rather than offloading products), and developing a long-term relationship based on trust. The customer brings the need to the table and the vendor brings the leverage points—ways of using products to accomplish different types of outcomes. Their interaction attempts to find a connection. For this to happen, the vendor needs to get into the head of the customers and learn what they really need.

The idea of consultative selling is not so easy to put into practice. I've heard complaints from skilled marketing specialists that a company's technical experts have had trouble with this process; they know what the product is intended to do and can't get out of this mindset to explore what the customer needs. On the other hand, the technical specialists complain that the marketing staff members have trouble learning the capabilities of a recently released product; they aren't well versed in its leverage points, so they can't do a good job of collaborative problem solving.

A data distribution company called us in because their technical specialists in the management information systems (MIS) department were in conflict with all the other groups in the company. The company was angry with how they were treated by the MIS department, how arrogant and unresponsive they were. The MIS staff members were contemptuous of people in other departments who kept bringing in problems, asking for software programs to solve their problems, and then rejecting those solutions even though the programs did just what was requested.

We found that the root of the problem was that the MIS specialists had gone into computer programming in college because they liked working on well-defined tasks. They liked being given clear problems by their professors, and figuring out creative ways to do the work. But outside of college, in this company, the MIS specialists were not being given clear-cut tasks. Most of the time the employees could only vaguely describe what they thought they needed. "These people are just wasting our time," was the common complaint in the MIS department.

We told the company that the programmers needed to do "consultative selling" with their own colleagues in the company. They had to help ignorant and fickle non-specialists figure out what they really needed. They had to learn how to instruct and guide as well as program. Somehow, the MIS department had to acquire skills in consulting with their co-workers.

Consultative selling essentially means entering into a partnership where the needs and goals are clarified through successive attempts to find solutions. It means bringing knowledgeability about leverage points into play, to see which ones can connect. It means discovering features of the desired outcome. It means discovering ways to adapt the leverage points. It means engaging in directed creativity.

Creativity involves flights of fancy. To better understand this, consider the very process of flight itself. We have reached the centennial anniversary of the invention of airplanes. We can understand a model of directed creativity by seeing how it applies to this invention.

POINTS TO REMEMBER

Tactics for Directed Creativity

1. Present the dilemma.

2. Send the team members off to work alone.

3. Re-assemble to exchange ideas.

4. Critique the ideas and identify new goal features.

5. Integrate the ideas into an improved problem description.

6. Conduct additional rounds.

7. Converge on a solution.

How to Improvise and Adapt Plans

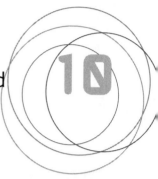

We're impressed by people who can make adjustments without losing a step. The adaptation of skilled workers is like the improvisation of jazz musicians—it builds on what has gone before while opening out to new possibilities.

But adaptation is not all joyful creativity. Usually it is about recovery, trying to escape a crisis that has suddenly loomed up. You can't plan an improvisation—you size up the situation and react. Therefore, intuition is essential for being able to improvise. We need intuition about *when* to adapt—to judge that a plan is falling apart. We need intuition about *how* to adapt—which routine or script to cobble into place to make the adjustment. We need intuition about whether to *trust* our adaptation—the changes we want to make may result in problems later on.

Our careful plans and procedures can crowd out intuition and discourage improvisation. Planners often try to specify every detail, leaving nothing to chance. Unfortunately, the more details there are, the harder it is to adapt, and the more brittle the plans may be—the more easily they fall apart when the situation departs from what was expected.

In their book, *Managing the Unexpected*, Karl Weick and Kathleen Sutcliffe point out the ways that plans can stifle adaptability. First, they make people insensitive to the anomalies that tell them it's time to adapt. The reason is that plans describe what is relevant and what is not, and anything irrelevant to the plan doesn't get much attention. Second, our plans may include contingency actions for coping with difficulties, but these contingencies were drawn up in advance and usually miss the context, the constraints, and the new opportunities that crop up at the moment the plan is being implemented. Third, plans are designed to have us repeat "optimized" patterns of activity but high reliability organizations cope with unexpected events by adapting to circumstances rather than by depending on plans.

We need to develop plans and procedures in ways that will still allow us to improvise and use our intuition. In other words, we should *plan to adapt*. We should expect to improvise, instead of trying to figure everything out in advance.

In Chapter 9 we saw that most projects have vague goals that are clarified as we go along. Similarly, the plans we develop—our attempts to solve problems—will likely need to be altered and improved as we learn more. Therefore we need plans that permit us to learn and to use our intuition.

However, adaptation isn't always a good idea. I know of service companies that decided there was more profit to be made in developing and selling software, only to discover, after expensive software coding, that they knew nothing about marketing or distributing software, or about maintaining and upgrading it.

So improvisation is not inherently beneficial. What's important is that you build up intuitions so you know when to make changes in a plan and when to leave it alone. Your intuitions act as your alarm system. They give you a sense of the gains from initiating a workaround as well as the efforts in carrying it off. And your intuitions alert you to the unintended consequences that arise from making last-minute adaptations. Your ability to adapt successfully is only as good as your intuitions.

To be adaptable is to respond rapidly and effectively to unexpected events. It means that you can quickly jettison your planned sequence of actions and replace them with a more appropriate reaction.

> ➤ DECISION GAME 10.1 THE ELECTRO-MISSION

You are a senior executive of a large company, and you've been called in at the last moment to evaluate a potential new project. Arthur, the director of a division in your company, has proposed to manufacture a concept for an "Electro-mission," a new type of very fuel-efficient emission trap to cut automobile pollution. The Electro-mission would be installed in hybrid cars running on gasoline and electricity. The concept has been developed into a prototype that was tested and has received all the necessary government approvals for installation.

One of the major automobile companies has agreed to make the device optional on their next model, but only if it is ready in six months. They don't want to lock themselves into a technology that could be obsolete in a year. Six months from now they want to see an assembly line that is up and running and ready to ship the product. If you can't deliver on time, the deal is off.

Arthur claims that he can do it. He has been working for weeks on this. He has developed lots of milestone charts showing when product cost accounting will be established, employee training plans will be finalized, production control, data gathering and reporting systems will be established, and so forth.

Here are the basics of his plan:

1. The manufacturing plans for Electro-mission are currently being reviewed and will be ready in two weeks.

2. The manufacturing will be done at a plant in California that was scheduled to be shut down.

3. To stay within budget, Arthur has decided he needs to manufacture most of the components himself, at the California plant.

4. Based on the preliminary manufacturing plans Arthur has already started to assemble a parts list.

5. Vendors have assured him they can deliver these parts in the next few months.

6. To get the price breaks he needs, Arthur has signed preliminary agreements with these vendors. The agreements will be voided if the project is canceled.

7. Arthur is assuming that the manufacturing plans will be approved so he's already directed a team to draw up specifications for the assembly line. These specs will be shipped to California by the end of the month.

8. Arthur estimates it will take another two months to reconfigure the machinery in the California plant and has hired the additional machinists who are needed to make the conversions.

9. The plant manager in California had already been reas-

signed when the shutdown was announced, and there is not enough time to find a new one, so Arthur is taking on this responsibility himself. He has not yet had a chance to visit the plant, nor does he have time to do so because he is so busy making all the other arrangements.

Your CEO has arranged for a team of specialists in the company to do an internal audit of this plan. Their conclusion is that each of the tasks is feasible as stated in the plan, as long as everything runs according to schedule.

Your CEO doesn't want to be rushed into a bad decision, but she also knows that the longer she delays and studies the plan the more she is crippling its chances. She has agreed to announce her decision tomorrow morning, and she confides in you that she will probably approve the plan.

However, she has had some last-minute qualms. Just to be on the safe side she is asking you, one of the people she trusts the most, to see how robust the plan is. She knows how busy you are, so all she asks is that you give her your opinion about whether Arthur will be able to adapt if things don't all go according to schedule. She isn't going to show you the detailed milestone charts, just the nine key aspects of the manufacturing plan that are listed above. She doesn't want you to tinker with the plan or schedule—it's too late in the game for that. "I know the plan *can* work. I have to figure out of it *will* work," she tells you. "Just five minutes," she says. "Tell me if you think we'll be able to recover if the plan hits any potholes."

Arthur's plan may look feasible—like many plans, if everything works out as scheduled the plan will succeed. Your task is to gauge where Arthur's plan is likely to hit a snag—and whether the plan is sufficiently robust to allow Arthur to recover. I imagine you've already spotted some weak points in Arthur's plan. For example, he doesn't know the capabilities of the workers remaining in the California plant. He's risking a lot by making preparations to modify the California plant before the manufacturing plan gets approved.

Arthur has clearly given up flexibility because he is so desperate to get moving. To determine if a plan is adaptable or not, you can go through a "planning-to-adapt" checklist. Let's use this planning-to-adapt checklist to help us assess Arthur's dilemma. (A short, bulleted version appears in the Points to Remember at the end of this chapter.) The criteria are features of a plan that can promote or stifle adaptivity.

IS THIS A MODULAR OR AN INTEGRATED PLAN? A plan is modular when different tasks can be performed independently of each other. An integrated plan is one where many tasks depend on the successful accomplishment of other tasks. Highly integrated plans are more efficient, but also more brittle. Plans that are more modular are less efficient but the advantage is that you can change one module without affecting the others. If Arthur could buy the subunits of the Electromission, he would just have to find a place to bolt these together. It's more complicated to work out the details of a new assembly line and it leaves Arthur's schedule vulnerable to delays. If any part of the assembly line breaks down, the whole line stops. Arthur's plan is highly integrated because there are a number of places where problems will quickly have a ripple effect on the rest of the plan. Modular plans are loosely coupled and have components that can shift around without creating much disturbance. Integrated plans are tightly coupled and have to be run exactly as scheduled—there's not much wiggle room. The more precise a plan is the harder it is to change because the tolerances are so narrow. Worse, the plan may be optimized for a narrow range of conditions. Under those conditions it will play out superbly, but outside of those conditions it will stumble. Another aspect of a precise plan is that every resource is tightly programmed. In contrast, a looser plan might leave some management reserve or some unprogrammed resources available, some flex in the schedules. Arthur's plan seems to be tightly coupled—there is dangerously little room for delays. Arthur could have increased his degrees of freedom by not selecting vendors until he had a firm manufacturing plan. He chose instead to go for the price breaks and traded away some of his flexibility.

WHAT'S THE POTENTIAL FOR REVISING GOALS? Some plans are intended to be run as described and others let you modify them based on feedback such as the rate of progress. This distinction can be cast as the difference between the act of cutting down a tree and trimming a hedge. Once you make a decision to cut a tree, you are pretty well committed to carrying it out. You can't cut halfway through and then change your mind. In contrast, trimming a hedge allows continual adjustment. One of the ways to manage uncertainty (see Chapter 7) is to create incremental plans so that you don't have to make the entire commitment up-front. You can see how you like the way things develop. Arthur's plan is more like tree cutting than hedge trimming. He isn't giving himself much leeway to learn from the initial runs of the product line.

A plan can assume the goal is fixed and proceed from there or it can allow for clarification and leave critical decisions open until partway through the project. Arthur's goal is pretty well fixed.

WHAT'S THE CONNECTION BETWEEN PLANNERS AND IMPLEMENTERS? It's easier to adapt when the people implementing a plan are working closely with the planners. The planners understand the boundary conditions and assumptions of the plan and are better prepared to make changes. When this connection is broken, the people who are doing the actual work are not prepared to notice the early signs of problems or to understand the consequences of making changes in the plan. In Arthur's case, because he is the planner and also is in charge of execution, he is in a better position to make changes if necessary.

HOW EASY IS IT TO INFORM OTHERS ABOUT CHANGES? Without reliable communications with distant team members, adaptation may be too risky. In the decision game, Arthur is to be running this show by himself. If he decides to change any part of his plan, he's personally going to have to notify everyone. That is going to slow operations down.

HOW EASY IS IT TO DETECT PROBLEMS? A good plan should enable decision makers to gauge their progress and notice potential difficulties. You should be more interested in reaching a good outcome than in following the plan. Unfortunately, we often estimate how we're doing by our rate of progress in carrying out the plan, and that can discourage us from making adaptations. Arthur needs to hit the milestones in the production plan. That may make it harder for him to spot problems until he's hopelessly behind schedule.

Is AUTHORITY CENTRALIZED? The more authority is centralized the longer it can take to detect problems, diagnose them, and react to them. In this case, all authority is centralized in Arthur.

The result of this survey is that Arthur's plan doesn't appear to be very robust. If anything goes wrong—and there is lots of potential—Arthur is going to have trouble recovering.

At this point, you might want to take some time and run the checklist on one of your own plans, either for a project you are currently performing or one you are preparing to carry out. The planning-to-adapt checklist is a tool for determining whether a plan is intended as a blueprint to be followed faithfully or a platform for improvisation.

Why Do We Plan?

Why do we build a plan in the first place? Plans serve several functions:

* *Solving a problem* A plan is a solution to a problem or barrier that is getting in our way. If we have a lot of experience, we may not need to plan at all. Plans are an effort to substitute deliberate problem solving for expertise, an attempt to build a script for situations where we don't have one.
* *Coordinating a team* The plan lets everyone know what they are supposed to do and where they fit into the tasks others are carrying out.
* *Shaping our thinking* The process of planning is a way for the planning team to get smarter. This is one reason why people enjoy planning so much, and why they persist in planning and adding more details even when it is time to take action.
* *Generating expectancies* A plan helps us know what to expect. It lets us anticipate how many resources we will need so we can spot shortfalls in time to do something about them.
* *Supporting improvisation* Plans can be viewed as platforms for adaptation.

This last function is key. Too often, planners intend for their plans to be carried out just as they were designed. To make that easier, the planners may add more branches and contingencies in an attempt to cover every eventuality. But these extra details and complexities just make it harder for the people executing the plans to understand what they are doing and why. And that makes it harder to make changes when necessary. Let's look in more detail at the idea of devising plans as a way to support improvisation.

Planning to Adapt

We need to be adaptive to deal with a chaotic and uncertain world. The more uncertainty we face, the more advantage there is in managing that uncertainty by building flexible plans—planning to adapt.

Further, if we plan to adapt we may avoid some of the frustrations that occur when we construct detailed plans and then keep changing them. By planning to adapt we are accepting the uncertainty and trying to manage it instead of trying to outthink it.

Strategic planning is the attempt to plot out a long-term course of action. For a number of years strategic planning was in vogue, and many companies invested heavily in that process. But, as Henry Mintzberg has pointed out in his book *The Rise and Fall of Strategic Planning*, the uncertainties were too great and the strategic plans quickly became obsolete. Thus, many of the leading advocates have quietly given up the grandiose and centralized notions of strategic planning found in the 1960s and 1970s.

Adaptation is not simply building a new plan to replace an old one. It is usually much more difficult than planning. Adaptation means modifying a plan in progress, and it's hard to take stock of a moving target.

Let's say your project gets reoriented after a few months. You may not know how much money has already been spent (vouchers may be late and your accounting department may be behind in issuing financial reports) or exactly what your team members have accomplished to date (they are too busy traveling to keep their trip reports current) or how far you have gotten. Under these circumstances, it is harder to make a new plan than if you were just starting out.

So when should we plan to adapt? Precise and detailed plans make the most sense in stable settings where the key variables are well understood. Outside of these conditions, it makes more sense to construct plans that leave room for improvisation.

To illustrate detailed planning versus planning to adapt, consider the concept of cybernetics. Cybernetics is the use of feedback systems to keep an operational system on course. Cruise control in our cars, for example, uses cybernetics to enable us to pick a driving speed and keep to it. If we set it while driving on a long, empty highway, we're not expecting to change our speed because we are confident that it's safe to drive at the predetermined speed we've chosen.

But we don't use cruise control in the city, where driving conditions are volatile and our desired driving speed may change unexpectedly. Even on the highway, we may turn off the cruise control when traffic gets too heavy because there's no way we could stick to a set speed.

The conflict lies between wanting to build procedures and plans while still leaving room for feedback. If there is a good chance of the unexpected, it's critical that we be ready to improvise.

The downside to leaving room for adaptation and improvisation in a plan is that the flexibility you gain carries a cost in the chaos you create. The more often you change your plans, the harder it is to predict what will happen next, and the harder for colleagues to anticipate and coordinate with you. Teamwork will suffer. We have all worked for leaders who wanted the freedom to change their plan every time they had a new idea. The first few times this happened, it probably felt good not to be constrained. By the fourth or fifth dramatic reorientation, chances are we started getting tired, and suspicious, and frustrated about all the resources we were spending for little return. By the seventh or eighth redirection, we wanted out.

Adaptation carries other penalties as well. Every time you change course, you open yourself up to the chance that you have missed some consequence of your new action. If you're under some time pressure, you may not be able to sort through all the implications of the change. That's why it's sometimes better to stick with your original plan, even though you know there is a better way to do things. Chapter 6 presented the example of the architect LeMessurier, who designed a skyscraper in New York. His colleagues made some simple changes to his design, such as substituting bolted connections for welded connections, because these would be less costly. The revision

In the 1980s, Japanese manufacturing companies made powerful use of robotics to perform a variety of functions. The "lights out" model of the factory had become a reality. These plants were able to rely almost entirely on robots, in some cases, so that it wasn't necessary to turn on the lights—no people were on the floor doing the work.

It therefore came as a surprise to learn that in the 1990s, some of these Japanese plants were dismantling their robotic systems. It seems that the robots could indeed outperform human workers. However, as plants needed to retool, to change their procedures, to make any sort of modification, it was turning out to be too expensive to reprogram or redesign the robots. Whereas human workers could be given revised tasks, the robots were not adaptive. Thus, in one factory, the workers are sometimes given only one day's notice to assemble new models of mobile phones. Previously, when the plant was completely automated, the engineers needed several months to do the reprogramming for a model change. A Toyota plant reduced its reliance on computers and found that it could equip an assembly line for a quarter of the cost it spent on a highly automated line, even though both assembly lines had the same capacity.

resulted in a dramatic weakening of the structure against crosswinds and a multimillion-dollar repair.

The adaptation by LeMessurier's colleagues was not a mistake. They maintained the agreed-upon engineering standards. The breakdown occurred because the adaptation had unintended consequences. The colleagues had no way to anticipate that LeMessurier was going to identify a new goal—improved resistance to crosswinds.

To sum up, adaptation isn't always necessary or desirable, but in a chaotic world, the *potential* to adapt is critical. We need to have the intuitive skills to recognize when it is time to adapt and to adapt skillfully.

Intuition and Procedures

Just as rigid plans can interfere with intuition and can block adaptation, so can procedures. The challenge is to find ways to use procedures without having our intuitions restricted by them.

Procedures serve a number of critical functions. They prepare inexperienced workers to handle emergencies. Constructing procedures protects against memory lapses and it enables team members who haven't practiced together to perform the same steps in the same sequence. Procedures let us work with technologies that are so complex that we cannot develop intuitions about them in a reasonable time. For instance, when operating our computers most of us just follow a set of procedures to get the computers to do what we want.

Procedures also can help us to adapt. For intuitive decision making, the scripts and routines we learn with experience are procedures that come to mind when we recognize particular situations. In scenarios where we need to adapt, though, there usually isn't enough time to figure out a new course of action. Instead, we plug in the script or procedure that seems most appropriate.

For example, in the battle of Gettysburg, Joshua Chamberlain was in charge of a unit at the Little Round Top that was about to be overrun by the Confederate troops. His men were out of ammunition. His response was to order his men to fix bayonets and charge downhill, using a wheeling maneuver that they had practiced on the parade grounds. He knew not to make up a new maneuver on the spot—it wouldn't have worked. Rather, he chose a well-learned maneuver and his troops executed it without having to think. He trusted his intuition—based on his experience—that the procedure would be successful and that his men could carry it out despite their fatigue and fear. His quick thinking thwarted the Confederate army's advance, and turned the tide of the battle.

In contrast, intuition wasn't able to save twelve smokejumpers in the Mann Gulch fire of 1949. The team had been retreating down a canyon when they saw that the fire had somehow ignited the trees at the bottom. They tried running uphill to escape but they were too slow. Furthermore, Wagner Dodge, the supervisor of the team, realized they weren't going to make it. On the spot he invented a tactic of setting a backfire that would spread uphill in front of him. Then, with the fuel burned away, he was able to dive into the ashes and take refuge. He survived. Dodge tried to get his men to join him but he was unable to explain the logic of his tactic. The rest of the crew all continued to try to outrace the flames. Unlike Chamberlain at Gettysburg, Dodge invented a brand-new tactic because none of the commonly understood procedures would have worked. But because there wasn't time for him to explain the new idea, most of the members of his team perished. Dodge was more innovative than Chamberlain, more adaptive, but he wasn't successful because, under time pressure and other stressors, too much adaptation can lead to disaster. Under these conditions, it is better to have some well-learned procedures in your hip pocket so that you can call a new play that everyone knows.

Therefore, my complaint isn't that procedures are a bad thing. Rather, I question the attempt to reduce all work practices to sets of procedures. Let's look at an industry that is adamant about procedures—the petrochemical refinery industry. The high risks in the event of an accident make it important that operators not make errors, even though the work can become tedious and mindless. The Occupational Safety and Health Administration (OSHA) imposes strict requirements for plants to document their operational procedures, and many plants hire full-time writers simply to keep the procedures up-to-date.

Greg Jamieson and Chris Miller, two human factors specialists, conducted a study of how these operational procedures are used. Their goal was to understand the "culture of procedures." They conducted field observations and interviews at four petrochemical refineries.

They found that the organizations they studied relied on procedures for a few primary purposes: as a source of guidelines; a way to meet OSHA's requirements; a training tool; a way to enforce the practices that had evolved in the plant; to capture expertise; and a way to store corporate memory.

The plants differed in their tolerance for incidents where the procedures weren't followed. In some plants, it was never okay to depart from the procedures. In others, it could be forgiven if the outcome was acceptable. In some, there was respect for controllers who realized that there was a better way to do things. And in some plants, the procedures were generally ignored, so it didn't matter.

Jamieson and Miller found that the plants had to balance a desire to make the procedures complete and comprehensive against the reality that no set of procedures would ever be complete and the procedures would have to be context-sensitive. Similarly, the plants had to gauge how much autonomy to give to the controllers. The more autonomy the controllers had, the harder it was for their teammates to anticipate their reactions and cooperate.

One of the key findings of the study was that a procedural approach has clear limits. The cost of maintaining the procedures, making updates and necessary revisions, can be very high. Even when plants invest in maintaining the procedures, operators often believe that the procedures are out of date, and this makes it harder to motivate the operators to use the procedures reliably. In virtually all the plants that Jamieson and Miller surveyed, the procedures weren't used very often. The operators either didn't have confidence in the procedures, or they believed they already knew what the procedures were going to say. And, of course, there was the problem that no set of procedures is ever sufficiently comprehensive.

Procedures have their functions, but they are not a substitute for expertise or for intuition. Intuition is needed to interpret procedures in context and judge which procedures to apply in case of ambiguity. If we dogmatically impose procedures, we run a risk of reducing the initiative of operators. Problems arise when we need those operators to react to emergencies and anomalies that are not covered in the procedures they have been taught.

How Intuition Helps You Adapt Your Plans

In situations where you want to increase adaptation, either your own ability or that of your team, there are a few steps you may find helpful.

PREPARE FOR ADAPTATION. Your stance regarding adaptation is important for enabling you to be more flexible. Are you poised to improvise, or are you locked into your plan? Intuition will help you manage your attention by signaling that you need to be more alert in situations where the risks are increased.

Planners often make the disclaimer "It's a mistake to fall in love

174   INTUITION AT WORK

with your plan." But of course we fall in love with our plans—they are our creations. Many planners are pained and frustrated when the plan starts getting changed. Yet, if you are not actively looking for counterindicators, you can miss the early signs of trouble, and miss your window for making changes. How open are you and your organization to making changes once you complete your plan?

SEARCH FOR EARLY SIGNS OF PROBLEMS. Intuition can help you spot problems earlier, to see that your actions are not going to be enough for you to reach your goals. You might realize that your margin of error is getting too small, and that you need to make some changes.

EXPECT TO REVISE YOUR GOALS. That means changing the priority of different subgoals or replacing goals with different ones. This is also a part of intuitive decision making. Your intuition—based on experience in the organization—has to warn you when your goals are no longer feasible.

RESIST THE "SUNK COST" EFFECT. Although you have already invested a great deal in the plan, the amount of previous investment is irrelevant to determining what makes sense today and tomorrow. Yet many of us get trapped in the investments we have previously made and are unwilling to throw these away. We may find ourselves escalating our commitment, throwing good money after bad, to try to salvage the original investment. Are you prepared to walk away from your original investment if you find a better way to get things done?

Some people refuse to adapt. They have found the routines that work for them and they aren't interested in changing. Dave Lehmann, an engineer who has become a turnaround artist for companies in trouble, sees executives and managers finding a script that works and sticking with it for the rest of their careers, rather than ever trying to rewrite it. He sees engineers who take pride in their skills and try to change their projects to fit their skills rather than trying to move beyond their skills to accomplish the project goals.

Tom Miller and Laura Militello, two of my colleagues, attended a meeting where artificial intelligence (AI) specialists complained about the unfairness of their sponsors. The AI professionals had developed all kinds of clever programs, but none was useful for the tasks they had been given. "They need to bring us different problems, ones for which our methods can work" was the complaint of one of the participants, and many others nodded in agreement. Talk about being close-minded!

Other people, like Arthur, in the decision game, don't prepare to adapt. Arthur isn't on the lookout for problems. He isn't interested in revising his goals. But he's going to get trapped by sunk costs if he lets the stigma of wasting resources discourage him from making any changes. In his favor, he seems well aware of the bottom line so that the plan is less important than bringing the product to market on time and within budget.

You, on the other hand, have the tools you need to formulate a plan that will let you rely on your intuition in order to successfully adapt. In addition to the planning-to-adapt checklist presented earlier in this chapter, you can also use some of the tools we covered in previous chapters.

You can perform a PreMortem (Chapter 6) to help you spot any troublesome signs for your plan.

You can also fill out a decision requirements table (Chapter 3) to see if you are ready to make difficult judgments, such as noticing that resources are being spent too quickly, or that the time programmed for certain tasks is inadequate.

You can build and play some decision games (Chapter 3) to try to become more adaptive. Treat these as yoga exercises to become more mentally flexible. By going through the decision games, you can practice making decisions on the spot, learning to ignore directives that have become obsolete and to use your own judgment and intuition.

You can use the decision-making critique (Chapter 3) to review your own adaptability. Try to see what might have been holding you up on previous projects.

You may find that you get yourself stuck because you don't know how to adjust—you don't know how to quickly reprogram assets, you don't know how long new tasks will take, you don't appreciate at the time how to alter some of your resources. If you see these limitations reoccurring, that means you need to gain better intuitions. Using the decision-making critique you can find out if your initial estimates of how long a task should take, and how much effort it should entail, are accurate. In this way you can build the patterns and action scripts that make adaptation possible.

This section has illustrated the different ways we use intuition: to make decisions, spot problems, deal with uncertainty, make sense of situations, generate creative ideas, and improvise. The next chapter presents a case study that illustrates how these activities all work together.

POINTS TO REMEMBER

Planning to Adapt: A Checklist

- Is this a modular or an integrated plan?
- What's the potential for revising goals?
- What's the connection between planners and implementers?
- How easy is it to inform others about changes?
- How easy is it to detect problems?
- Is authority centralized?

Molding Your Intuition: A Case Study

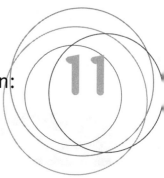

11

L ia DiBello had never been in a foundry before in her life, but moments after she put on work boots and a hardhat to tour a financially strapped iron foundary, she had an intuition about how to save it from going bankrupt.

By seeing where Lia's hunch came from, how she communicated it to the managers of the foundry, and how she designed a tool that altered their own intuitions, we can learn a lot about intuition at work.

None of the dozen managers running the business agreed with Lia's hunch when she first told them about it, but they were in a difficult position. For the past three years the company had been losing about $3M a year—on annual revenues of around $60M company-wide. They were $8M in debt. The banks, preparing to foreclose, had steadily increased their demands for collateral and the owner had already put up $3M of his own estate. Each month, the banks studied the statements and stiffened their terms. Nothing the plant managers had tried had made any difference.

In desperation the foundry managers heeded Lia's advice. Within a month of making some simple changes they were turning a profit. The company reached almost $500,000 in gross profit in the third month alone. It was breaking its own production records, and doing it all with fewer hourly workers. The percentage of on-time deliveries had soared from 37 percent to 86 percent and the scrap rate dropped in half.

Where did Lia's intuition come from?

Background

An iron foundry relies on essentially the same process that was used by our Bronze Age ancestors to make tools and ornaments. A mold is created and molten metal is poured into the openings and allowed to cool. The mold is removed and the metal tool is ready to be finished and used. Of course, the techniques used today have been developed since the Bronze Age. The metal is iron, not bronze, and the procedure for making the molds has become very intricate. The molds are still made of sand because of its high melting point, but the mixture of compounds added to the sand has become very sophisticated.

Years ago, foundries made all sorts of equipment, but cheap and lightweight plastics have now become widespread. Today, foundries cast products that have to be heavy, durable, and heat resistant. These include engine blocks for bulldozers, food processing equipment (such as industrial mixers used to make 40,000 batches of cookies), and compressor components (pumps, turbine housings) for power plants.

Foundries are under pressure to compete for business with foreign labor markets. One way is to find better ways to build the molds. The more detail in the mold, the less the cast-iron product will require welding to add components or machining to remove unwanted parts of the product. These operations take time and energy—if the mold can reduce the need for such operations, the product can be made less expensive. That's why mold making is a fine art.

There are hundreds of companies doing this work, primarily located in the Midwest. The company that called Lia in had seven plants in the United States. Three of these—all in one location—were ringing up most of the losses.

And I should give you some background on Lia DiBello herself. Her Ph.D. research examined the way people use tools to perform conceptual tasks. She is particularly interested in the way large organizations use software programs—costing millions of dollars—to perform scheduling for operations and maintenance. One of her early clients and success stories was the New York Transit System, where she first got in the habit of donning the work boots and hardhat to investigate the intricacies of bus and subway maintenance. Lia and her colleagues have been doing this for a decade now. In the industry, perhaps 70 percent of the materials requirements planning (MRP) software systems are judged as failures and are often returned to their developers. Lia has worked on more than twenty projects for introducing complex software schedulers, and none have failed. Today she works for the City University of New York, and also heads her own company, Workplace Technologies Research, Inc.

What Did Lia Know and When Did She Know It?

The company had been losing money ever since 1998. By the end of 2000, the owner realized that neither he nor the plant managers would be able to recover from their downward spiral. The company had tried changing leadership, bringing in new plant managers from industries with better management skills. They were changing plant managers every few months. Nothing was helping.

The chronology of how Lia solved the company's problems falls into five phases: the time prior to Lia's first visit; her first visit to the foundries in April 2001; her second visit in June 2001; the preparation of an exercise later in June; and the use of that exercise in July 2001 to reframe the thinking of the plant managers and workers.

1. *Previsit* Lia and her colleague Sterling Chamberlain first heard about the company from a financial specialist who was advising the owner. Even as she listened to the story, Lia doubted that the problem was about finances or organizational structure. Lia heard that customer complaints were mounting—customers were not happy with the ability of the plant to deliver products on time and were turning to other foundries. She learned that foundries usually have little trouble finding customers, so she suspected that if the company was losing money, it was probably because of their managers' execution, not their finances.

2. *Lia's first visit in April* The company arranged for Lia to visit five of its foundries in three days in April, 2001. Within minutes of walking into the first foundry, Lia formed a hunch of what was going wrong.

Upon walking into that first foundry on her tour, Lia found that the plant floor was even more bewildering than she expected. It was a noisy, dirty, and dark place, but she supposed that was normal for a foundry. The floor itself was made of concrete but was covered by sand from the molding process. There were fires to watch out for: The workers would coat the molds with a solvent and then use a torch to cut extra pieces off, but they wouldn't necessarily turn off the torch (why waste time in turning it off and then on again?), leaving it on the sand. And sometimes masses of the solvent would catch fire and be left to burn themselves out in the sand. Or molten ore would spill out; workers simply let it burn and eventually cool down. She had to be careful where she walked, so as not to step into a fire. She also had to keep an eye out for the overhead cranes, and for forklifts.

More important than what she was seeing was what she *wasn't* seeing. Lia was struck that there was no visible way for the workers to know what to do next. The people on the floor were each working in a space of their own. They were doing their own jobs and not monitoring the flow of work around them. There were no visual aids, no charts on the walls.

Lia had worked in many other manufacturing companies and operations, and the lack of structure at this particular foundry jarred her. She wondered how anyone was supposed to know if they were meeting a schedule, so she asked for data concerning on-time rates. Someone showed her a list of the items being worked on at that time. The list on the shop floor did *not* include any information about the dates that the items were due to be completed. Lia asked to see the scheduler's report from the production system. That list had a column showing the customer promise date. She noted that many of the items on the list had been due a month or more earlier. That meant that the deadline had already been missed! No wonder customers were frustrated.

Lia asked some workers, "How do you know what to make?" She was told they got a list once a week. She asked how they sequenced the items on the list. She was told that they would make whatever they could, given the materials at hand. Again, this was a telling comment. They weren't thinking about a schedule or due date. They were just trying to build molds and pour molten iron to make more products.

Lia tracked down the weekly list. It obviously wasn't a highly studied document—she found it sitting on the foreman's desk, covered with dust. She had found another part of the puzzle. The workers had very little data and weren't even using what they were given.

Lia asked several people on the floor, "What is the nature of your job?" She made a startling discovery. The workers realized that the plant was in trouble, so they were trying to help by building as many products as possible. To the people on the floor, the goal was to keep busy and work hard. They weren't concerned with what they made—they assumed everything would get used eventually. But to be worth their salary they needed to be working hard and fast. The company was paying them and they wanted to give the company its money's worth.

One foreman told Lia that his job was to make fifty molds a day. And he reached that goal. True, some of the molds weren't on the list he was given, but he didn't always have the materials or tooling he needed to build those molds. Rather than sitting idle and waiting for resources to come in he preferred to keep busy and make more molds out of the materials on hand.

The molds are big black cubes—all the intricacy is inside, where the iron will be poured. In walking around the plant, Lia felt she was in a sculpture garden. The plant was filled with a variety of molds of different shapes and sizes. The molds were everywhere, dominating every setting. For a bulldozer engine block the molds might be six feet high by eight feet long by six feet deep. To know what is inside the mold—the product it is designed to make—people put a two-inch square Post-it note listing the pattern number. Sometimes the paper got incinerated so the finishers didn't know what they were making until they broke open the mold.

In listening to the workers describe how they made molds, Lia realized that they were doing mental simulations. They were picturing themselves as the metal going through the mold. They were imagining how they would flow, how they would be cooling off, where they might get blocked. The mold makers had figured most of this out through experience.

Lia saw one part of the puzzle very clearly. If the customers were unhappy because they didn't get their castings on time, but the plant floor had no way of knowing the due dates for the castings, how could the foundry possibly meet the due dates? The workers didn't have information about what to make, when they needed to finish each casting, or how many units to make. There was a weekly list but it didn't contain due dates and wasn't used anyway.

The foundry was also insensitive to time, and this too puzzled Lia. She had been told that the company might pay a penalty for late delivery of a casting or that an order could be canceled if it wasn't delivered on time. Some castings on the weekly list of products were already six weeks late. The foundry was losing customers who complained that the castings were never on time. The reason the customers were using a casting process was to get a more complete product so it would take less time to assemble downstream, and less time to deliver to *their* customers. This business was all about time. If the foundry was not delivering on time, that was negating the rationale for making the complex molds in the first place. Customers usually had several foundries making products at the same time, so that if one foundry was late, a customer could pull the order and give it to another foundry. In contrast, if a foundry was 100 percent on time, it could increase its prices, eliminate penalty costs, and increase its volume. So much depended on time, and yet the plant seemed oblivious to any schedule.

From her other projects, Lia had learned to look for a few key questions: When are things due to internal and external customers, what is due, how much should be made, and to what level of quality? Timing is not always important. But in this case, timing was very important.

After some more probing, Lia discovered why the foundry was so insensitive to time. Historically, the foundry was always late, but customers had never minded before. However, the situation had changed about three years earlier. The automotive industry and others had switched to using plastics so the opportunity for the foundry to produce a continual flow of parts for these industries had disappeared. In their place was a new type of customer for whom timing was critical. For example, a company making bulldozers for construction sites needs to deliver these on time because construction often takes place in a narrow window during the year. The foundry knew that its world had changed and tried to solve the problem by hiring different managers.

The Company's View

The plant managers had a sense that their problem was in execution, but they had only their default ways of solving it; they tried to be on time by pushing production harder or making more stuff. They had no idea that it might be valuable to let the workers know more about the schedule. To them, the workers simply needed to do their jobs without asking questions. They didn't understand why, when they badgered their workers about being on time, the response they got was, "We're up to our limits. We can't work any harder." This only reduced the respect the leaders had for their workers.

3. *Lia's second visit, in June* Lia came back in June for a second visit, bringing her associate Sterling Chamberlain as well as a few specialists in building high-level business process maps. These maps show how a company currently does business and calculates the costs involved in the process. Lia had scheduled a day and a half for a group of ten middle managers and shop floor managers to sit in a focus group and fill in these maps.

Once the maps were finished, the plant managers were asked to draw circles around where they thought were the bottlenecks.

They circled "cost problems." And they explained that the sales representatives were quoting prices that were too low. Lia thought that was ridiculous. The real problem was that the cost of making the castings was too high. If they raised their prices instead of improving their execution they would lose even more customers.

They circled "being on time." But the members of the focus group didn't know why working harder wasn't getting them closer to on-time deliveries. Their mental model was the same as the workers': If we work faster we'll be on time.

They circled "patterns not being retrieved on time." The patterns were directions for making the molds, and with 2,000 patterns in the plant there could be problems finding the right one. To Lia, that didn't sound like a critical issue.

They circled "materials running low." That meant that no one was carefully monitoring the materials that they were ordering.

They circled the "mold-making process"—they weren't sure it was being done right. But they didn't know what was wrong with the current procedure or even what the current procedure was.

Watching them draw the circles, Lia felt more confident in her original intuition that the plant could not be on time because the workers had no way to track the schedule. The items circled were all parts of that pattern. Materials would run low if you didn't have a way to forecast your needs. Patterns wouldn't be retrieved on time if you waited until the last minute to go looking for them. The underlying problem was that the workers didn't know what to do when.

Yet the managers in the focus group didn't see that these were all different aspects of one underlying problem. They had correctly identified the key elements of the problem but could not recognize the larger pattern these created. They were all stuck in their offices, wondering why the plant was having trouble. They weren't looking for the answers on the plant floor.

During the focus group session the managers were asked why the foundry was going over budget. Their answer? "Maybe we don't have enough customers. If we had more customers we could more easily sell all the things we make." Listening to this, Lia realized that even the managers were caught up in the mentality of making as many molds as possible, even if people hadn't ordered them, with the belief that someday someone would want them. It was a ridiculous way of working.

All of this extra, unneeded stuff—the cores and molds—just sat around. Sometimes the managers remembered that they had already made a mold that a customer requested, but other times they forgot. They just let these cores and molds pile up in storage areas all through the plant—and it was a very big plant. A mold might be buried four layers back and they'd need a crane to get at it. Sometimes it was easier to just make it again.

The managers didn't see the problem they were creating by endlessly spewing out unneeded products. They believed that as long as everyone worked harder, they could solve their problem. Besides, they didn't want to have the workers sitting idle. There was little lost in having the workers make a duplicate of a mold they already had made. Further, the managers didn't realize how many units weren't being used.

As the focus group was working, Lia took several opportunities to escape onto the plant floor. During these walk-throughs, Lia crystallized her intuition that the workers needed to see a schedule and she formulated an idea of what should be on the schedule.

When she came back to the focus group and looked at the process map, she confirmed her suspicions. It was costing the foundry $1.09 per pound to make the castings and they were selling the castings for 98¢ per pound. They were losing at least $3,000,000 per year from this imbalance alone.

Further, the business process mapping showed how expensive it was to use extra materials for reacting to emergencies. They were paying time and a half overtime rates for 40 percent of the labor hours. Customers with clout would demand immediate service for castings they needed urgently, and the reactions to these drills would disrupt the rest of the cycle. No one had calculated the costs of their reactions before.

The Solution

So Lia listed all the questions that should be answered on a "To be cast" report that could be shown to the workers every day.

_____ *1.* When is the item due to be delivered to the customer?

_____ *2.* When does the item have to go in for cleaning?

_____ *3.* When does the item have to go to Center Street for final preparation?

_____ *4.* When is the pour date?

_____ *5.* When is the mold due date?

_____ *6.* When is the core due date?

_____ *7.* When is the tooling due date?

_____ *8.* Is the pattern ready to be used and back in its storage slot?

_____ *9.* Are the materials available for making the core and mold?

The managers in the focus group reacted fiercely to the suggestion that Lia and Sterling made for this "To be cast" report. They hated it. They thought it was unnecessary, impractical, and of no use. To their minds, it was unnecessary because the workers merely had to do their own jobs, not worry about what others were doing. (Lia knew this was wrong. To ensure tight coordination and schedules, workers have to track each other and make adjustments on the fly.) It was impractical because the foundry wasn't set up to provide all the data needed in the "To be cast" report. (Lia believed they had most of the data and could make good estimates for the remainder.) The managers also argued that these types of detailed reports, perhaps 136 characters wide and many rows long, were simply too hard to read. (Lia and Sterling knew that if the workers appreciated the importance of the reports, they would use them.) It was of no use because it wasn't going to address the need to get the workers moving faster. (Lia, of course, felt that the managers had the wrong mental models and moving faster should not be the objective. The workers needed better direction not more time pressure.)

The foundry managers rejected the idea of the "To be cast" report and insisted that what was needed was a set of detailed instructional lists for each of the positions on the floor.

Lia and Sterling were not surprised by the managers' reactions. In many settings they had seen managers who had little faith in their workers, particularly in their workers' ability to do conceptual tasks such as tracking complex schedules. Therefore, Lia was not swayed by the resistance of the foundry managers. Her intuition was that she had seen it before and that this attitude was part of the problem.

At this point, Sterling took over. He explained that it would take too long to build detailed instructional lists for the various positions (which, as Sterling was well aware, was not entirely true). The banks weren't going to wait. The simplicity of the "To be cast" report made it easy to set up in just a few days. Reminded of how desperate their plight was, the managers finally caved in.

4. *Designing the intervention* Lia and Sterling returned to San Diego after this second visit and tried to figure out what to do next. They had five working days, June 25–29, 2001, to design an intervention.

The way Lia and Sterling work is to design a simulation exercise or game in which the organization works in teams to physically build or assemble something concrete. Examples would be simulation games for repairing buses that involved working on miniature buses, and for assembling refrigerators that had the workshop participants putting together tiny refrigerators. But what type of simulation should Lia and Sterling run for the foundry?

First, Lia and Sterling knew they had to get the foundry to understand what "on time" means and requires. It is not the same thing as working faster. It is about delivering castings when promised.

Second, Lia and Sterling were convinced that the foundry workers needed to have access to the "To be cast" report, even though the managers didn't think it was appropriate or necessary.

Although their managers did not have much confidence in the workers' ability to learn and plan, Lia had watched them when she walked around on the floor during the June visit. She had an intuition that they could make good use of the "To be cast" report.

Lia's intuition was that whatever game they created had to center around molds. The whole plant was filled with molds. She felt that a game involving molds would feel valid to the foundry workers and would help them see how the game referred back to their work. "We have to make molds," Lia told Sterling. Sterling argued it was too hard to figure out the physical arrangements of mold making on a miniature scale for the game. Lia was not swayed. "We *have* to make molds," she insisted.

For the next few days Lia and Sterling and their team hurried around testing different types of materials and flasks and pourers to arrange a simple tabletop mold-making exercise. They compiled lists of things to be molded and assembled sheets of customer due dates. They set up similar financial parameters to the ones the foundry was facing. They set selling prices and penalties for late deliveries. They made sure that the game did allow a team to make a profit, but only if they coordinated, planned, and adjusted.

5. *Changing the mental models in July* The entire intervention took three days, July 24–26, 2001. On the first day the foundry managers and key workers set themselves up as a team—except that they decided it would be interesting to have the shop floor workers do the planning, selling, and budgeting and to have the managers do the mold construction so each could see what the other was up against.

They ran through the simulation—and they crashed. Only 20 percent of the molds were finished on time. No matter how hard they worked they could not avoid losses. The workers felt sorry for their bosses, who were killing themselves trying to finish up more and more molds. To make up for their shortfalls the team would accept hot "add-ons" which were special orders that came in late and at a higher price. The result of throwing these into the cycle was to increase the lateness for all the other molds in the process. The team was in a daze, merely reacting to everything that came along. Just as in actual operations. When the exercise was finished everyone was exhausted and the foundry personnel were discouraged. When Lia debriefed the teams, she showed how they were being hurt by not paying attention to the internal due dates. She provided feedback curves for their actual performance compared to the ideal performance that was possible. She illustrated the cost of their not being on time with their customers.

The team members started to talk to each other about how they might do better. They started trying to coordinate their schedules by asking each other, "When did you need the cores?" When they heard, "A few days earlier than we got them," the response was, "I wish we had known that."

The next day was used to conduct another business-cycle mapping session. This time the session centered on the business process used in the game. The team worked out a solution to how they could coordinate better. Basically they reinvented the "To be cast" report that Lia and Sterling had been preparing. This is how Lia and Sterling work their magic. Rather than trying to convince organizations to give up their flawed mental models and to accept a new one, the simulation game and follow-up review lets them understand why their mental models aren't working and makes them eager to try a better way.

The third day was used to roll out the "To be cast" report and try it in another cycle with the miniature-mold-making exercise.

The team was shocked by its own performance. It achieved a 20 percent profit margin, compared to the large losses incurred on the first day. It was 100 percent on time. Plus it added 50 percent additional orders to the original scheduled set. And it had enough time on its hands to work out unexpected and innovative strategies for speeding up the cycle by altering the mold-making process.

When the participants returned to the business of the foundry they were all believers in the "To be cast" report and the need to get their work done on time. While they did not achieve the 20 percent profit rate they showed in the simulation game, their 6.8 percent profit rate was more than sufficient to stave off the bankers and exceeded the normal 2 percent average for the casting industry. The company has been profitable ever since.

The scrap rate went down from 12 percent to 6 percent. One reason is that they are now working more slowly, not more quickly. They are more careful because they are freed of the compulsion to make as many molds as possible. And they are not storing unnecessary molds on the floor where they get damaged and become scrapped. For every 1 percent they reduce their scrap rate, they make $5,000 a day. They never understood that before.

Today they would have trouble going back to the old mental model of making as many molds as possible. They would refuse to work if the "To be cast" report was taken away. "How can we do our jobs without that report?" they would ask. Exactly.

Section III

INTUITION

Ways to

Safeguard It

Executive Intent: How to Communicate Your Intuitions

➤ **DECISION GAME 12.1 TAKING A STAND**

You are the head of a division at IMPART, a company that manufactures precision parts. One of your larger customers, George Johnson at Callabash Industries, has not covered his obligations for some time—the oldest bills date back six months. Jennifer, your manager, tells you she's losing her patience and doesn't want to ship Callabash any more parts until the payments are cleared up. In talking to Walter, a colleague in the industry, you find that George has also let his bills from Walter's company go unpaid for many months. Further, Walter tells you he knows of two other companies in the same fix.

You and Walter agree to a show of force. You both will call a meeting at George's office, along with representatives from the other two companies. This will be a creditor's meeting, prior to getting any lawyers involved. You will demand a repayment schedule, with all current bills to be settled in total in the next three months, and progress payments along the way. If this doesn't happen, you'll impose joint sanctions. You will not supply any more parts to Callabash (and you have some leverage here because you know George is depending on parts from both your company and Walter's). And you will freeze Callabash out of future projects.

You inform Jennifer of the meeting. "Good," she says. "Make sure you don't come back without a signed agreement, a written repayment schedule, and firm penalties for noncompliance." By this, Jennifer means:

a. She's more interested in getting paid than in doing more business with an unreliable customer.

b. The most important thing is to get a legally binding document, to avoid the constant drama of pleas and threats, even if you have to compromise on the amount of repayment.

c. She wants this customer to be humiliated for all the anguish he has caused your company.

d. Stand tough with this customer, but don't let it affect your relationship to other divisions in the same company.

e. She is glad you are taking action instead of just letting the problem fester.

Which interpretation do you think is the true fit? Take two minutes to form your impression.

What? Having trouble? Jennifer's intent wasn't entirely clear, was it?

Here is where intuition comes in. If you have worked with Jennifer for a few years, you may know how she thinks. You have a shared background. There is a way in which you feel you can read her mind—that's the basis of your intuition about what she wants. A new employee, however, would have trouble making a selection from the five interpretations offered above. The words aren't clear so you'd need the shared experience—the intuition—to decipher Jennifer's meaning.

And now let's go on to the next phase of the game:

If George makes the following offers, which, if any, would you accept?

I'll write you in for a share of a new project that we just signed. Your share will be larger than the amount I owe you.

I'll pay you 70 percent today, right now, but that's it.

I'll pay you everything, but not for another six months.

I'll give you half now, half in three months. But nothing in writing—we're trying to protect our credit rating.

The reason the first step in this game was for you to describe Jennifer's intent is because describing intent is what guides us when managing uncertainty. If you don't know what Jennifer wants you can't be sure how to respond to George's offers. And if you're Jennifer, you've just made your employee's job harder because you weren't able to explain what you expect—you weren't able to translate your intuition into words.

One of the difficulties in using intuitive decision making is that you may struggle to express exactly what your intuition is telling you. It isn't enough to make great decisions if you can't get them implemented. We run into this problem on both ends: when we try to communicate our intent to our subordinates and when we struggle to interpret the intent expressed by our bosses.

We need to find ways to *communicate* our intentions clearly to our subordinates. When they don't understand the reasons behind our instructions, they're ill-equipped to respond to unexpected problems or questions. That's what made it hard to figure out how to respond to George in the second phase of the decision game.

And when we are *receiving* directions and intentions from someone else, such as Jennifer in the decision game above, we have to reach beyond the words to determine what the person wants.

Here's a common scenario: You sit in a meeting where a supervisor has been describing what he or she wants. The people around the table nod their heads, you included. The supervisor seems satisfied. You all walk out, and, with a backward glance to make sure the supervisor is not near, you ask each other "What are we supposed to do here?"

Even if the words seem clear at the time, you may not realize the ambiguity in your boss's instructions until much later. You thought you knew what your supervisor wanted, but as you got enmeshed in whatever project you've undertaken you discovered that there were some questions you should have asked when you had the chance. The decision game in Chapter 3, "Care Package from the Board," illustrates what can happen when you have to act on your own without a good sense of what you should be trying to accomplish.

To reiterate, the intuition of both parties is affected when the intent isn't presented clearly. If you're trying to get someone to carry out a task, you may compromise your intuitive decisions if you don't convey the vision or purpose of that task. Even worse, you will likely compromise the intuition of the person you are trying to direct. You need your subordinates to be able to adapt effectively. The more con-

> *EXAMPLE 12.1* COVERING FIRE

In 1993, riots broke out in Los Angeles following the announcement that a jury had issued a verdict of not guilty for the police officers who beat Rodney King. The Army National Guard was called in to help the Los Angeles Police Department, the California Highway Patrol, and the L.A. County Sheriff's office.

In one incident, law enforcement officers had determined that criminals were taking refuge in a residence. The decision was made to conduct a raid on the house. The Sheriff's Department was going to rush the house and make a forced entry. The National Guard troops were placed in support and they were directed to provide cover. Everyone was in agreement with the plan.

The sheriff's men got ready to make the assault. Just prior to their attack, they signaled to the National Guard that this was the time—they were going in.

Thereupon the National Guard troops began firing their automatic weapons at every door and window in the house.

The sheriff's officers were stunned and called a halt to the proceedings. The two sides quickly huddled. They discovered that "covering" for someone means one thing to the Sheriff's Department (watching for antagonists and shooting at them if they appear to be threatening) and another to the military (pin down the enemy while the assault force makes its move).

fused they are about what they are supposed to accomplish, the harder it will be for them to use their intuitions.

When we fail to make our intentions clear, we can be surprised at the way others interpret our simple directions.

As mentioned above, one way to reduce confusions such as the one in this example is to work with others, practice with others, and get to a point where words, terms, concepts, and routines become commonly understood. These shared experiences will help teammates build up intuitions about what the other really means.

However, building up shared experiences with others may not be sufficient if people aren't skilled in getting their intentions across as described in Example 12.2.

Evidence such as this suggests that building up shared experiences with others isn't enough to strengthen people's abilities to intuit another person's intent.

> *Example 12.2* WHY DID HE DO THAT?

Colonel Lawrence Shattuck (now at West Point heading the United States Military Academy's Department of Behavioral Sciences and Leadership) performed an experiment on communicating intent as his Ph.D. dissertation at Ohio State University. As an officer in the Army, Shattuck was in a position to study how officers communicated and interpreted intent. When military plans are constructed, they include a section called the "commander's intent" statement, which explains the purpose of the plan.

Shattuck obtained a set of brigade-level orders and got permission from four different battalions to run his study. In each battalion, Shattuck gave the higher-level orders to the battalion commander with these instructions: Imagine you received these orders from your higher echelon, the brigade commander. Please convert these into orders for your own subordinates. Shattuck had the battalion commander issue his orders and his intent to his company commanders, both verbally and in writing.

For each battalion, Shattuck studied the revised orders to find a place where an unexpected but plausible event could derail the operation. Then he interviewed the company commanders individually.

Shattuck hit them with the unexpected event he had found. His challenge was "if this event happened, how do you think your battalion commander wants you to react?" Shattuck videotaped them as they responded. He did this with each of the three company commanders in a battalion.

Following this, Shattuck went back to the battalion commander and presented him with the same type of challenge, but in reverse: If this unexpected event occurred, how would you expect your company commanders to respond, given the way you described your intentions? Shattuck wrote down what the battalion commander said. And then Shattuck played his trump card—he showed the commander the videos.

The battalion commanders' typical response when they heard what their company commanders would have done was "Why would he do that?" In only 34 percent of the cases did the company commander's response match the expectation of the battalion commander. And when Shattuck told the company commanders what the battalion commander expected, their typical response was "How did he expect me to know that?"

There are skills, however, that you can learn that will help you do a better job of communicating the reasons behind your intuitive decisions. First, however, it may be useful to clarify what "executive intent" is, and why it matters.

The Functions and Features of Executive Intent

Executive Intent is what you want to accomplish when you've asked someone to perform a task. The concept of executive intent is adapted from the military term "commander's intent" that's included in plans that are disseminated into the field. Military leaders have learned how easy it is for plans to take a wrong turn when subordinates aren't clear about what the plan is supposed to accomplish. Despite the importance of describing intent in the corporate world, it has not received the same level of attention as in the military.

If you just tell subordinates what you want them to do, without telling them why you need it done, you have kept things simple, but you have also made your plan more vulnerable. The reason for telling your subordinates why you want something done is to promote their independence and their ability to improvise. If subordinates don't understand your intent there's a greater chance for an unexpected obstacle to throw the plan off because they won't know how to adapt appropriately. They will have trouble making tradeoffs between goals, and this is important because we rarely have only one active goal at a time. With several simultaneous goals, we often find that some of our goals are conflicting. We have to find a way to resolve this conflict with a tradeoff. The better your subordinates understand your intentions, the easier it will be for them to resolve goal conflicts the way you would want.

When they understand the intent, subordinates can react to the events without having to wait for your permission. Subordinates who understand your intent can recognize opportunities for achieving your goals, even if they weren't part of the original plan. The subordinates can set priorities and make trade-off decisions. They can use their intuitions, instead of being locked into the procedures and steps of your plan.

In addition, if the subordinates see that one of your assumptions is faulty, they'll know they should check back with you rather than mindlessly carrying out the task.

Here's an actual communication from Allied Signal describing its top priorities for 1996:

- ◆ Make customer satisfaction our first priority.
- ◆ Drive growth and productivity through integrated world-class processes.
- ◆ Make all of our commitments, including net income and cash flow.

The company claims that customer satisfaction is its number-one priority. What does that mean? How will the managers know when they've achieved this goal? Is customer satisfaction measured by the amount of investment the company makes or in the results it achieves? Is it based on the number of complaints it receives? On the average rating on those customer satisfaction cards it mails out? Is customer satisfaction found in the result of telephone interviews with small samples of customers? Will senior managers see it as they watch employees interact with the public?

In Chapter 9 we saw that for many projects, our goals are going to be incompletely defined. Because we do *not* want to paralyze ourselves by trying to capture the goal perfectly before we can get started, we have to describe the goal as well as we can and expect to clarify the goal as we go along.

Back to customer satisfaction. Let's say you, like the company, want to make customer satisfaction a priority, but you don't know how to articulate what that means to you. You can begin by telling your employees that you want the company to improve how it responds to the problems raised by dissatisfied customers, and that if the company doesn't do something different, customer loyalty is going to diminish and, ultimately, profits will suffer. The overall goal is to leave each customer convinced that the company cares about whether the customer was happy with the service, and feeling that they were treated with fairness and respect. You can't define those things precisely, but that is what you are after. You can give examples, both positive and negative, if anyone has questions.

Even if your goal is imprecise, when you help subordinates get on the same wavelength as you, together you will stand a better chance of adapting your plan of action when the need arises.

Informative Directions

W hen stating your goal, you want to provide meaningful information. That means avoiding vapid slogans. Your stated intent has to describe to your subordinates the outcome you want to reach (if you can describe one), the problem you are trying to avoid or solve, or the improvement you want to make.

Here is a way to gauge whether your stated intent is useful: Ask yourself if there is an alternative outcome that you're not interested in pursuing. If you can't think of an alternative, then you aren't telling your subordinates anything useful. A football coach telling his team that he wants to win the next game isn't really providing any new information.

The decision game at the beginning of this chapter, "Taking a Stand," illustrates what can happen in the absence of information. The manager, Jennifer, uttered what seemed to be a directive: "Make sure you don't come back without a signed agreement, a written repayment schedule, and firm penalties for noncompliance." Yet we saw how much ambiguity remained. Her statement, which seemed pretty clear on the surface, didn't do a good job of reducing your uncertainty—it was simply an expression of encouragement.

The defining feature of information is that it reduces uncertainty. If I say that I want our company to be profitable this year, that isn't offering very much information. What else would I want? It only counts as information if there is a *reasonable alternative position* that I am *rejecting*. To say that "Customer satisfaction is my number-one priority" is public relations, not information.

If, however, I say that customer satisfaction needs to improve and that I would trade .5 percent of profits for an increase in customer satisfaction ratings of 10 percent, that *would* count as information. If I can't tell you what costs I am willing to bear to achieve better customer satisfaction, then I'm just blathering. So many statements describing intent are really just cheerleading exercises. They drape the company in the flag of being "number one," being world-class, making quality a priority—and it means nothing.

For executive intent to have an impact you have to give a brief description of the task and explain why it is necessary.

Karl Weick, at the University of Michigan School of Business, has presented a script for giving directions:

> Here's what I think we face.
> Here's what I think we should do.
> Here's why.
> Here's what we should keep our eye on.
> Now, talk to me.

I have formulated Weick's approach into an acronym: STICC: *situation, task, intent, concerns, calibration.*

SITUATION (Here's what I think we face.) Describing the events or the changes that are prompting your call for action ensures that everyone sees the problem the same way. If we don't we better figure out why. Your description of the situation has to grab your subordinates' attention. It has to make them realize why this communication is happening. You want to inform your listeners why they need to pay attention, and why this is going to matter to them.

TASK (Here's what I think we should do.) This statement should be fairly brief in the initial telling. You can elaborate later, once everyone understands the big picture and your intent.

INTENT (Here's why.) This is where you explain the reason you need your staff to perform the task. If you have a vision of what the end result should be, you should describe it now. The intent is different from describing the situation—it's the purpose of the task, the way you want to resolve the situation.

CONCERNS (Here's what we should keep our eye on.) This is an optional step, but it's best if you tell your staff members what they need to monitor more closely. You may want to point out potentially tricky parts of the task so teams can prepare for them.

CALIBRATION (Now, talk to me.) This is key: You must make yourself available for questions so you can be sure that the members of the team understand their roles.

Example 12.3 shows how STICC can come in handy for daily interactions as well as when making long-term plans.

Notice in the example the key was starting out with a description of the situation they were going to be facing—why this is going to matter to them—rather than the problem I was having. And I gave the in-

---

> **EXAMPLE 12.3 WIELDING STICC**

I rent a car from a small airport late Friday night. Once on the road, I notice that the car has a very annoying clatter. I need this car for the next few days, but I'm not looking forward to driving it. Then I realize that, fortunately, I have to drop someone off at the same airport Sunday afternoon, so I can just exchange the car at that time for one that works.

I call the telephone number, and wade through the thicket of voicemail options only to be diverted to emergency road service. This isn't what I want. I try again and explain that I am having trouble with a car. Again, I'm transferred to emergency road service. I call a third time, telling the service rep that I rented a car there and it isn't working well. Again, transferred to emergency road service. It is time for STICC.

I call the car rental desk at the airport one last time. This time I say:

- I am going to be replacing my rental car at your location around 2.00 P.M. (*Situation*)
- When I arrive, I want you to have the paperwork available to make this change and the new car ready. (*Task*)
- Because I want to replace the car with as quick and smooth a transition as possible. (*Intent*)
- If someone else is at the desk, I hope there won't be any confusion. (*Concern*)
- Do you see any problems here? (*Calibration*)

The conversation is short and satisfactory. The replacement on Sunday goes off without a hitch.

INTUITION AT WORK

tent for why I wanted the customer representative to have everything ready. I didn't explain why I wanted to replace the car. The noisiness was not relevant to the clerk except as a box to be filled in when I arrived at the airport. The noise problem didn't connect with the task I was requesting—to have the paperwork prepared by the time I came back.

Another tip for communicating intent is that sometimes you can add an antigoal, something you don't want to happen. In the car replacement example I could have stated my intent in the form of an antigoal, "I don't want to have to wait." I did include an antigoal as a concern: "I hope there won't be any confusion."

The fifth statement in STICC—calibration—ensures that everyone is on the same page and offers a chance for suggestions and other comments. The way this calibration is made is critical. I have seen cases where someone asks, "Any questions?" and then one second later follows up with another task. If you want feedback, you have to show that you mean it by waiting, and by looking at people. Assume that people aren't sure of what they are supposed to do, and ask them, "What are your questions?" to prompt responses. Too often, people listen to instructions and, because they have understood all the words, they don't look ahead to anticipate possible confusions. In this step of STICC you are trying to get people to shift from passive listeners to active listeners. You want them imagining how they are going to carry out your intentions.

You can go further to ensure calibration. You can run a short Pre-Mortem session to see what people are thinking.

Let me make this suggestion more forcefully. If you are sending your team off on an important task, it is worth the extra time to do a PreMortem on the task and the intent. Give everyone a few minutes to write down the ways they think they can become confused and mishandle your request. Then use their feedback to sharpen your statement of intent. This small investment at the beginning can save lots of hours and meetings later on.

In workshops where I have taught the executive intent concept, I include a PreMortem exercise. I break the participants into small groups, and in each group, the members take turns issuing intent statements. They use the actual intents and tasks they are going to request when they get back with their work teams. The other participants do the PreMortem. The feedback is followed by a discussion of how to craft a better statement of intent.

The PreMortem exercise helps the participants when they issue their requests. It also provides training.

In one such group the executive intent statement came from the director of internal training, who wanted to get a list of vendors she could use to conduct refresher training:

SITUATION She was preparing to launch a new training initiative.

TASK She was going to direct her team to research different geographical regions by looking at training companies available in all the regions, and composing a list of vendors the company could use.

INTENT To do some refresher training of the company's technical staff in all regions.

CONCERNS She admitted that she wasn't clear about what she needed, and she feared that as a result her team would spend too much time on the research and they'd lose their window of opportunity to provide the refresher training.

CALIBRATION The PreMortem exercise turned up many problems because her intent statement was so vague. The people in the group wanted to know things like:

* What are the boundaries of the types of training that interested her?
* Are there companies you don't want us to use?
* Do we negotiate rates with them or leave that to you?
* Do we want to use their facility or have them come to us?
* What type of training classes do you want us to observe?
* Should they be one-on-one or group classes?
* How soon do you need the information?
* Does it take priority over the other stuff we're doing?

It was an eye-opening experience for her. Prior to the exercise, the director of internal training felt that she was a good communicator of intent. The PreMortem showed her that she wasn't. Many of these questions centered on the situation, constraints, and concerns. Her intuitions about what she would need to convey in the future were strengthened through this type of feedback.

In another session, we worked with a company that was partnering with some larger firms. Debbie, the person issuing the intent, was frustrated because she wasn't getting much guidance from one of these partners about how to formalize contracts more quickly, to resolve issues about rates, markups, intellectual property, and so on. A task force working out these details was just poking along.

SITUATION The task force hadn't prepared guidelines for joint bids, and a joint bid needed to be submitted the following day. The task force was going to meet that afternoon.

TASK To get the conditions of terms decided for the bid due tomorrow. To get someone in the larger company to take charge of this.

INTENT Debbie wanted to get the task force to prepare general guidelines that she could use, but her immediate need was to get her bid submitted the next day.

CONCERNS Debbie wanted the task force to get moving, but didn't believe she had the clout to make this happen, and she didn't want to come across too sternly while everyone was still learning how to work together. She was also worried that without guidelines, the bid would fall apart, thus weakening the collaboration process.

CALIBRATE The PreMortem session helped to clarify that it was impossible to obtain useful guidelines from the task force in time for this bid, but the larger company would still want the upcoming bid to be issued in time. The intent had to focus on the specific bid needed by the following day.

At the end of the exercise, Debbie felt she had a good intent statement that she could give at the beginning of her afternoon meeting— getting the bid in on time, rather than opening up a larger discussion about the need for guidelines. We checked with Debbie the next morning. Her meeting had gone very well. Her intent statement had set the tone and set the agenda.

Table 12.1	Guidelines for Executive Intent Exercise

1. Each person identifies a directive he/she is going to issue upon returning to the office. The participants can use the STICC format if they want, but the emphasis should be on the communication of intent more than on the other aspects of STICC. If people use the STICC script, they should not bother with the last component because this exercise itself is the calibration.

2. One person volunteers to present his/her directive to the group.

3. That same person leads a PreMortem with the group: "Suppose that in two weeks [or whatever time frame is appropriate] we discover that people have misinterpreted the intent of the directive and have gone off in the wrong direction. What they achieved wasn't what you had wanted. In three minutes write down all the outcomes they might have mistakenly pursued and the reasons this could have happened, given the statement you have been given."

4. The group presents its responses. (See PreMortem instructions in Chapter 6.)

5. The group discusses ways to improve the intent statement.

Table 12.1 is a suggested format for running a PreMortem exercise around executive intent.

There is still another way to calibrate everyone's understanding of intent—by seeing how people would react if the plan breaks down. Too often, we assume that the plan is going to work perfectly, that the task can be carried off without any complications. But one reason you are explaining your intentions is to help people improvise when they run into trouble. So, why not make that an exercise up-front, as you're explaining your intent?

To try this approach, just prepare a simple scenario in advance—just a few sentences, nothing fancy—and ask your team what they would do if this occurred. Or you can take someone's question, like "How should we respond if [that] happens?" and turn that into the exercise. "Okay, let's say that has happened. Now, you write down what you think you should do, and I'll write down what I expect you to do, and then let's compare notes."

In my own company, every new project starts with a kickoff meeting for the team members, including the customer. And the first item on the agenda for the kickoff meeting is usually a description of the project leader's intent along with the customer's intent. That way, everyone knows why we are doing the project, and what counts as success.

In keeping with the idea of muscular intuition (explained in the Preface) learning a tool such as STICC is less important than developing your intuitions about what others need to know in order to implement and adapt your decisions. But if you can get a feel for your subordinates' mental models, the way they make sense of situations, and what can lead to their confusions, then you'll have an easier time explaining your intentions.

What happens if the subordinates haven't yet developed good intuitions? Perhaps they have not yet had many experiences and haven't developed the mental models or learned the patterns and action scripts they need to successfully adapt when carrying out your plans and trying to achieve your purposes. What happens if you haven't been able to bring them up to speed as quickly as you needed? That is the topic of the next chapter: boosting the intuitive decision-making skills of your subordinates.

Coaching Others to Develop Strong Intuitions

eaders train their successors. That's part of their responsibility. They train their teams to bring people up to speed, and they train their successors to take over when they move to more senior positions.

In his book *The Leadership Engine*, Noel Tichy argues that one of the most basic features of successful organizations is that they have a culture of teaching. The leaders pass on their knowledge and energize others to be teachers. The result is an organization of teachers at all levels, starting at the top. Dick Stonesifer, who ran GE Appliances for five years, personally coached his executives. The opposite attitude is shown by companies that bring in consultants and academicians who aren't leaders themselves, who are proficient at business-speak, but not at teaching skills that are critical to the business. For the knowledge to stick, the teachers have to be the leaders in the organization.

Another of Tichy's examples is Roger Enrico, the CEO of PepsiCo.

the two years before he became CEO, Enrico devoted more than 120 days exclusively to coaching and mentoring the next generation of PepsiCo leaders. He personally designed a program called Building the Business, and over 18 months he ran the program 10 times, with classes of nine participants each time.

Enrico had realized that PepsiCo could only remain successful if the current leaders took on responsibility for training other leaders. The results were not only an improvement in leadership and decision-making skills, but an improvement in Enrico's own skills. In addition, his subordinates got to know Enrico so that they were able to work with him more effectively once he took over as CEO.

And of course there is Jack Welch, former CEO of General Electric. "For 15 years [Welch] has made biweekly visits to GE's Crotonville executive training center . . . His schedule is also filled with hundreds of video conferences, meetings, factory visits, and workshop sessions."

Not only CEOs but a wide range of experienced workers, managers, and colleagues are getting in on the act. One estimate is that 70 percent of all workplace learning takes place outside the classroom. Men's Wearhouse, rated as one of *Fortune* magazine's "Best 100 companies to work for," boasts that it doesn't have many trainers on staff, and doesn't call on outside consultants to provide training. Instead, it holds managers accountable for developing the skills of the people who report to them.

So what can be wrong with this picture? Simply this: Intuition is likely to get lost in the shuffle. As you become more expert, you are likely to find it harder to explain how you performed a task. Explaining yourself is simple when you're just following someone else's rules. But once you build up patterns, action scripts, and mental models of your own that enable you to anticipate potential problems and react accordingly, it gets much tougher to explain them to others.

If these intuitive skills are so critical to expertise, how are they to be passed on? All of Peter Senge's materials extolling the virtues of a learning organization or a teaching organization aren't enough if you don't have the tools to improve the intuitions of others.

When people don't know how to transmit intuitive decision-making skills, they like to give speeches. They expound on their favorite theories. They make up procedures, even if they themselves don't follow those procedures.

Too many experienced decision makers don't learn to transmit their intuitive skills. They are like the pilot in Example 13.1, and keep their coworkers in the dark.

How many valuable teaching opportunities slip away, how many chances to boost expertise are ignored like in Example 13.1? Communicating your intuitions to others is a difficult skill. In the previous chapter we saw how important it is in the near term to describe intent and directions so that others can use their intuitions to effectively adapt as they work. In this chapter we look at the long-term issues of contributing your expertise to helping others to develop and use their intuition.

Getting Inside People's Heads

As I've said earlier, one reason that it's hard to share our intuitive skills is that we don't always know what we know. People make judgments all the time based on nothing but a hunch, but rarely do they understand where that hunch came from.

Fortunately, there are ways to help people unpack their intuitions. Methods of cognitive task analysis have been designed for just this purpose. You'll just hit a brick wall if you ask an expert, "How do you know that?" Either the expert gives you a blank look, or gives you a lecture that sounds very intelligent but doesn't answer your question. In my research, I've found that I get better results when I stop asking cause the captain was writing it up so the maintenance crew could check it out and repair the problem. I pressed him. "You don't have any idea at all what was going wrong?" He insisted, sounding very sincere, that he was clueless. It was a bizarre malfunction and he himself would be curious to find out the problem the following day.

After about twenty minutes the captain arrived, climbed into the seat next to me, and the van started driving us to our hotel. Despite the lateness of the hour, my snoopiness had not diminished. "So," I asked him, "what happened back there, with the yawing?" He shrugged, to show me he wasn't concerned. He explained that at the speed they had been traveling, he had decided it wasn't going to be safe to abort the takeoff. He figured it was probably something like the nose wheel sticking. He had expected the yawing to stop once they lifted off. And that was exactly what happened. When his theory was supported, he made a mental note to be careful upon landing to keep the nose wheel off the ground until he had slowed down. That was why we felt the yawing at the very end.

And that was when I got scared. It hit me that these two men had just spent forty-five minutes in the dark, nothing to look at, sitting side-by-side, and they had never discussed the problem.

general questions ("How do you know . . . ?") and instead inquire about specific incidents. I'll ask the expert to tell me about another time when a similar type of situation arose. Then I stretch the incident out on a timeline and identify the judgments and decisions that were made. I question the expert about the cues and patterns that were available. Then I ask the expert to compare this account to the way a novice (such as me) might have approached it. After a good interview, experts sometimes express their appreciation because they have learned for themselves what really happened.

In order to explain and share your intuitive skills you should focus on the aspects of expertise that we discussed Chapter 2: the hard-to-detect cues, mental models, and the patterns and action scripts that you recognize. However, you usually apply these types of knowledge without thinking about them. That's why it's hard to describe them to others. And that's why you do better talking about a specific incident, because subtle aspects of your expertise become more visible.

My friend Doug Harrington is a former Navy pilot. He was a good one, and he loved his work. But in the middle of his career, he almost washed out of the Navy.

Doug had been flying F-4 aircraft and had become an instructor pilot. He was a natural teacher and had a gift for helping young pilots overcome their fear of landing on an aircraft carrier. True, the carrier is moving away from you and changing the angle of the landing area of the flight deck. True, the waves are moving the deck up and down, and sometimes sideways. True, you sometimes have to make these landings at night. But all of this can be managed, and Doug was patient and firm and effective.

Then it came time for Doug to transition from the F-4 aircraft to the A-6. He quickly learned the dynamics of the A-6 and was ready to complete his carrier landing qualifications so that he could join his next unit. To qualify, Doug had to complete six carrier landings during the day, and then another four at night. This didn't seem like much of a hurdle to someone with Doug's experience base.

So there he was, coming around the final turn for his first daytime landing in an A-6 airplane. He carefully lined up his airplane and prepared to come in for a perfect landing. Except that the landing signal officer told him to "come right." This was odd—he was nicely lined up. He moved slightly to the right, even though he was sure the landing signal officer was making a mistake. "Come right, come right," said the voice on the radio. He moved the plane a bit farther to the right, but not enough. The landing signal officer waved him off. He had to go around and try again.

Somehow, Doug got the plane down. Somehow he completed all of the six daytime landings. But none of them was pretty. Each was a struggle. Doug was told he would not be trying any nighttime landings. He would have to repeat the daytime landings the following day. If he messed these up, he was done. He would have failed to qualify for the A-6, and his flying career in the Navy would be over.

Everyone felt awful for Doug, and many of his friends tried to help him. "Doug, you've got to bear down tomorrow." As if Doug wasn't really trying very hard. "Doug, you have got to make those landings perfect!" As if Doug didn't understand that today's landings had been a disaster. "Doug, you've just got to concentrate." "Doug, this is really important." "Doug, just do it the way you always do." "Doug, don't let this throw you." And in the midst of all of this, Doug was in a daze.

Late that night, there was a knock on his door. It was the senior landing signal officer. Doug couldn't take any more help. He told the man that he needed to get a good night's sleep and that he was tired of listening to people—they were making his confusion worse than ever. The man refused to be dismissed. Doug tried a harder line. He told the man that he didn't want to hear anyone else tell him what to do. "I'm not here to tell you anything, Doug," the man said. "I just want to learn some things." Disarmed, Doug let the man into the room.

The senior landing signal officer was true to his word. He didn't offer any advice. He seemed genuinely curious. He asked Doug to walk him through the strategy he was using to land the airplane.

"I'm just doing it the same way I always have. I put the nose of the airplane on the center line, and come in."

That seemed to make the senior landing signal officer even more curious. "You're used to flying . . . what airplane?"

"An F-4," Doug answered. "I was an instructor pilot."

"I know. And tell me, how are the seats configured on the F-4?"

"I sat directly behind the trainee."

"So your nose lines up with his, and both line up with the nose of the airplane."

"Right."

"Now tell me about the A-6."

"I sit in the left-hand seat, next to the A-6 instructor pilot."

"So your nose is *not* right over the nose of the airplane."

"No, but my seat is only a foot and a half, maybe two feet from the center. We're pretty squished together in there."

"And what you are trying to do is put the nose of the A-6 down on the center line, like you have with the F-4."

"You got it."

The senior landing signal officer had the information he needed, and his face showed it. His frown of concentration turned into a relaxed smile. He explained that although the distance may not seem large, the angular effect was greater than Doug realized. The man had Doug hold a pen in front of his face, like the nose in the F-4, close one eye, and pretend to line up for a landing against the vertical line of the door. That was ground truth, a perfect line up. Then he had Doug

cont.

Example 13.2 (cont.)

move his head about six inches over to the left, and see how many degrees he had to shift the pen over to the left to make it line up with the door frame.

"That's why you keep telling me to come right, come right," Doug realized.

"That's it," the senior landing signal officer agreed. "Forget about the nose of the airplane. It's throwing you off. Just put your own nose on the centerline. You'll be off by a couple of feet, but that's well within the margin of error here."

Doug's landings the next day were successful. So were the ones that next night. Each time, Doug ignored the nose of his airplane and just positioned himself on the centerline.

The landing signal officer saved Doug's career: Instead of telling Doug anything, he just listened.

This chapter describes some methods and ideas that may help you teach others about your intuitions—so that you can become a more effective coach and leader. The idea of coaching someone's intuitive decision-making skills is different from the common use of "executive coaching" because that term has such a strong sense of personal development. My focus is on-the-job training. I am convinced that you can help people develop the intuitions they will need on a daily basis, particularly in tough cases, but it isn't easy. The landing signal officer in Example 13.2 was an effective coach in action.

A Nation of Coaches?

It would be nice if we all had the coaching abilities of the senior landing signal officer. Most of us do not. A casual expedition to a Little League game, or to watch parents coaching young children in soccer, would show how limited many of us are at coaching others. We may think we are effective coaches—but only because we don't really know what effective coaching is.

I was once working with a group of firefighters, captains who were themselves training officers. One captain informed me that he was a great coach. I asked what made him so good. He explained that he had a simple, foolproof strategy. "I tell them what they are supposed to do. And if that doesn't work, I tell them again. And if I need to, I tell them one more time. But after that, I'm done with them, and they know it." This seemed like a pretty simple strategy to me. Especially when I compared it to the strategy that another captain described: "I explain how they should do it, and if that doesn't work, I demonstrate it to them, talking while I go so they can see what I am doing. And if that still doesn't work, I ask them to perform the task and explain what they are trying to achieve, so I can get a sense of their strategy." Both of these men believed they were good coaches. If you compare the two strategies, I think it's obvious which one was the real coach.

Think of the coaches you've seen, particularly the poor ones. Try to remember the things they did that got in the way of your understanding of what they were trying to teach you. We've all seen plenty of examples of incompetent coaching. When I work with firefighters, I often give them an opportunity to act out poor coaching by trying to "help" me put on the turn-out gear in ninety seconds. With the military audiences, I do the same by inviting poor coaching for putting on a gas mask. The workshop participants seem to relish a chance to imitate some of the favorite examples of abusive and unhelpful coaches.

Most people either ignore teaching opportunities or mishandle them. Several years ago the Army funded my colleagues and me to study effective and ineffective coaching, to see why some people are able to get across intuitive types of skills and others fail. We studied music instructors, nurses, executives, and sports coaches. Here are some of the barriers we identified that prevent people from being good coaches.

AFRAID OF CRITIQUING OTHERS We know that others can be sensitive to criticism, just as we are. Therefore we don't offer helpful criticisms if we can avoid it. And when we can't avoid it we are vague so we don't hurt the person's feelings. Unfortunately, vagueness doesn't help the person learn how to do better. One tactic you can try is to focus your criticism on the specific behavior you noticed ("When you described your goals to the team I was a little confused and I thought some of them were confused as well. I wrote down the way you phrased it . . ."). This type of comment is less challenging than a critique of the people themselves ("Your problem is that you're not very articulate").

LACK OF TIME We are so busy cleaning up after other people's mistakes that we don't have the time to spend with them to help them avoid those mistakes in the future. Or else when we run training exercises, we cram a whole two-hour exercise with activities, perhaps leaving ten minutes at the end for critiques. One rule of thumb is to earmark at least half your training time for a follow-up discussion.

DIFFICULTY IN DESCRIBING SUBTLE SKILLS We concentrate on procedures, not on intuitions. Your subordinates have to learn procedures, but they also have to learn which procedure to use, whether it is working properly, and how to modify it. These are hard things to explain so be prepared to use examples to illustrate the stumbling blocks they could run into.

POOR TIME MANAGEMENT If we see six areas of weakness during a training session, do we work on all six in the twenty minutes we have available, or just pick one or two? We tend to hit all six, with the result that the discussions are pretty shallow. Skilled coaches only cover one or two topics, and save the others for later.

Caroline Zsambok was one of the lead investigators in our research on coaching. Caroline once surveyed a group to find out their reactions to on-the-job training and coaching (see Table 13.1). She was struck by the similarity of complaints expressed when people described their frustrations in providing coaching (the left-hand column) and when they described their frustrations in receiving coaching from someone else (the right-hand column).

People were frustrated when coaches weren't available, but they resented the need to take time out of their schedules to help coach others. The difficulty of knowing if the trainee was catching on mirrored the trainee's fear of asking questions and exposing ignorance.

Master Coaches

The most important part of our research on coaching has been to describe what sets the masters apart from others. Across different fields and settings, we found that the master coaches excelled on a few important levels. Figure 13.1 shows what these are.

You can strengthen your coaching skills by working on all three of

Table 13.1 Two Sides of the Same Coaching Coin

FRUSTRATIONS IN PROVIDING COACHING	FRUSTRATIONS IN RECEIVING COACHING
Providing the big picture	*Understanding the big picture*
Explaining interrelated pieces and how they relate to the big picture	Not enough information about the "big picture"
Patience and pacing	*Patience and pacing*
Having to repeat instructions	Was afraid to ask too many questions
Being patient	Didn't always feel confident I could do what was expected of me
Couldn't assume trainees already knew things (or overestimating their level of proficiency)	Felt stupid when I made mistakes
Understanding that a learning curve exists	Feeling totally incompetent
Uncertain whether employee was really understanding everything	Trainer beginning at too high a level
Understanding different learning styles	Not understanding terms or knowing people
Materials and info overwhelmed trainee at times	Being talked down to
Not knowing the audience	
Feedback	*Feedback*
Providing consistent feedback	No feedback
Conflicts	*Conflicts*
Resistance or challenges due to difference of opinion	Clash in trainer's value system
	Not feeling like I could voice my opinion
Workload	*Workload*
Finding extra time to do the training	"Okay, you've got it! See ya" attitude
Interruptions of my own work	Person not being available later for questions
Instructional skills	*Instructional skills*
Learning good presentation techniques of my own	Trainer not experienced in instruction
Organizing the lesson	Unprepared trainer
Explaining complex concepts	No format to the instruction
Breaking down complex tasks into manageable subtasks	No documentation or references
Deciding which were the critical bits to be trained	Incomplete communication and direction from trainer
Having relevant examples ready	Lack of knowledge from trainer
Motivation of learner	*Motivation of learner*
Keeping someone's interest in a mundane subject	Too much downtime; boredom

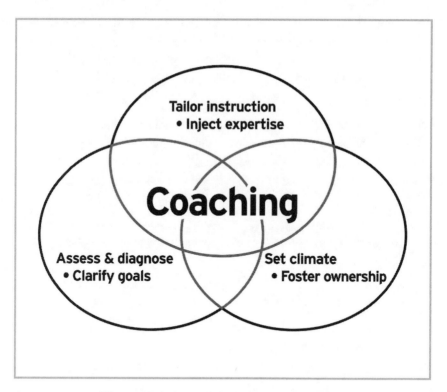

Figure 13.1 A Model of Master Coaching

these dimensions. This is particularly true when you want to coach people in the subtle, intutive skills that you've acquired through your experience.

Assessing and Diagnosing

Instead of jumping in with solutions to a student's problems, master coaches paid careful attention to where the person was falling short. Then they tried to diagnose why this was happening. Thus, a highly skilled music teacher, the head of a very successful high school orchestra, related an incident in which a cello student seemed to be less skilled than on an earlier observation. The teacher listened and watched, and speculated that the girl was working hard to keep her wrist flexible, and this was distracting her from making instantaneous corrections in the way she was striking the notes. So the problem was not what was happening (a lot of notes that were too sharp or flat) but what wasn't happening (the slowness of the corrections). In the example of Doug, the Navy pilot, the landing signal officer started out with an assessment and diagnosis before offering any suggestions to how Doug could overcome his problem.

Part of the process of assessing and diagnosing is to be able to set realistic goals. The coach, and the trainee, will make the most progress if the goals are reasonably within the trainee's grasp, and if the trainee appreciates their importance. For example, some colleagues of mine have studied the instruction given to new drivers. Teenagers are taught rules about how many car lengths to stay back at a time when it is all they can do to keep their vehicle between the lines on the highway. They are instructed about the proper use of the rearview mirrors when their eyes are still glued on the tailpipe of the car ahead. They are taught arcane information about the appropriate way to handle traffic circles at a time when they are still afraid to change lanes. Too many times we try to pack the information in, without considering if any learning has occurred. It's as if we believe we can't be blamed for someone's failure so long as we have presented the information.

The process of assessing and diagnosing is critical for training intuitive decision-making skills because it prevents the coach from maintaining an inflexible posture, such as the fire department captain with the foolproof technique who thought all he needed to do was explain what he wanted. When you are earnestly trying to assess another person, you are modeling some of the sizing-up skills that are important for that person to learn if they are to develop intuition. Doug's experience with the landing signal officer not only made him a better pilot, it made him a better coach.

Tailoring Instruction

Teaching is more than just lecturing. You can coach people by giving them opportunities to gain experience, or by giving them a chance to hear themselves as they describe to you how they are performing the task. Doug Harrington was learning about landing the A-6 as he described his strategy to the landing signal officer. One of the least efficient means of coaching is lecturing about how to perform a task. That's why skilled coaches have a large repertoire of ways to tailor instruction. In studying master coaches, we compiled a list of dozens of strategies and techniques. Here are some of the most effective instructional practices.

◆ Demonstrate the task to the trainees and think aloud so they understand what you are trying to do and why you take the steps you do to accomplish it. To assist in building intuitive decision-making skills, you can emphasize the cues and patterns you are noticing, the action scripts you are using, and the ones you are not applying.

◆ Discuss what could go wrong and how you might notice these early cues. Think of this as a mini-PreMortem.

◆ Let the trainee make mistakes. Instead of warning the trainee to avoid mistakes, you can build a richer mental model by examining the consequences once a mistake is made. If this is too risky or would take too long, you can discuss what the consequences might be. Mistakes are valuable in filling in our mental model.

◆ Ask the trainee to think aloud while performing the task. By asking trainees to make predictions and describe what they expect to happen, you can encourage their intuitions. You can also take the trainee's perspective. Instead of dismissing their mistakes, explore what the trainee is trying to do in order to find out why the person is having trouble.

◆ Have the trainee instruct the coach. You can learn where the trainee's mental models are flawed, and both of you can hear what the trainee isn't sure about.

◆ Help the trainee explore alternative action scripts. The point here is for trainees to learn to do a task in different ways. You don't want them to prematurely settle into a routine. By having them explore alternative routines, you can help them build richer mental models and also help them be prepared to adapt to unexpected obstacles.

◆ Ask open-ended questions. In contrast to closed questions ("If you have to make this type of repair you call for backup, right?") an open-ended question has more than one "right" answer, and invites the trainee to reflect (e.g., "What could go wrong when you have to repair this type of fault?").

- Notice improvements, rather than just discussing weaknesses.

- Manage time effectively. That usually means selecting two, never more than three, major issues and spending time on these rather than rushing through ten points in fifteen minutes.

- Go beyond procedures. This is the core of coaching intuitive decision-making skills. You want them to gain an intuitive feel for the task instead of mechanically carrying out procedures. Master coaches are able to describe the cues, patterns, and action scripts they use for judging when procedures are not working. Or at least, they can show the trainees that it is possible to develop these intuitions. One U.S. Navy instructor who was a specialist at using electronic signals to identify airplanes told us that when he was just starting out, an old hand showed him that it was possible to distinguish between the electronic signatures of certain commercial and military airplanes. The young man couldn't hear any difference, but once he knew it was possible, he practiced diligently. Every time an airplane flew within range, he studied the signal. And eventually, he was able to make the distinction intuitively.

Setting the Climate

The third feature of master coaches is in the attitude they create. Their attitude is a respectful one rather than a punitive or evaluative one. They don't ask, "Can you learn this?" but, "How can we find a way for you to get better?" They approach the lesson as a collaboration between teacher and student.

As a result, the trainees feel responsible for improving their skills. If you want to develop someone's intuitions, you need to work with an active, engaged learner, not one who is defensive and passive.

Once we put on a coaching skills workshop with fire department captains and structured it so that we had three blocks of time, each separated by a few weeks. The reason for this schedule was to let the captains practice the methods we were teaching them and get back to us with their questions and problems. We wanted the coaching methods to become part of their repertoire, rather than a one-shot jolt of instruction.

During the second session, one of the captains asked us if he could apply these methods toward personnel problems and conflicts as well as skills coaching. We didn't think so. We didn't want to make claims that the coaching methods could accomplish all kinds of things, and had no reason to believe that the methods could be used for personnel issues.

A few months later, however, in the final session of the series, the captain came back and informed us that we were wrong. He had had a firefighter in his department who was a real attitude problem. The man refused to listen, refused to obey orders, and was defiant. After the previous coaching session, the captain's crew had gone on a fire run and the problem firefighter had once again messed up.

Normally, the captain would have confronted him about it: "How many times have I told you not to do it that way? You're incompetent. I'm writing this up so that I can document my case when I throw you out of the department."

However, this time the captain decided to try some of the coaching methods he had just learned. When they were back in the station, the captain arranged to be alone with the firefighter. The captain said, "I was surprised at how you handled this last run. I'm wondering what your reasoning was." (This is based on the tactic of taking the trainee's perspective.) The firefighter explained what he was trying to do, and the captain realized that it made sense. Just because it wasn't what the captain expected didn't mean it was stupid. The captain explained why he expected a different strategy, and described its advantages, but acknowledged the strengths of the strategy the man had used.

"And you know what?" the captain told us, in the third workshop session. "We've been okay ever since. That firefighter didn't have an attitude problem. *I* was the attitude problem. So these coaching methods *can* apply for personnel problems!"

The three aspects of master coaching—assessing/diagnosing, tailoring instruction, setting the climate—should help you become a better coach. And don't forget the core methods of the intuition skills training program. You can use the decision requirements table as a diagnostic/assessment tool to establish the trainee's needs. You can use decision games both to diagnose your subordinates' abilities and as another method for tailoring their instruction. You can also use the decision-making critique as an instructional tool—to review the way you or the trainee handled an incident.

Getting Coached

𝕐ou won't always be the coach. Sometimes you will be the one who needs coaching. What can you do to get the assistance you want? Perhaps if you're lucky you will have a boss who is good about passing on expertise. But too often your boss will be somebody like the pilot in Example 13.1, who didn't share any of his insights with his co-pilot.

When you do gain access to a skilled decision maker who is not energetic about providing any coaching, how can you make effective use of this opportunity? It's probably going to be up to you to start the interaction. Based on the model of master coaching, there are some suggestions.

Actions to Take

• Probe for specific incidents and stories. This is not the same thing as listening to war stories. It means selecting incidents where intuition was needed, and expertise was challenged, and then digging into the details.

• Ask about cues and patterns. Try to find out what the expert was noticing while making sense of the situation. You want to uncover types of discriminations that the expert has learned to make, types of patterns the expert has learned to recognize. The decision-making critique can suggest lines of questioning.

• Follow this with "what if" questions. You can use hypothetical variations of the incident to dig even deeper.

• Ask the expert to contrast how a novice would have approached the incident. You can nominate yourself as the novice: "What mistakes would I have made in interpreting that information? What would I have been likely to try here? What patterns did you see that would have confused me?"

• Press the expert to learn something while talking to you. Instead of allowing the expert to recite familiar material, try to get the expert to reflect on a challenging incident and see it from some new perspectives. Ask the expert to reflect on subtle cues and patterns. You may find that this type of probing helps experts realize how they accomplished a difficult part of the task. This type of learning on the part of the expert is a good sign that you are getting at some important aspects of the expert's intuitions.

- Don't ask for general advice. Too often, you'll get slogans and adages. You'll hear things like, "Make customer satisfaction your number-one priority," but you won't find out how to do this.
- Don't encourage experts to expound on their "general theories." Many experts love to share their theories of the universe. These theories aren't necessarily part of the experts' intuitions. The expert may be trying to filibuster as a way of avoiding tougher questions. Sometimes these general theories of how to do the job can give you a helpful overview, but if the lecture isn't getting you what you need, ask for specific examples.
- Don't settle for information that is readily available. You can read it on your own time. Your time with the expert is too precious to be wasted in this way.
- Don't continue if either party gets bored. That's a sign that you aren't getting at useful insights.

In 1999 the Navy asked my company to use our explorations of intuitive decision making and on-the-job training to prepare a program to improve coaching. With all the time that sailors spend at sea, there are lots of opportunities for on-the-job training, but few opportunities for classroom training. There is also a lot of expertise on board a ship. The question is how to transfer it to the people who need it. Our task was to coach people in how to become better on-the-job coaches, and how to learn more from coaching sessions.

The program that my colleagues designed was aimed both at the coaches and the trainees. We helped the experts see how they could do a better job of providing coaching, using methods I've outlined in this chapter. In addition, we helped the trainees see how they could ask questions and take more control of their own learning, drawing more from the experts. The collaboration was designed to increase what the trainees knew, improve how they thought about problems, and improve their ability to carry out routines.

The Navy coordinated with us to evaluate the effectiveness of this program. Not only were the trainers using a wider range of strategies during feedback sessions, they covered more relevant topics than the sessions of the control group. More important, the trainees who went through this program were interpreting situations more like their trainers, compared to their control group counterparts.

So it's clear that coaching skills can be taught. Further, it seems to help to prepare the trainees as well as the coaches. Both parties need to appreciate that coaching should be a collaboration.

Not only can you be working with your subordinates to expand their patterns, action scripts, and mental models, but you can also be alert for ways to put these types of knowledge into action. To help someone develop intuitions, you can sensitize them to different types of tough decisions. You can help them learn where they have to direct their attention, so that they can spot the problem signs while there is still time to do something about it. You can help them appreciate different types of uncertainty, and to expand their repertoire of reactions. You can assist them in sizing up situations. You can help them construct new options. You can prepare them to adapt and improvise.

When sharing your intuition skills with others:

- Demonstrate the task while thinking aloud

- Discuss potential problems

- Explore consequences of mistakes

- Have trainee think aloud while performing the task

- Have trainee instruct the coach on how to achieve the task

- Explore alternative action scripts

- Ask open-ended questions

- Notice improvements

- Focus on two to three issues per session

- Encourage trainee to go beyond the procedures to develop an intuitive feel for the task

Overcoming the Problems with Metrics

14

ecause our intuitions can mislead us we often want to track events using objective measures. To do this, we develop metrics that will record what we need to know, whether it is a rate of change, a degree of progress, or some other feature that will help us make decisions. Metrics are yardsticks measuring important characteristics of performance. For example, the metric of batting average tells us something about the skill of a baseball player. The metric of market share tells us the extent to which a company dominates its industry.

Intuition and hunches can't really help us figure out overhead rates or make budget projections. Intuition comes to us through emotional reactions and perceptions, not through numbers. Our hunches just pop into our minds without leaving any auditable trail about how they were formed. In contrast, metrics provide a firm documentation for our decisions. If someone questions us, we can point to the numbers to explain ourselves.

Unfortunately, metrics are not always more trustworthy than intuitions. Too often, what is hard about hard numbers is that they are hard to obtain, hard to interpret, and hard to apply. Quantifying the elements of a situation doesn't guarantee that we will make a good decision.

Metrics can even *interfere* with intuition. The hard numbers don't necessarily add up to a story that explains the sequence of events that may be puzzling us. We could live with this interference if the metrics helped us do a better job. Unfortunately, metrics are as likely to *mislead* us as to help us.

Nevertheless, we cannot dispense with metrics. They force us to

Jerry Kirby, the CEO of Citizen's Federal Bank for twenty-five years, relied heavily on metrics to spot problems and size up situations. He worked hard to make sure he had the right benchmarks in place for his bank as a whole, and for the major departments. The four metrics he relied on most heavily were ROI (return on investment), ROE (return on equity), ROA (return on assets), and Efficiency Ratio (revenue minus expenses, divided by the number of employees).

He used these benchmarks to assess if the service provided by a department was efficient and profitable. And he would conduct his review every quarter in order to see if a department was getting better, worse, or staying the same. If a department kept getting worse, he would check it again the next quarter, and eventually ask whether the bank should be offering that product or service.

Kirby knew that the department heads, as champions for their activities, could get emotionally involved. The metrics helped Kirby keep the project reviews objective.

square our intuitions with reality. For example, they'll keep us from retaining a project leader whose skill at projecting an image of confidence masks the reality of missed deadlines, overspent budgets, and disappointing rates of progress.

This isn't as easy as it sounds. Jerry Kirby, in Example 14.1, was trained as an accountant. Therefore, he knew where the numbers were coming from, he had set up these benchmarks for others, and he was careful to factor in conditions such as a business slump or recession that might be skewing the numbers. He appreciated that a service might be running into trouble because of a lack of marketing support, or because the managers weren't up to the challenge. The benchmarks were put into place to catch his attention, not to make his decisions. That is why CEOs such as Kirby want their chief financial officer to have experience managing operations so they aren't simply reporting the numbers without appreciating what goes into the numbers.

So the challenge is to find a way to blend intuition and metrics. This is the same challenge we discussed back in Chapter 4, blending intuition with analysis. We don't want to abandon metrics but we don't want to be fooled by them either. We need to find ways to use metrics effectively to support and correct our intuitions, so that we can benefit from two different ways of interpreting events.

The Functions of Metrics

We rely on metrics for a number of reasons:

SETTING GOALS We can use metrics to define goals. A technique such as "management by objectives" relies on our ability to measure the degree to which goals are being accomplished so that we can tie our judgments of good and poor performance to progress in reaching outcomes.

SETTING TRIPWIRES We can use metrics to set alarms for ourselves. "Once a contract has spent 85 percent of the available funds, it needs to be reviewed." "When cash reserves decline four months in a row, initiate an investigation."

SPOTTING TRENDS Metrics can help us monitor changes over time.

SENSEMAKING Metrics combine lots of data to give a bottom-line picture.

REGULATING PERFORMANCE Metrics provide us with feedback that helps us adjust performance. If you are running a race, you want to know how fast you are completing each mile, and what your pace is. That way, you can be careful not to peak too early.

ENSURING COMPLIANCE In situations where we don't want subordinates to use their judgment, we can sometimes establish a metric for them to use. This allows the subordinate to act without thinking, and without having personal responsibility. "When the price of the stock reaches $54, buy 2,000 shares for me."

MAKING COMPARISONS Metrics can help us contrast different activities by putting them on a common scale. Thus, Kirby could compare

> *EXAMPLE 14.2* THE ECONOMIC EDUCATION OF A MARINE GENERAL

Retired Marine Corps General Anthony Zinni is currently a special envoy to the Middle East. Prior to his retirement, Zinni was the commander in chief of Central Command. A few years before this appointment we had a chance to interview him about earlier missions in places like Somalia and Russia. One theme that repeatedly emerged was the need to make sense of metrics in order to understand local economies.

In Somalia, Zinni landed with his Marine contingent, and tried to carry out the mission of reducing tensions and violence. Three months into the mission, Zinni asked his subordinates whether they were succeeding. One data element they had to work with was that when they arrived, the price of a Russian AK-47 assault weapon was $50, and now, three months later, the price had risen to $300. This seemed like good news—it meant that their efforts to confiscate weapons was having an effect. Their actions were creating a scarcity that was driving the prices up. Then someone else argued that maybe the price was so high because there was a much greater demand—maybe insecurity was now so much greater that more people than ever wanted high-quality weapons. And there was Zinni, not trained as an economist, needing to figure this out. (He eventually brought other indicators to bear, and judged that the price change was due to reduced supply, not increased demand.)

In a mission in Russia, Zinni had wondered whether conditions were getting better or worse. A data point was that the price of meat was going down. Therefore, more people should be able to obtain meat. However, closer analysis showed that the price was falling because so few people could afford meat, and also because farmers could not afford to feed livestock and were slaughtering them, thus increasing the supply. What seemed like a promising observation was just the opposite—a cause for concern.

the return on investment for the different departments in his bank to see what was driving his profits.

EVALUATING AND REWARDING PERFORMANCE Metrics can help motivate performance, such as paying by the item produced rather than the number of hours worked.

Promoting fairness Metrics can help us develop fair policies. An example would be monitoring the number of mortgage loans made to minorities. If bank officers had to use credit ratings and other objective criteria instead of their own judgment, they might not build up expertise in making credit judgments, but they would be less likely to deny credit due to racial prejudice. Another example would be instructors basing final grades on test scores, instead of awarding extra credit to the teacher's pet. In these ways, metrics can help to develop a meritocracy.

Helping us build stories and mental models We can use metrics to understand the issues that challenge us. This points the way for blending metrics with intuitions. When we use metrics to build richer mental models, we are gaining expertise.

Example 14.2 shows the difficulty of just relying on the economic indicators without understanding how they were obtained—the stories behind the numbers. We will return to this theme later.

Metrics Can Mislead Us

Just because someone has run the numbers doesn't mean that we have to believe the conclusion. Numbers aren't necessarily more credible than intuitions based on experience. Here are several examples that pit data against intuition: Example 14.3 cautions us about putting too much faith in hard data; Example 14.4 cautions us about relying too much on metrics.

Once we know what the metric is, we can usually find a way to "game" it—to show that we are doing well according to the official yardstick even though we are not making progress toward the larger objectives. One famous failure of managing by the numbers was the attempt of Robert McNamara to manage the Vietnam conflict using statistical control methods he had developed at Ford Motor Company. The result was attrition warfare that emphasized counting bodies, instead of trying to outmaneuver the adversary. Soldiers started inflating body counts to create an impression of success.

No one would argue that a poor selection of metrics can create difficulties. But the problem is more basic—metrics have *inherent* limita-

Several years ago, one of the original information technology companies re-leased a product that helped customers use its database records to locate other individuals. Included in these records were not only the normal name and ad-dress information, but also the social security numbers for tens of millions of people. The ensuing uproar surrounding this invasion of privacy resulted in an avalanche of telephone calls. But after a few days the number of calls peaked and leveled off. For some managers, the curve of phone calls suggested that they had gotten through the worst of it, and soon the problem would blow over. However, the tone of the calls that did come in was as venomous as ever. Exec-utives who had been listening in on some of the calls refused to believe that the problem was going away, despite the data. Their intuition told them that the problem was as serious as ever and perhaps even getting worse.

The number crunchers carried the day and the company continued the product as designed. Subsequently, the company found out that the curve of telephone calls had appeared to flatten out because the local telephone com-pany's switching equipment had run out of capacity and was rejecting calls due to lack of available circuits. The actual number of protest calls had reached a level several times the number that were actually getting through.

The end result was that the company eventually had to turn off the new service. The skeptical executives' intuition had turned out to be correct.

tions. There are two basic problems associated with metrics even when they are used skillfully: the loss of *history* about how the data were collected and analyzed, and the loss of *context* for understanding the metrics.

THE LOSS OF HISTORY A strength of metrics is that they present us with a snapshot without bothering us with the details of the process by which that snapshot was acquired. This loss of history speeds up communica-tion. However, the fact that the method for obtaining data isn't usually shared means that we have to judge the numbers on face value. When someone provides us with metrics in the form of summarized data, we can't follow the logic that person has used in compiling the data, which makes it very difficult to be sure if we can trust the numbers.

Burger King was growing tired of running in second place in the fast food race, behind McDonald's. Although the Burger King hamburgers received higher taste test scores than McDonald's, the McDonald's french fry was tops in consumer ratings. The Burger King fry was regarded as soggy, limp, often cold. This was a barrier to attracting more customers, and it was also a revenue weakness because french fries offer one of the higher profit margins on fast food menus. Burger King decided to launch an attack on the McDonald's potato supremacy.

The market researchers at Burger King determined that consumers like french fries that are crunchy on the outside, soft on the inside, and that stayed hot. The scientists figured out how to coat the potatoes with a layer of starch to retain heat and increase crunch. McDonald's was not coating its french fries, so Burger King believed it had a chance for a breakthrough and announced it through a $70M marketing campaign. On January 2, 1998, "Free Fryday," Burger King distributed fifteen million orders of french fries across the United States.

The national advertisement campaign would be effective only if all of the Burger King franchises across the country were capable of delivering the new model of french fry. Each supplier had to be provided with new equipment, and 300,000 restaurant managers and staff members had to be trained and "certifried" to prepare the new fry. Burger King prepared a nineteen-page french fry specification document, and it included an unusual requirement: "For each mouthful of french fry, the degree of crispiness was to be 'determined by an audible crunch that should be present for seven or more chews . . . loud enough to be apparent to the evaluator.' "

At first, the new french fries were a hit. But after six months, the quality of the fries began to go downhill. One reason was the seven-chew audible crunch metric. With a seven-crunch minimum, restaurants started to add more batter, more starch, just to be safe. As a result, the potato flavor became weaker, and the fries got cold more quickly. The seven-crunch metric was superseding other criteria that were more important. Eventually, Burger King conceded defeat. Thirty months after introducing the product, Burger King rapidly phased it out. A new version is being introduced, with less coating. And the seven-crunch metric has been withdrawn.

THE LOSS OF CONTEXT A strength of metrics is that they give us streamlined data. By abstracting the situations, metrics let us make comparisons in different settings. The numbers are intended to be taken out of context.

The trouble is that seeing the metrics out of context can cause us to misinterpret information. Further, the advantage of metrics—that they give us a simple answer—is also a disadvantage because simple metrics are almost always inadequate and misleading.

The simpler the metric, the more likely it is to mislead us. Effective CEOs, like Jerry Kirby, have learned to rely on a range of metrics rather than a single yardstick and have learned to use the metrics to raise flags, not to make decisions. But they are the exception. More typically, number crunchers are asked to reduce their analyses to single dimensions, to make it easier on the decision makers. Too often, time pressure and lack of expertise press business leaders into a "How did we do last month?" mentality, looking for a thumbs-up or -down.

Therefore, we have a conflict—the need to present all the facets and nuances of the data, versus the need to boil those data down. "Just give me the bottom line" is a phrase we have all heard or expressed.

For some CEOs, their bottom-line metric is cash flow. For others, it's retained earnings. At Apple Computer, it was the marginal return per computer sold—how much profit they got from each sale. During its prime, Apple was able to keep this profit margin high. This metric contributed to the disasters that befell Apple in the late 1990s. Apple lost market share by charging such high prices, which meant less incentive for software developers to write programs for the Mac, which created a downward spiral of smaller market share, fewer games and other types of programs.

Executives and managers also like simple metrics because they make it easy to set goals for staff members. We have already seen how Burger King used Management By Objectives to establish a criterion for its ill-fated french fries.

In many cases people and organizations just adjust to make their simple metrics work for them. For instance, airlines are now evaluated for their on-time arrivals. They have responded by lengthening the flight times to give themselves more of a cushion to meet the objective. It now can take more official time to go between cities than it used to. Airlines also count pushing back from the gate as leaving, to count as an on-time departure.

Sometimes the way we fudge simple metrics does create problems. This phenomenon is called "perverse incentives"—its effect is the opposite of what is desired by the people who set performance targets, as employees find unforeseen ways to meet the targets.

The United Kingdom unwittingly created perverse incentives when it set performance targets to make public services more accountable. The British government decided it needed to reduce hospital waiting lists, and set a performance target to cut the number of people waiting for treatment by 100,000. The medical service reached this target, but did so by distorting its priorities. Because minor disorders are handled more quickly than major ones, hospital managers pressured surgeons to give smaller problems priority over larger ones.

Simple metrics blind us to the larger context and make it difficult for us to use our intuitions. There are no single or simple metrics that cannot be gamed, resulting in consequences detrimental to the organization. Perverse incentives are the rule, not the exception.

Imagine that you are the CEO of a small business and have been traveling for the previous two months, essentially out of contact with your office. Upon your return, the head of the accounting department greets you with the news that your cash flow has improved. You are only using $525,000 of your line of credit with the bank. The ceiling is $725,000. That leaves you a cushion of $200,000. Now is the time to purchase that accounting software package that your executive board has been pushing.

Do you agree? Hopefully not. You need to learn the stories behind the numbers. What has the line of credit been doing—increasing or decreasing? Are the revenues in the coming month expected to exceed the expenses? Is the $525,000 current as of last week, last month, last quarter? Were there any atypical expenses or income that could distort the picture?

The numbers may be your last profitable moment, or they may signal a long period of prosperity. Without digging further you can't tell.

I don't believe we should be shielded from data. Rather, we need better navigation tools to drill down into the data to get the story and the context behind the numbers.

Metrics and Stories

e can synthesize metrics and intuition by using stories. A story describes how things came about—how a few primary influences caused the outcome we are trying to understand. We can use stories to add context to the metrics—and the metrics help us impose discipline on stories.

In Example 14.2, General Zinni could only interpret the metrics by filling in the stories about the cost of the AK-47 in Somalia, and the price of meat in Moscow. Zinni did not want to proceed with his mission simply on the basis of impressions and opinions. A metric such as the cost of the AK-47 had to be fitted into a narrative about how his operation was succeeding. After Zinni built a story around the metric, he discovered that different, less optimistic explanations were also possible. His mental model of the possibilities had become richer.

Think of metrics as the pieces to a puzzle. Without a story, a chance to see the big picture, we can't form an intuition about how to put these pieces together. We can compare each piece to each other piece but that's a laborious process. However, if we use the picture on the box to know what the pieces are supposed to show after they are assembled, it'll be much easier to get a rough, intuitive idea of where the individual pieces belong.

We can blend metrics and stories to accomplish several different functions.

a. *Sensemaking.* We can use metrics and stories to make sense of a situation. Like a puzzle, we need both the picture (the story) and the pieces (the metrics) to proceed. General Zinni believed that the United States forces were making the situation in Somalia more stable. Otherwise, Zinni would have needed to rely on his memories of how jumpy the Somalians appeared to him when he arrived, to see if they appeared more relaxed after he had been there a while. These types of impressions based on memories can help flag apparent anomalies, but they aren't a reliable basis for gauging rate of progress. And that was why Zinni was seeking metrics—to test his intuitions.

b. *Competing stories.* If we have competing stories we can search for the metrics that will help us select one of the stories. In doing a puzzle we may realize that a grouping of pieces can go in two different places. So we start looking for specific pieces that will resolve the ambiguity. In the Somalia example, Zinni discovered he could not rely on the cost curve of AK-47s because the same data would support the opposite story—that he was making the situation worse, not better. Conflicts like this help us adjust our confidence in the stories.

c. *Goal setting.* We can use metrics and stories to communicate goals. In working with others on a puzzle, we could point to the picture on the box to give the team members their assignments. In business, if we just rely on the metrics as objectives, we run into the problem of perverse incentives. An intent such as "Make customer satisfaction our number-one priority" doesn't mean much unless it is accompanied by some metrics to show how we plan to measure success. And posting a metric without providing the purpose too often encourages fudging. We need both.

d. *Evaluating metrics.* We can use stories to evaluate metrics by explaining where the data came from. Often we find that the confidence we place in metrics disappears as we discover how they are collected. Here, we need stories to interpret the metrics. One retired professor described to me how he still remembered a time in a graduate class when he was reporting some findings he had read about, and wrote a number on the blackboard. The professor asked him, "Where did that number come from?" And he had to admit that he didn't know. "Thereafter, when I saw a number in a paper, or a metric of any sort, I made sure I knew where it came from! So have many, many students whose committees I have been on."

e. *Evaluating stories.* Metrics don't have to replace our intuitions. They let us perform analyses that inform and help us correct our intuitions. If the metrics surprise you, don't try to explain the numbers away. Take the numbers seriously and be critical about your intuitions. The numbers can lead you away from a fixation on an incorrect interpretation.

Too often, metrics are not used to perform any of the functions listed above. During military exercises, commanders sometimes ask, "Are we winning?" They want to know if they are competing well against the adversary. Staff members are prone to respond with numbers: "We have destroyed this many tanks, and that many airplanes, and our own losses are . . ." This isn't what the commanders want to know. They are trying to form a judgment, an intuition, about how well they are doing. Numbers are only part of the impression. Primarily, the commanders' sense of progress is based on whether they are increasing their ability to adapt and be flexible, and reducing the adversary's adaptivity. They may have destroyed a lot of tanks and airplanes because the adversary saw a chance to take a strategic pass, and launched a desperate and successful attack.

Schwarzkopf's skill was in being able to look beyond the facts, and to imagine what must be happening on the battlefield (see Example 14.5). There was no metric to read, but once Schwarzkopf had a few pieces of data, he could assemble a story, and that was how he was able to interpret the events. If Schwarzkopf had waited for all the official reports to come in, for the data to be scrubbed, for all the metrics to be calculated, it is likely that he would have squandered the momentum of the attack. The data he was using weren't part of the official information collection plans but that didn't stop him from using those data to build his story of the collapse of the Iraqi front lines.

We see the complementary strategy in Example 14.6, which relates how Alan Greenspan tried to make sense of productivity changes in the 1990s.

Greenspan wasn't going to take numbers at face value. He could use his mental model of the economy and his ability to spot patterns to build a story that cast doubt on some of the numbers. Then he

In 1996 pressure was mounting on the Federal Reserve to increase interest rates. Corporate profits had been rising, and unemployment had dropped to 5.5 percent well below the 6.0 percent level that had historically triggered higher inflation. Alan Greenspan, the chairman of the Federal Reserve, had to balance the effects of a rate increase—slowing the economy—against the needs to fight inflation.

But Greenspan didn't believe that inflation was going to be a problem. Over the past year, the core inflation rate reported by the government was less than it had been for several decades, only 2.6 percent. His review of the data suggested that workers were not going to agitate for higher wages, despite the low unemployment; he believed that many workers worried about job insecurity and were reluctant to take actions that might force them to change jobs. Workers had gotten sizeable raises in the early 1990s, and now seemed to be more attached to their jobs, and more productive. It was a pattern that seemed to emerge during 1994 and 1995, and was continuing.

The hypothesized productivity gains fit into another puzzle. Business profits were growing sharply, but prices were stable and so were wages. The only explanation Greenspan could find was that productivity was going up as well. Companies were investing their profits in new technology and making themselves more productive. However, the data showed that productivity—the output per hour for a worker—was going *down*. It didn't make sense. Profits couldn't go up if prices, labor costs, and non-labor costs stayed the same, and

cont.

could selectively dig for the more detailed numbers that let him build a better story of what was really going on. The story and the measures both needed to inform each other, as in the parable about Marco Polo:

Marco Polo describes a bridge, stone by stone.

"But which is the stone that supports the bridge?" Kublai Khan asks.

"The bridge is not supported by one stone or another," Marco answers, "but by the line of the arch they form."

Kublai Khan remains silent, reflecting. Then he adds: "Why do you speak to me of stones. It is only the arch that matters to me."

Polo answers: "Without stones there is no arch."

Example 14.6 (cont.)

productivity went down. He was sure of the other parts of the equation—the profits, the prices, the labor and non-labor costs—so productivity had to be going up.

Greenspan was having trouble fitting these data points together and explaining them to his colleagues on the Federal Reserve Board. He was seeing things that just weren't there, according to the numbers. Greenspan's conclusion was that the numbers had to be wrong.

He instructed the staff of the Federal Reserve to "disaggregate" the numbers in order to get at the story behind the story. Instead of seeing the overall data for productivity growth, he wanted to see it for different types of businesses such as farms, manufacturing companies, mining companies, public utilities, financial services companies, auto repair companies, health services, and retailers. He wanted to understand the story behind each of these economies.

The results showed that productivity was generally *increasing*, except for the service businesses where productivity had been falling. But it was clear that these data for the service providers were flawed. Approximately a third of American companies fall into this category, and there was general agreement that productivity in the service sector was increasing, not decreasing. Moreover, these flawed data were dragging down the overall productivity numbers.

By getting underneath the aggregated statistics, Greenspan was able to buttress his story of productivity growth, and counter the pressures to raise the interest rates, thus helping to keep the economic expansion going for several more years. Unemployment dropped below 4.5 percent by the end of 1998, and inflation dropped with it, down below 2 percent.

Representing the Metrics

It's important to present data and metrics in a form that supports intuition. Otherwise, there will be unnecessary conflict between the two. For example, many statisticians and decision researchers have complained that people don't know how to use base rates. A base rate is the general rate of occurrence for an event.

Test your own judgment on this example:

The probability that a woman of age forty has breast cancer is about 1 percent. If she has breast cancer, the probability that she tests positive on a screening mammogram is 90 percent. If she does not have breast cancer, the probability that she nevertheless tests positive is 9 percent. What are the chances that a woman who tests positive actually has breast cancer?

What is your estimate?
Now try this problem:

Think of 100 women. One has breast cancer, and she likely will test positive. Of the 99 who don't have breast cancer, 9 will also test positive. Thus, a total of 10 women will test positive. How many of those who test positive actually have breast cancer?

This doesn't seem tricky at all. But it's the same problem. Instead of using probabilities, this version relies on simple frequencies. You can see that the answer is that only one out of ten women who test positive actually has breast cancer.

Gerd Gigerenzer, in his new book *Calculated Risks: How to Know When Numbers Deceive You,* shows that people can usually do a good job of making estimates, as long as they are given the data in a form that supports their intuitions.

We are exposed to lots and lots of statistics. Our job, as informed citizens and consumers, is to make sense of them. Gigerenzer describes a study of 1,000 Germans who were asked what "40 percent" means. They were given choices: (a) one quarter; (b) four out of ten; (c) every fortieth person. Around one-third of the people tested got it wrong. (The answer is [b], four out of ten.)

Gigerenzer makes the claim that probability data are poorly suited to our intuitions. Yet we have little trouble analyzing the same data when they're presented as frequencies—tallies of counts, such as "Of the ninety-nine who do not have breast cancer, nine others will also test positive," instead of "If she does not have breast cancer, the probability that she nevertheless tests positive is 9 percent." This is because our minds are adapted to natural frequencies, especially when we can visualize them.

Gigerenzer has shown that AIDS counselors often get confused by probability data. As a result the counselors routinely misinterpret the results of screening tests. Some counselors interpret a positive test result as a definite sign of AIDS, even though there is a good chance that the client doesn't have AIDS at all—the AIDS tests are not completely accurate, just as breast cancer results are not completely accurate in the previous example. Several cases have been documented of people committing suicide after getting positive results on their AIDS screening tests, even though they actually did not have AIDS. An inaccurate representation and interpretation of data can be hazardous to your health.

Fantasy Baseball

Across America, there is a vast underground conspiracy that enslaves otherwise productive members of society in a cult of statistics and metrics. I'm referring to fantasy baseball. In 1992 I decided to study this conspiracy up close to get a better idea of how it works. I agreed to participate in a fantasy league that was formed in my own company. In the interests of science, I sustained my observations throughout the following decade. And rather than be a passive uninvolved spectator, I have actively fielded my own teams. Some might think of this as an addiction, but to my mind, true dedication to science demands no less.

To preserve some veneer of research, the members of our league have occasionally filled out data sheets recording our rationale at the time we've made decisions. We have also conducted some systematic debriefing sessions to identify reasons behind the good and poor decisions we've made. Fantasy baseball requires frequent decisions about alternative options: which player to acquire, which player to release.

The association between baseball and metrics is not altogether whimsical. No sport is as amenable to metrics as baseball, or as compulsive about maintaining and applying statistical analyses. And, within baseball, there are few avenues as well designed for our needs as fantasy baseball, because fantasy baseball has stripped out all of the irrelevancies, such as the actual physical play, or the interference created by agents and owners. It's a pure exercise of metrics.

For those readers who would like a brief description of fantasy baseball, here it is in one paragraph: When the baseball season starts the members of a fantasy league draft real major league players onto their imaginary teams. The selection of players usually involves some sort of auction. Usually each team has slots for about twenty-five players, so that would mean around ten pitchers and fifteen hitters. Once the season begins, each "owner" compiles points using predetermined statistical categories. From your hitters, you want to achieve the following: home runs, RBIs (runs batted in), runs scored, stolen bases, and batting average (number of hits divided by number of times at bat). There are corresponding categories for pitchers. Each week, the league owners calculate how many home runs, RBIs, runs scored, stolen bases, and hits per opportunity their players rang up, much the way a bookkeeper might tally up financial results. Owners whose teams did well (scored a lot of runs, had a lot of hits to raise their batting averages, and so forth) move up in the standings. Everything is computable.

Here are some observations my colleagues and I have made over the years:

1. *Fantasy baseball involves multiple metrics, and this can trap someone who relies solely on intuition.* I remember being very pleased when I drafted Tony Gwynn, perhaps the best hitter of his generation, because Tony usually had the highest batting average, or at least was in the top three. However, when I looked more carefully, I noticed that Tony didn't hit many home runs, or steal many bases, or have many runs batted in. And toward the end of his career he had a fair share of injuries, taking him out of the lineup too often. Just because Tony had received a lot of deserved praise as a hitter, that didn't make him a valuable asset. Fantasy baseball showed us that we could not trust our intuition. We had to keep our eyes on the numbers. And we could not fixate on a single number. We had to track a range of metrics to get a true picture of a player's worth. *In business, it is also risky to rely on a single metric which assures you of a one-dimensional view. It takes more work to gather and track multiple metrics, but they can give you a better picture of performance.*

2. *Baseball is about base rates.* Base rates are the long-term averages. Some researchers have found that decision makers don't always do a good job of taking base rates into account. In fantasy baseball, this is the sign of a sucker, someone who sees a hitter do well for a few games

and believes that the hitter will keep it up for the whole season. For example, if a month into the season a player is hitting over .400 (a very good average), some people begin speculating that the player can achieve this for the full season. However, no one has hit over .400 for a full season since Ted Williams did it in 1941. It is very unlikely. Short-term successes cannot be interpreted as typical performance levels. Base rates matter—how well has this person hit in previous seasons? *Business executives also have to be careful to take a longer view or else they may jump to conclusions based on random fluctuations in sales.*

3. *But which base rates should we use?* Here, fantasy baseball illustrates the problem with trying to rely on base rates. Do we use the hitter's average for the past week as our best guess of his current capability? Too short. How about his performance over the year? But sometimes players can have a good or a bad few months, being lucky or recovering from a nagging injury. So, what about the previous year? Or the player's entire career? This doesn't take into account a player's ability to improve. How about using several previous years and perhaps relying on trends? This is exactly the argument Steve Wolf made in trying to trade me Mickey Morandini. Figure 14.1 is the "Morandini curve" that Steve drew to argue that Morandini was going to hit .282 in the coming year, after batting .241, .249, and .265 in the previous three years.

I was skeptical. The trend would have Morandini achieve a level that he had never previously accomplished. What is your assessment of Morandini's likely average: .282 as Steve suggested, .265, the level of his previous year, .252, the average of his three previous years, or something else? The existence of base rates does not constitute a solution. Having too many base rates is not much better than having too few. (In 1993, Mickey Morandini batted .247, lower than any of these base rates would suggest. However, in fairness to Morandini, he did bat .292 in 1994, and even reached .296 in 1998, his highest level yet in eleven years as a major leaguer.)

Executives are surely familiar with the frustration of trying to determine the appropriate base rates. For example, consider the debate in 2000 about why the euro was undervalued against the dollar. Compared to its starting level in January of 1999, the euro had fallen 27 percent against the dollar, down to $.86. However, if the euro had been in existence in 1985 it would have traded at $.69. So whether the euro is up or down versus the dollar depends on how you set up your base rate.

4. We need to use stories to make sense of the base rates. On another occasion Steve Wolf saw me hesitating about picking up Hal Morris. Morris had a very nice batting average, but didn't have much power. I didn't mind the lack of home runs. However, I was going to need a hitter who provided more runs batted in than Morris had ever achieved. No matter how I looked at the data, no matter how I scrutinized his past performance, I didn't see Morris driving in enough RBIs. Then Steve mentioned that for the coming year, Morris was going to be moved in the batting order from second to third. When you bat second, your job is to move the lead-off runner over. You can bunt or sacrifice, it doesn't matter which. It is better to hit a slow ground ball so the fielder gets you out at first and lets the runner move, than to hit a sharp ground ball that can be turned into a double play. In batting third, however, your job is to swing away and drive the runner in. So the shift in batting order rendered Morris's data less relevant. And, in fact, Morris did go on to get a lot of RBIs from the third position in the batting order.

Now, perhaps my failure here was that I neglected to consult the appropriate base rate. I should have somehow factored in the increase in RBIs scored when the same player shifts from number two to number three in the batting order. But how was I to know this without a

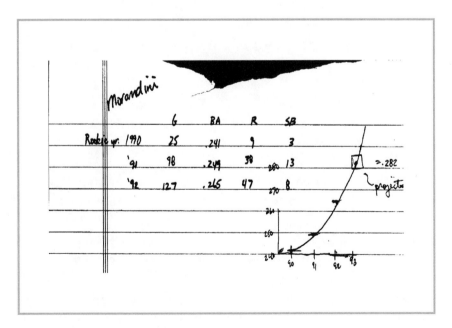

Figure 14.1 The Morandini Curve

causal model, a story? Without a story, I would have to go scrambling every time any change was announced: a new lead-off hitter, a replacement in the number six hitter, a new photo on the player's trading card. Changes are occurring all the time. How do I know which are important? I could take a data-driven approach, and study all the changes, factoring in only those that seem to have an impact. This seems pretty cumbersome. Instead, I believe I need to rely on stories to alert me to the changes that probably make a difference.

In looking at a pitcher over time, we might notice that he was less effective with every start for the past several games. This might be an aberration (short-term trends aren't reliable). Or it might portend an injury. Thus, Steve Wolf heard a rumor the general manager of the Cincinnati Reds was in the market to trade for some starting pitchers. That aroused Steve's suspicions. He checked and saw that Jose Rijo (star pitcher for the Reds at the time) had not pitched particularly well in his last few outings. Even more worrisome, Rijo had not gone more than six innings in any of these starts. This was enough to prompt Steve to trade Rijo, who continued to struggle for a few more games before admitting injury and going on the Disabled List.

The need for stories is painfully evident in the commercial arena. As I write this section, the drama of Enron is playing out—a $60B company less than a year ago has suddenly collapsed. One of the ways that Enron kept investors fooled so long is that it focused on one metric: earnings per share (EPS). This is a key number used by both analysts and investors. It is also easy to manipulate. Enron used a number of strategies such as setting up off-balance-sheet entities that were used to account for almost 30 percent of Enron's EPS in 2000. Some analysts probed for the story behind the metric and became skeptical. But most investors were content to take the EPS numbers at face value, and suffered the consequences.

5. *Fantasy baseball is as much about solving problems as making decisions.* We quickly learned that we had to be careful about how we replaced players who were put on the Disabled List because of injury. At the beginning, we treated these as decisions—who is the best remaining player to pick up? Later, we realized that we could treat these roster changes as opportunities to solve problems. Thus, David Klinger and his son Josh had to face the loss of third baseman Matt Williams, who broke his foot after being hit by a pitch. Here is the note that Dave wrote for our data log: "Matt Williams, the world's greatest baseball

player, broke his foot . . . I [am] picking up Kingery of Colorado for him. I am moving Jeff King to third and putting Kingery in my swing spot." The rationale? "Kingery is playing every day and hitting about .300. He can't hurt us. Also, he is an outfielder who, when Williams comes back or any other transaction allows it, can stay on the roster (if he continues to play well) and knock off Burks if he [Burks] doesn't come around."

Thus, the transaction was about building in some flexibility for the future, while taking care of current needs. If there had been another third baseman who had had slightly better statistics than either Kingery or King, then a calculative approach would have made that player the one selected. Dave and Josh Klinger traded some current performance for flexibility and the opportunity to divest themselves of a player—Burks—who was worrying them.

Business executives frequently transform decisions into problem-solving platforms as they bring in other concerns, other opportunities, other types of agendas. Only a neophyte would seek to make a decision on its own merits and screen out additional considerations.

The discussion of metrics in baseball, and this chapter in general, echoes the themes of Chapter 4. Intuition and analysis/metrics are not conflicting and incompatible forces. Neither is sufficient—both are necessary. Each is an imperfect means of understanding situations. Our job is to find ways to synthesize both of them in order to transcend each one.

Smart Technology Can Make Us Stupid

Information technologies are intended to make us more productive, but their use carries a penalty. The computer programs, the decision support systems, the search engines, databases, and shareware we use can diminish our intuition and expertise. They can make us stupid.

I don't have any concrete ideas for avoiding the damage inflicted on us by information technology. The best I can offer is to help readers become aware of the risks that information technology poses to our intuitions and our expertise.

I consider myself an advocate of information technology. For more than a decade I've worked with professionals such as Dick Stottler and Andrea Henke, who run an applied artificial intelligence company in San Mateo, California. I've had a chance to see how valuable these technologies can be. But like any tools, information technologies can be used well or misused.

Hospitals are filled with poisons and sharp instruments—researchers have estimated that thousands of people die unnecessarily in hospitals each year from careless misuse of tools, be they medicines or scalpels. Yet we wouldn't want to close hospitals down. Concerned professionals are doing everything they can to make hospitals safer.

We don't want to reject information technology any more than we would want to close down hospitals because they are dangerous places. We are never going to give up our computers and go back to typewriters. We know that computers do a better job than we could of rapidly solving the equations for estimating interest payments. We accept that our arithmetic skills have declined now that we use calculators. We remember fewer phone numbers now that we can set up speed dialing. Technology often leads to a loss of skills that are no longer practiced, but the trade-off is usually worth it.

Yet sometimes the trade-off is too risky. The trade-off is only worth making if the new combination of human + computer can outperform the human alone. Problems arise when (a) the new combination underperforms because the technology interferes with our intuitions; (b) the human + computer combination only outperforms humans in limited settings and otherwise breaks down; or (c) we've lost our intuitive skills by the time we discover the limitations of the technology.

Information technology can inflict three levels of damage. First, it can *disable* the expertise of people who are already skilled. Second, it can *slow their rate of learning*, so that it takes much longer for people to build up their intuitions and expertise. And third, it can *teach dysfunctional skills* that will actively interfere with the people's ability to achieve expertise in the future.

Everyone is familiar with the first level. Information technology disables our expertise by simply preventing us from finding the data we need to make decisions. We see this in displays that make it hard to read information because there is so much packed onto a computer screen. The more attention we have to spend on figuring out how to navigate through a decision support system, the less is available for staying on top of the situation.

To understand how information technology can inflict more lasting damage by slowing the rate of learning and teaching dysfunctional skills, consider a standard strategy people use to cope with excessive amounts of data: the "waterfall" model of data interpretation. The idea is that the clerical staff reviews and filters the data, moving it forward and transforming it so that the top managers just have to work at the level of understanding, the distilled essence of the data. Information technology relies on this model to spare us from the flood of data. The technology developers seek to use algorithms to transform the data into information, knowledge, and understanding.

This waterfall model made sense to me until my company had a chance to study skilled weather forecasters. In 1997 we were asked by the Air Force to figure out what made the good forecasters different from the rest. The Air Force wanted us to use our cognitive task analysis methods to get inside the heads of their best people. We interviewed over fifty weather forecasters in this project, including the

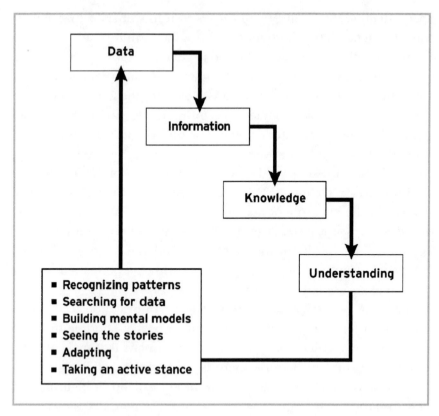

Data

Information

Knowledge

Understanding

- Recognizing patterns
- Searching for data
- Building mental models
- Seeing the stories
- Adapting
- Taking an active stance

Figure 15.1 Who Is Going to Turn Data into Understanding?

forecasting team that was brought in for the 1996 Atlanta Olympic games.

We found that the journeymen are good at their routines. They come in to work, check out the computer analyses, write these up, and send them to pilots and air traffic controllers. They are happy to use the available metrics provided by computer support systems.

The expert weather forecasters are different. As they leave their houses in the morning, they are sensitive to dew on the handrails of their front stairs. They notice the footprints they make as they walk across their lawns. As they walk to their cars, they look up at the clouds to get a sense of what the day is going to bring. When they get to work they don't want to see the computer runs. They don't want the previous forecaster to brief them on what to expect. The experts spend time looking at the data from the previous six hours or so, building up their own mental models of what has been happening since they left. Only when they are comfortable that they understand the whole picture will they look at the computer outputs. It's clear that expert weather forecasters want to build their own pictures and they want to work directly with the data. Here's why:

- Their expertise is about seeing trends and *patterns* in the data. Their repertoire of patterns enables them to spot negative cues—things that should have happened but didn't. They can only see these nonevents by reviewing the data themselves and not relying on someone else's interpretations.
- Their expertise helps them know where and how to *seek* more data. Too often, decision makers try to define in advance what data they will need. As a situation unfolds and a story is constructed, decision makers learn what data are really important. The appropriate level of detail cannot be defined in advance—it depends on what they're searching for. In addition, the story helps alert decision makers to data and metrics that might not have been factored in to how they originally perceived the dilemma.
- They need to build their own *mental models*, not rely on others'.
- They need to understand the *story* of how the data were collected.
- Experts need to *adapt*—to feel free to change the way they study data as they learn more about the situation.
- Their expertise depends on the *active stance* they take, actively searching, actively building mental models, actively adapting.

All of these functions of expertise were compromised when the seasoned forecasters were fed preanalyzed data. That's why they refused to look at the computer-generated forecasts or listen to the briefings from the forecasters on the earlier shift until they had a chance to review the data from the previous six hours and build their own understanding of what was happening. These expert forecasters were showing the same active stance we see in experts in most other fields.

Using this framework we can see how information technology compromises our expertise and our intuition by disrupting or blocking each of the functions that I have just listed.

Intuition depends on our ability to notice patterns, to judge typicality, to spot anomalies, to have a feel for what is happening around us. Information technology can eliminate this ability because it automatically provides us with the data and information rather than letting us work with the data ourselves. The data flow rate is simply too much for us to handle by ourselves; given the high flow of information, this mechanism is almost required by our current technology. For the most part, we don't even realize what we've lost, but the old-timers, who used to log the data in manually, can tell the difference.

The journeymen in Example 15.1, of course, were happy with the smoothing function. They didn't know to pay attention to the whorls and wiggles and therefore didn't miss them.

Another example of how technology can actually impede us from

---

> **EXAMPLE 15.1 THE DISPLAYS THAT WERE TOO SMOOTH**

One of the expert weather forecasters we followed complained bitterly about a new computer system that had replaced his old machine. The new system could show trends and plot curves and do all kinds of computer tricks. And that was the problem. If the temperatures in a region were very variable, some high and some low, the computer would smooth these out to provide a uniform temperature curve for the region. The program developers had wanted to provide operators with a sense of the trends, and to do that they had filtered out the "noise."

But the expert had always depended on seeing these areas of turbulence. To him, they signaled some sort of instability. Whenever he saw this cue, it triggered a reaction to watch these fronts much more carefully because it was a sign that something was brewing. As this forecaster said, "In reality, the fronts 'wiggle' as they move across the land. And it's in those whorls and wiggles that weather happens."

The new system had erased this cue, making him less sensitive to the way the weather was developing and hurting his ability to do his job.

---

doing our jobs as well as we could comes from a project in which my colleagues and I studied the decision skills of AWACS weapons directions (AWACS stands for Airborne Warning and Control System; those militarized versions of the Boeing 707–320B commercial jets distinguished by the addition of a large, rotating rotodome containing the main radar). We heard from old-timers that previously, when they were ground controllers, they watched the radar screens and marked the targets on a screen with grease pencils. They felt that back then they used to have a better feel for what the radar screens were telling them than they now did as AWACS weapons directors, where the computers automatically entered and tagged the aircraft. The old-fashioned hand-marked screen had helped them to create their own big picture.

I have seen this sort of problem myself. I'm old enough to remember the "good old days," when computers weren't widely available. When doing statistics, we had to calculate the tests and analyses of variance using mechanical calculating devices. Yes, it was a pain. But when I taught statistics, my students were highly attuned to their data because they could see how different subjects contributed to the variance or skewed the distribution. The students entered the subjects' data on large sheets, and as they wrote down each number, they could compare it to the numbers preceding it. They could spot anomalies, catch errors, and form new hypotheses. Once computer programs were used to perform data analysis, though, it became easy for students to generate results without understanding exactly what had happened and why. Students would enter their data and report that the experiment had worked. But close questioning revealed the students often didn't know which group was achieving a higher level of performance in a study that compared a control group to an experimental group. They knew that the difference was statistically significant, but they couldn't say what the difference was.

Think about the information technology being built into our cars. The cars of today have traction control devices that can sense when the tires are not adequately gripping the road, and, in the case of a slippery road they will automatically transfer power to the tires that are maintaining traction. But many of the cars equipped with traction control don't tell the driver that there is a traction problem. These cars allow us to drive in ignorance of the true situation. While driving, we may believe we are safe, but the system knows that there is a problem. This is not a failure in the technology. It's a failure of the car designers to recognize the importance of the driver's judgment. It would be easy to design a system that announces the auditory message "traction activated" to let us know that something is wrong, giving us a chance to reappraise the road conditions and adjust our speeds. But this isn't done. Instead, the system makes the adjustment, and does it in a way that prevents us from using our judgment and expertise. Some cars will make an announcement, in a message that appears on the dashboard, but we can read it only if we take our eyes off the road in difficult driving conditions. The result is that during dangerous driving conditions, our cars are often smarter than we are.

The cars of tomorrow will probably be worse in this regard, not better. We read about systems that monitor the distance to the car ahead, automatically slowing our car down when we get too close. No effort is made to pass this information to the driver. Such information could be useful in stressful situations such as blizzards or heavy rainfalls, when the visibility is poor and we are forced to follow the taillights of the car ahead. It wouldn't be difficult to make information technology and drivers partners, but too often the emphasis is on making them compete for control of the car. A smart system slowing our car down is yet another way to make us stupid. Because we don't know why the car is slowing (could be a problem with traction, could be water in the gasoline), we might be tempted to increase our pressure on the accelerator to counteract the effect, thus creating the very same dangerous conditions that the technology was trying to avoid.

Experts don't need or want to see all the data. But they want *access* to the data, and the opportunity to investigate it more thoroughly, if necessary. If information technology breaks that connection it not only disables our intuitions, but also makes it harder for us to build new intuitions.

Information Technology Can Limit How We Search for Data

Information technology can flood us with material. One way experts cope with this challenge is to take control of their own searching, like the skilled forecaster in Example 15.2.

This example illustrates another difficulty with the "waterfall" system of dispensing data—it assumes you can predefine the data as essential or nonessential and let low-ranking assistants or the computer compile the data. In fact, there is no "basic" level of detail; the appropriate level of detail depends on what you are searching for. In this case, the relevant data didn't even appear in the most recent report.

Because it's so hard to predetermine what counts as relevant data,

---

> ### Example 15.2 The Ghost Storm

An Air Force weather forecaster described a time in Korea when he announced that in two hours the Air Force base would have only one-mile visibility, snow showers, and a 1,000 ft. ceiling. However, none of the other forecasters believed him because the conditions at the time were perfectly clear.

He had noticed that the upper air charts from the previous twelve- and twenty-four-hour periods showed a movement in the shortwave range, and his mental model of the winter weather patterns in the area made him suspect that clouds might soon be coming in off the Yellow Sea. But the movement in the shortwave range had disappeared in the most recent chart. He knew the shortwave movement effect couldn't simply go away, so he figured that the computer must have smoothed it out because there aren't many data sources over the sea.

He decided to ignore the recent chart, choosing instead to mentally simulate how the wind shift was likely to be progressing and when it would take effect. He manually reanalyzed the upper air chart, extrapolating forward from the twelve- and twenty-four-hour reports. By doing the analysis by hand, he was able to see the radical shift in weather approaching.

The other forecasters believed the computer data and blew the forecast. In just two and a half hours the weather went from "clear and a million" to a 1,200 ft. ceiling and snowing. Five aircraft had to be diverted.

---

experts like Alan Greenspan—a master of sensemaking—have become skilled at drilling down to find the right cues, the critical data elements. We saw this in the example presented in Chapter 14 which showed how Greenspan interprets data. In Example 15.3, we can see how Greenspan actively searches to understand events.

> *EXAMPLE 15.3* HOW ALAN GREENSPAN MAKES SENSE OF SITUATIONS

Alan Greenspan, the chairman of the Federal Reserve, has to judge whether the economy is strengthening or weakening, so that he can decide whether to raise interest rates, cut them, or leave them alone. Trends in the economy take six to twelve months to become clear, and often they emerge only after it's too late to do something about them. That's why Greenspan attempts to spot these trends as early as possible. For instance, it wasn't until August 1, 2002, that economists positively identified a recession that began in March 2001. Greenspan saw the recession coming much earlier. He started to aggressively cut interest rates on January 3, 2001, from 6.5 down to 5.0 by March 20, to 4.0 by May 15, and eventually below 2.0. Greenspan saw how serious this business downturn was, and took strong action to strengthen the investment climate way in advance of the official statistics.

Greenspan's approach relies on a blend of intuition and analysis. He has access to thousands of data sources, yet he complains when organizations reduce their flow of data and information. His experience lets him know how these numbers were obtained, which numbers to review, and how to interpret them. He taps into the actual data: How fast are specific suppliers filling the orders from factories? This is a signal that inflationary pressures are building up. What is the current status of worker insecurity? To assess this he may look at the data on the number of newly unemployed who say that they left their last job voluntarily. To gauge inflationary pressure, Greenspan monitors the weekly tally of new claims for unemployment benefits. He also looks at the amount of overtime worked, auto sales, and purchasing activities.

Many policy makers want Greenspan to rely on a more general, easier-to-understand set of guidelines, such as increasing interest rates when unemployment drops below 6 percent. But he won't—to do so would interfere with his intuitions.

Greenspan tries to sense the direction of the economy without relying on briefings from subordinates about what they think the economy is doing. Why should they have a more informed judgment than he does? He doesn't rely on summary metrics—facts and statistics that others have synthesized, such as overall productivity growth—because those hide the real trends. Instead, he tracks more detailed data, such as changes in inventory rates in different companies in a single industry or productivity changes in different sectors of the economy. Because he knows so much about different parameters, different industries, and different companies, Greenspan can use data to verify or discredit unlikely stories. He can make his diagnoses the way a physician would, seeing for himself, listening to the vital signs, drawing on his patterns and sense of typicality. By looking at industries, and at companies or even plants within companies, Greenspan can construct stories that explain what the data really mean, and thus determine what action he should recommend. That was how Greenspan was able to warn the country about "irrational exuberance" in the stock market in December 1996, when the Dow Jones was at 6,636, on its way to 11,722 on January 14, 2000, before falling back toward 8,000 in 2001/2002.

Consider again the metaphor of solving a puzzle. Skilled puzzle-solvers don't passively sort through every piece. They actively look for pieces that will fill in gaps.

Here is a counterexample to Alan Greenspan, a patient who embodies what can happen when our ability to seek out and interpret information is taken from us.

In 1995 the neuropsychologist Oliver Sacks wrote about a case of a fifty-year-old man who had lost his vision in early childhood due to thick cataracts and had recently regained his vision through a simple cataract removal operation. Sacks studied this man, "Virgil," and realized that there was still a major disability. Virgil now had fairly good acuity. He could see shapes and colors. However, during the decades of blindness he had lost the ability to *see*. That is, he was content to passively receive a succession of images, but he did not naturally look at things, or look for things. Upon being introduced to people, he did not really look at their faces. "Virgil would look, would attend visually, only if one asked him to or pointed something out—not spontaneously. His sight might be restored, but using his eyes, looking, it was clear, was far from natural to him; he still had many of the habits, the behaviors, of a blind man." Sacks concluded that the patient was mentally blind.

Information technologies have a very strong tendency to reduce users to passive recipients of data, particularly users who are not intimately familiar with the way hardware and software is designed, which makes them reluctant to try to work around problems or strike out on their own. With the emergence of information technology we may be creating a new breed of decision makers who become mentally blind in that they will have lost their ability to look, to search.

Information technologies make it hard for us to become Greenspans, and turn us into Virgils.

Think about how we search the Web. We plug some terms into our favorite search engine, enter "search," sit back and wait to read the hits. Finally, we get them, some which are helpful, some which are not what we need, and many which are downright puzzling. Do you ever wonder where these hits come from? Was it the terms you used, a limitation of the search algorithm, or a clever strategy used by someone to attract more hits? You can't know. And you don't have any way to find out. If we sent assistants to the library we would be outraged if they brought back such a high percentage of irrelevant information. But with Web searches, we endure the irrelevant stuff. We have no way to question the search strategy, yet we don't complain. Over time, we move one step closer to becoming Virgil.

Decision makers don't like to be constrained by rigid search categories—we want to change categories in mid-search depending on what we turn up. For example, you might want to learn more about work my company has done in intuition skills training by looking at the projects listed in my company's database. You could start by searching projects by size (either dollars or duration of the project) if you had an idea of how a typical training project was run. If that didn't work you might notice on the roster for one of our projects a familiar name—Debbie Battaglia—and remember that you once got some decision training materials from her. So now you call up all projects on which Debbie is listed. But there are a lot of reports written on these projects, interim reports and final reports. You don't want to read them all. Then you remember that the information you want is probably in a report that we wrote for the Marines, so you change your focus to include sponsors, aiming at the intersection between projects Debbie has done and projects the Marines have sponsored. But you come up empty. However, you have noticed that many of the reports covering decision training that have Debbie's name on them also list Jenni Phillips as an author, so you try replacing Debbie with Jenni in searching for work sponsored by the Marines, and now you get what you need. This is *not* a neat or orderly method. But it may be the best way for you to conduct an effective and flexible search.

The results of one phase of a good search will likely suggest the feature you want to search in the next phase. An effective search strategy is like a snake that keeps twisting and wriggling, changing shape as you learn new things.

Sometimes, though, there are more "new things" than we can process. Information technologies are exciting because they can quickly present enormous amounts of data to decision makers, which sounds wonderful until we realize that there's no way we can absorb such excessive data rates.

The truth is that human beings aren't well suited to absorb a flood of information. This is how information technology insidiously reduces the quality of our decisions.

How much information is "too much"? Several research studies of weather forecasters have shown that, after they settled on the key five to ten pieces of information, additional information didn't help them, and even got in their way and reduced their accuracy. A 1992 study of expert meteorologists discovered that as the amount and quality of the information increased, there was a substantial *decrease* in agreement among the forecasters regarding their predictions of turbulent weather.

Studies like this suggest that information technology can turn us into Virgils by providing us with more information than we can swallow and digest.

Information Technology Can Weaken Our Mental Models

Our mental models get richer as we gain experience in an area. The categories we use to understand the world—the distinctions and connections we make—evolve. Some distinctions will get abandoned, others will get differentiated further. For example, if you have moved to a new product division and are sorting through the customer base, you might start with some basic categories such as the size of the customer's orders and the type of business in which the customer is engaged. Once you're more familiar with the division you may instead opt to use a set of categories about the ways that customers use the product.

If information technology keeps our thinking locked in the same categories that we started with, it can do some serious damage to our ability to build better mental models. Consider a situation where we are preparing for a new project by setting up spreadsheets in advance, so that, as the data come pouring in, they can be automatically sorted and analyzed. However, we presumably are collecting the data in order to learn something, and that learning will likely lead us to new and better categories and distinctions. If we have to set up our categories in advance and retain them, how are we going to learn? I once posed this question to an analyst working on a research project, and was quickly rebuffed—"I have to set up my categories in advance; otherwise I'll be buried in data." Learning—which you'd think would be the goal of someone conducting a research project—was the furthest thing from this analyst's mind.

When we set up categories in advance and expect to keep them in place, we soon forget how those categories work. As a result, we may not notice the implications when something changes. In the Marine Corps exercise "Hunter-Warrior," the command post staff was getting bombarded with emails. Everyone was copying everyone else. They decided to set up news groups, so that Marines only had to check the one or two news groups relevant to their responsibilities and only had to post new messages into one or two news groups. This helped a lot. But one day, a very sharp young captain went around the consoles, asking his fellow-Marines if any of them had gotten any reports from helicopter and F-18 pilots recently. None of them had. The captain did some more detective work. He found that someone had changed a news group. As a result, the pilot reports were being dumped into a news group that was no longer active. And as a result of that, no one in the command post had received a single pilot report for the previous twenty-four hours. Worse, no one realized it until the captain started getting curious about the omission. Everyone else was content to do their job, read their emails, and send responses. They placidly stayed in their passive, somewhat disengaged stance, and did not ever get into the active mindset that would make them wonder what had happened to the pilot reports. They were in a receive-and-respond mode, not an active searching mode.

Information Technology Hides the Story of How It "Thinks" About the Data

Information technology doesn't let us see how it does its reasoning: how it has collected and analyzed data, how it has arrived at its recommendations, and how it "thinks." In Chapter 14 we saw how important it is to have an accurate story of how metrics are collected; the same holds true for the actions and recommendations put forward by information technology. We can't interpret them and we can't use our intuitions to trust or modify them because there's no way to make sense of the data and decisions information technology issues.

Information technology can hide the pedigree of the data, so we don't know how old they are, how credible they are, how often and what types of transformations they have undergone.

Imagine that you are performing a task in coordination with another person—say it's with me. If I want to help you, I will give you lots of information about what I need from you, where I'm confused, how I'm viewing the work at hand. I will be a real partner to you. If I want to foil your work, I'll be inscrutable. I won't give away any clues about how I am thinking, or what I am planning to do.

Think of information technology as your partner. If it's inscrutable, you can't coordinate with it.

In some circles this is seen as a strength. Designers may purposely try to make the workings of a system invisible to us so that we won't be distracted by the details of the software codes behind the programs we use. And in some ways that might be helpful. But sometimes, the user very much needs to know what the system is doing. If the mechanism is hidden, the user's attempts to work with and work around the system are stymied.

Many websites are inscrutable. Have you ever tried to buy something off the Internet? The website may make sense to the designer, but it sure doesn't work for the customer. Analysts have been amazed to find that 60 percent of potential customers, presumably eager to make a purchase over the Web, give up. Why? Because they can't figure out how to get the information they want. They can't anticipate how the site will react and so they're afraid to move forward. A website like this is not a partner. It's a potential trap.

In commercial aviation, the flight management systems (i.e., the autopilots) are notorious for being inscrutable. Earl Wiener studied pilots who worked with these systems, and he heard the common reaction: "What's it doing? Why is it doing that? What's it going to do next?" Pilots know the system is doing something, but it is not telling what its plans are. Some airlines simply instruct their pilots to turn off the flight management systems during emergencies or complications. The reason is that it's hard enough to handle an emergency without also having to worry about how the computer is going to interfere. Pilots can get distracted trying the read the "mind" of the computer in order to anticipate its next move.

Some people do know how to "reverse engineer" the mind of their computer. One Navy technician I met described his sophisticated computer system as "a liar" because it sometimes gave erroneous results. These malfunctions drove the new operators crazy, but they didn't bother him because he knew why it made those mistakes, and he knew when and how to compensate for them.

However, most of us can't do this and don't even try. We never develop much intuition about the computer systems with which we work. Instead, we passively accept what the computer does, and try to muddle through on our end without making any serious blunders.

I've found that the more clever and advanced the information technology, the worse our frustration becomes. For example, some software developers are using algorithms to overcome the problem of information overload. These algorithms inspect and synthesize the data for us, to spare us the effort of having to sort through all of the data ourselves.

The problem with this is that we can't get inside the algorithm to inspect how it is thinking, or to see the data it is using, and so we are disconnected from the context in which these data were culled. In addition, we're now forced to trust the skills and strategies of a programmer we know nothing about.

Sometimes, decision makers rebel when they are disconnected from the context of how the computer is thinking. For example, the Air Force developed artificial intelligence programs to automatically generate Air Tasking Orders (ATOs) that specify which airplanes are to fly which types of missions each day along with the supporting details of every flight. Ordinarily, generating ATOs takes days and requires large amounts of staff effort. The artificial intelligence programs could produce the ATO in just a few hours. The Air Force planners, however, didn't like the new system. In 1995, my colleagues Tom Miller and Laura Militello were asked by the Air Force to investigate the problem.

ATOs are quite thick and detailed, so it was no surprise that Tom and Laura didn't observe anyone ever evaluating a staff-generated ATO once it was finished. Rather, they noticed planners evaluating the ATO *while* it was being prepared. One planner would suggest an approach, others would debate the suggestion, point out limitations, perhaps make some improvements. When the ATO was finished, the planning team would have a thorough appreciation for the nuances and special issues with which they had all been wrestling, and the staff would be well prepared for any unexpected problems that arose.

But when the artificial intelligence software produced the ATO, the users lost their opportunity to conduct an evaluation. The ATO would just appear, and the planners had no way to appreciate the rationale behind the order. No wonder the users weren't comfortable with the new technology. It threatened to force them to carry out plans they did not trust or understand—it didn't allow them room to use their intuition. Their response was to reject the technology.

Unfortunately, when I explained to the Air Force Scientific Advisory Board why the decision makers were unwilling to rely on the computer-generated plans, one of the senior members of the panel responded, "They'll just have to learn to trust the system!" As far as he was concerned, anything that slowed the adoption of information technology had to be stamped out, regardless of the effect.

Information Technology Can Make Us Less Adaptive

Information technology makes us less adaptive by pressuring us to follow the prescribed procedures. The programmers design their system to work best if we approach a task as a set of steps to carry out in the correct order, not by improvising or making adjustments. Our role, to their mind, is to give up using our judgment and intuition skills and just operate the system. We should all assume that the task will be performed as planned, mistakes won't happen, and adjustments won't be necessary. Therefore, the system can look very easy to operate, as long as everyone follows the script.

One way information technology reduces our adaptability is by exacting harsh penalties when we depart from the procedures that have been established. Information technology can bombard us with error messages and warnings, or it can just lock up like a petulant child who has not gotten its own way.

Information technology discourages adaptations by being difficult to modify. Recall the example in Chapter 10 about how some companies are dismantling their manufacturing robotics systems because they are too cumbersome to reprogram.

Information technology can reduce adaptability by introducing a type of advanced information technology called an "adaptive system." The premise of an adaptive system is that the technology adapts to the needs of the decision maker. Adaptive systems can sense who the user is, what the user wants, and what preferences to set up. You've probably read about one type of adaptive system in magazines—the home of the future that will supposedly recognize you when you walk through the door, set the rooms at the temperature you prefer, start your favorite music playing, and so forth. If your spouse gets home first, then the smart home will tune itself according to a different set of preferences.

You would think that adaptive systems would make it easier for decision makers to be adaptive, but I suspect they will have just the opposite effect. Adaptive systems put us under the control of the computer. The computer is the partner who is doing the adapting, not us. After the information technology learns all of our preferences, then we better *not* change. If we do any adapting of our own, we will confuse the computer and create all kinds of problems. No, the best thing for all involved—both us and the computer—is for us to stay frozen in our typical routines.

Remember how I insisted that feedback is essential to building intuition? Well, it actually depends on what kind of feedback. It might surprise you to know that the low-cost rapid feedback we get from computer systems can actually work against us. Immediate feedback does speed up learning during training sessions. However, research by Richard Schmidt and Gabriele Wulf shows that this reduces the amount of eventual learning. As long as we are getting the rapid feedback, we do well and our learning curve during *training* will be fine. However, once we leave the training environment, we have to figure out how to get our own feedback. We need to monitor our own behavior. Information technology is wonderful for giving us low-cost rapid feedback during training, but it deprives us of the skills we will need once we leave the training environment.

And, look at what happens when children play with computer chess programs. It's a real challenge to beat the program. However, the programs usually also come with an advice generator. Naturally, the child passively seeks advice from the system every time a tough situation is encountered. The computer suggests a good move, the child tries it, plays further until another quandary is reached, then asks for more advice. Instead of playing chess against the machine, the child is really just passively carrying out the machine's recommendations, a servant to the machine.

Information Technology Can Make Us Passive

Information technology can diminish the active stance found in intuitive decision makers and transform them into passive system operators. Information technology makes us afraid to use our intuition; it slows our rate of learning because we are too timid to explore new strategies.

Unhappily, I'm a perfect example of this problem. For reasons too painful to recount, this book was produced in Word rather than WordPerfect. Instead of being able to go to the "reveal codes" function to take control of formatting, I was reduced to accepting whatever formatting quirk the program decided I needed. I was forced to depend on Veronica Sanger, my production support specialist, to sort it all out. Lucky for me, Veronica is very good at what she does, and my editor had no complaints with the formatting of the manuscript.

Simple passivity is bad enough but it can degenerate to the point where decision makers assume that the computer knows best, and stop trying to figure out what to do. In the world of aviation, this condition is described as "automation bias." Airline pilots and dispatchers make worse decisions if they have access to an intelligent system that generates recommendations. They stop engaging in the task and just follow the system's recommendations about what they should do, even in those cases where their own judgment is better than the system's solution.

What Can We Do to Protect Ourselves?

I take the assault on our intuition by information technology very seriously. We've been warned about the effects of computer use on our hands, and have federal guidelines to reduce these repetitive strain injuries. Our heads also deserve protection. We need to find ways to defend ourselves against repetitive brain injury, to sustain our intuitions and to safeguard our expertise.

Why are information technologies being developed in ways that compromise our expertise and intuitions? There seems to be a clash between different perspectives. For most software developers, who consider our minds as simply biological computers, there shouldn't be any conflict. If thinking really just boils down to computing, then information technology is just supplementing our own computational ability.

But our thinking is not only computing. It involves pattern matching and sensemaking and all the cognitive processes discussed in this book. There is a fundamental difference between the way we think and the way computers think.

Information technology specialists often try to design technically impressive systems, viewing the users as the potential weak link in the cycle. They sometimes see the operator as a way to feed the system, and strive to design a system that offers minimal opportunities for the operators to stray from the intended strategies. Programmers often get nervous when decision makers do something radical, like try to adapt in ways that they (the programmers) had not anticipated. For the programmer, the ideal user is one who follows the rules, operates the controls, and lets the system do its job.

Sometimes, we hear people describe a utopia in which people do what they are good at, and machines do what they handle best. This utopia seems plausible, because computers can do the tasks that we struggle with, such as maintaining vigilance for long periods of time, noticing tiny discrepancies, searching through lots of data, performing complicated calculations, and so forth. The promise is there for computers to perform the precise and reliable operations, and leave it to us to be creative.

But that isn't the way it works. Don Norman, a prominent observer of the interface between people and technology, draws on his experiences at Apple Computer and Hewlett-Packard to describe the way things have really turned out:

> technology has decided that machines have certain needs and that humans are required to fulfill them. The things we are good at, those natural abilities, are hardly noticed. Machines need precise, accurate control and information. No matter that this is what people are bad at providing, if this is what machines need, this is what people must provide. We tailor our jobs to meet the needs of the machines.

Bert and Stuart Dreyfus issued this same warning back in 1986:

> at all levels of society computer-type rationality is winning out. Experts are an endangered species. If we fail to put logic machines in their proper place, as aids to human beings with expert intuition, then we shall end up servants supplying data to our competent machines. Should calculative rationality triumph, no one will notice that something is missing, but now, while we still know what expert judgment is, let us use that expert judgment to preserve it.

So what do we do? First, we must try to understand the bases for our own expertise and intuitions. We cannot safeguard what we do not value or notice. I hope that this book—which shows how much we rely on intuition and explains how intuition is based on the patterns, action scripts, and mental models we have acquired through experience—will be helpful in this regard.

Second, we should stay alert to the ways that information technology is interfering with our intuitions. If we carry on, oblivious to the problem, then by the time we wake up and discover what we have lost it will be too late.

Third, we can demand from programmers more in the way of support and less in the way of dominance. When we select systems, when we are consulted about systems being designed to help us, when we change our work practices to incorporate information technology, we can insist on design methods that respect our intuitions. We can learn to do a better job of articulating our recognitional skills and sense-

---

> *EXAMPLE 15.4* COMPUTER MODELING OR COMPUTER MEDDLING?

After we finished our research investigation of weather forecasters, Rebecca Pliske, who led the effort, gave a paper on our results at a conference. The audience was primarily made up of forecasters, and Rebecca described what set the experts apart from the others. One of the characteristics she mentioned was the need of the experts to build their own mental models.

The next presenter showed the new system his company had designed to make the job of the forecasters easier. This system included a sophisticated and comprehensive model of the weather phenomena. It was going to do a massive analysis of all kinds of variables and provide the forecaster with a comprehensive set of predictions.

Although she is not a combative person, Rebecca could not stop herself from commenting once the presentation was finished. She said that this was exactly what the skilled forecasters did *not* want. They needed to build their own mental models, and they needed help seeing and keeping track of the data. They did not want to be turned into clerical assistants to the computer model this person was pitching.

The audience applauded Rebecca's comments. And then they cheered. There is very little cheering in professional meetings, so this response was significant. It suggests how strongly experts feel about the importance of building their own mental models.

---

making skills, instead of passively standing by while these are swept aside by software developers who are programming us at the same time they are programming our machines. Specialists in the field of cognitive engineering are working to establish methods for advocating for the needs of decision makers as part of the development of advanced computer support systems.

It is possible to develop sophisticated forms of information technology that are compatible with intuition. Approaches such as cognitive engineering are attempting to codify the strategies that will help software developers work with human factors specialists to improve the design process. Cognitive engineering begins by determining the types of strategies and expertise that decision makers employ to accomplish a task in order to design the computer support around these requirements.

We don't have to be concerned with whether our machines are smarter than we are—in some ways they are, in others they aren't. And we needn't gnash our teeth over each new computer triumph, such as the victory of Deep Blue over Garry Kasparov. Of course computers are going to get better and smarter, and I admire the development of a new type of intelligence.

My concern is simple: I don't mind that computers are getting smarter than us because they are growing in intelligence. I *do* mind that they're getting smarter than us by making us stupid. And that's what can happen. That's the trend we have to resist.

Becoming Intuitive Decision Makers

The intuition skills training program described in this book is designed to help you join the ranks of Lia DiBello; Jerry Kirby, the CEO of Citizens Federal Bank; Darlene the NICU nurse; the structural engineer William LeMessurier; and the firefighters and military leaders we've encountered along the way. None of these individuals were born with outstanding intuition. All of them practiced their craft for a decade or more, learning how to see the world more clearly, to see the possibilities and the pitfalls.

What does an intuitive decision maker look like? If you believed in *magical intuition,* an intuitive decision maker would be someone who is open to feelings and impulses. That description certainly fits the individuals singled out above. But it also fits lots of people—it doesn't capture what impresses us about this roster of intuitive decision makers. If your perspective was one of *rational analysis,* an intuitive decision maker would be someone who is illogical, impulsive, and superstitious. That doesn't describe these individuals at all. In contrast, the *muscular intuition* perspective sees an intuitive decision maker as an expert. And that's how I view the people I just identified. Here are the characteristics of the intuitive decision makers celebrated in this book:

- Their performance is markedly better than we would expect by chance.
- They have a good sense of what is going to happen next.
- They can explain how the current situation has developed.
- They are aware of their fallibility. If you question their interpretation or forecast, they can come up with a different one.

- They are confident, particularly in the face of time pressure and uncertainty. They can anticipate problems in time to avoid or defuse them, and relish the challenge when the plans fall apart because it is an opportunity to find new solutions.
- When unexpected events happen, they know how to work around them. They know the routines, and they also know the limits of those routines and so they are not trapped by them.
- They are still trying to improve. They know they are not perfect. If you ask them about mistakes, they can tell you about recent ones because they have been mulling over those mistakes, trying to figure out how they should have done better.

Three Strands: Practical, Theoretical, Experiential

One strand of this book is aimed at practicality—an intuition skills training program consisting of methods for developing, applying, and safeguarding intuitions. The program is based on the premise of muscular intuition that you can speed up your learning curve. You aren't being criticized for defective thinking processes, or being asked to change the way you make decisions—that only adds to your confusion. Rather, you are being encouraged to approach problems the way you always do, armed with a more solid experience base.

The second strand offers you a theoretical framework: that intuitive decision making stems from experience, and that we can define how intuition works—through pattern matching, repertoires of action scripts, richer mental models—and that we can understand how intuition operates—by letting us detect problems, manage uncertainty, make sense of situations, and improvise. This theme shows how intuition is the translation of experience into action.

The third strand of the book is the use of exercises and decision games to help you experience the different aspects of intuitive decision making.

The approach I have taken to intuition is woven from all three of these strands. It is a set of *tools* that will continue to expand. The tools are based on a *theoretical framework* for acquiring decision-making skills, a theoretical framework that emphasizes the accumulation of *experiences* over the establishment of procedures.

Chapter 3 described the three core tools in the intuition skills training program: the decision requirements table, the use of decision games, and the decision-making critique. The rationale for these tools is that we can treat intuitive decision making as we would any important skill that we wish to train: We clarify the training objectives (the decision requirements), we provide appropriate practice (the decision games), and we ensure feedback (the decision-making critique).

These methods are intended to help you become an intuitive decision maker in some fundamental ways: by learning more *patterns* and *action scripts*; by learning to notice *subtle cues* you might have previously missed, like the way master mechanics can tell from the vibrations whether or not a machine is working well; by learning to quickly judge situations as *typical*, as you recognize more situations; by learning to spot *anomalies* more quickly; by acquiring a better understanding of how things come about—sometimes referred to as a *mental model*—so that you can understand the different influences and how they operate; by taking a more *active stance* as you search for problems, manage uncertainty, and build more flexible plans. Subsequent chapters added to the set of tools for carrying out these functions. Some of these tools will help you apply your intuitions more effectively, and some will help you overcome barriers to intuition.

Do You Have a Non-intuitive Attitude?

The concept of muscular intuition asserts that you can take control of your own intuitive decision-making skills. Through practice and feedback you should be able to improve your ability to size up situations, spot problems, manage uncertainty, and plan more flexibly.

But that is only going to happen if you exercise these skills. You would not engage in a physical conditioning program in which you went running once a month. That wouldn't achieve anything. Similarly, your intuitive decision-making skills will only improve if you work on them.

Some of you may do that, but I fear that others will finish this book and go back to their old habits. Here are the excuses and attitudes that you must avoid if you're going to take the intuition skills training program further. (I have listed in parentheses the chapter where the belief is rebutted.)

1. *Experiences automatically compile into expertise. I don't have to do anything special.* (Chapter 3) This belief is a justification for laziness. Merely having experiences is not enough. True experts take their skills seriously, and they set goals for themselves about how they want to improve. They organize their practice sessions around these goals, to work toward some accomplishment in each session. In order to develop expertise, you need to get repetitions and feedback. Chapter 3 offers tools to help you take control of your learning curve.

2. *It's too discouraging to relive failures—better to just move on.* (Chapter 3) This is another excuse for avoiding the hard work of figuring out what went wrong. This excuse is connected to the belief that you should be making perfect decisions, and avoiding mistakes. Worse yet, this excuse misses the fact that mistakes and failures are some of the best opportunities for learning. They are doorways into the discovery of richer patterns and mental models. In addition, the reliving of failures should not be hard work. I know that when I've failed, really failed, I cannot just repress it. I am stricken by it, and the only way I can emotionally neutralize the failure is to figure out what I should have done. Once I discover this, the pain of the failure seems to disappear and to be replaced by the hope that I will get another chance.

3. *I already have too much on my plate to spend time working on my intuition skills.* (Chapter 3) Maybe so. But perhaps you feel overworked because you're going about things the wrong way. If you could learn more efficient decision-making strategies you might dig yourself out of the hole you are in. You need to improve your intuition skills because your current decisions aren't working. They are taking too much time and forcing you to do too much damage repair.

4. *I'm already a good decision maker, why else did I get promoted?* (Chapter 3) Here are four names—perhaps you have heard of some of them: Tiger Woods, Michael Jordan, Jerry Rice, Tony Gwynn. In case you haven't, Woods is a noted golfer (the best ever, at this stage of his career), Jordan was/is a basketball player (the standard of comparison for all others), Rice was a football receiver (often considered the

most skilled of all time), Gwynn was a baseball player, generally recognized as the best hitter of his generation. When these athletes achieved prominence, after they were recognized for their brilliance and idolized and showered with media attention, they all refused to become complacent. Woods took the startling action of changing his golf swing—no golfer had ever successfully made this type of change

> *EXAMPLE 16.1* THE LAST PERSON IN THE WORLD WHO NEEDED TO IMPROVE HIS GOLF SKILLS

From 1998 to the present, Tiger Woods has been recognized as the best golfer on the professional tour. Nevertheless, he decided that he needed to overhaul his game.

Specifically, he was unimpressed with his swing. Watching videos, even videos of his commanding victory in the 1997 Masters tournament (where his lead was twelve strokes at the finish), he could see that the mechanics of his swing were flawed. He was using his timing and athletic ability to compensate. He realized that as he got older, he would be less able to compensate, and could see how his performance was likely to slip over the years.

A few other golfers have tried to remake their swings, and none have succeeded. But Woods was determined. Working with his coach, he learned how to keep his clubface square with the ball for a longer period of time, and to keep the club under greater control throughout the swing. Woods and his coach estimated that his play would decline immediately while he learned the new style, and that for months he would not be competitive with the leaders. He prepared himself to see reports about how his early success was a fluke.

And he did go downhill. For the next nineteen months he only won a single tournament. He struggled to learn the new swing, and was often frustrated. However, he still believed that he was becoming a better golfer than when he was winning.

Finally, the new swing became automatic. He could count on it. And his game came together again. He won ten of fourteen events during 1999. He also dominated in 2000 and 2001, and won his third Master's title in 2002. And he still is looking for areas of weakness that he can work on, to turn them into strengths.

INTUITION AT WORK

before. Jordan worked hard to develop a fadeaway jump shot, and to improve his defense, as insurance for the inevitable decline of his athleticism. Rice developed and adhered to a conditioning program few others could manage. Gwynn became notorious for studying game films of his own batting swing, and of opposing pitchers, all through the years when he was winning batting titles. None of these athletes needed to intensify their preparations. All could have coasted, but they chose not to. Why should you?

5. *There is no payoff for becoming a good decision maker—no one notices*

> EXAMPLE 16.2 THE MACHIAVELLIAN MARKETEER

Many years ago, I had arranged a meeting with the vice president of marketing for a major corporation. I had developed a strategy for using analogues as the basis of marketing projections. The strategy involved ways to identify previous products for which there were data on development and sales, and techniques for adjusting these data to yield a forecast for the current product.

I explained the technique to him, and he agreed that it might increase the accuracy of the marketing department's estimates. But before I could get too excited, he told me he had no interest in trying out the new method.

"Think about it," he explained. "When I am asked to make a prediction of how many units of a new system we will be able to sell, I go along. I know that my prediction will be used for a while, then stored someplace and then become forgotten. My prediction may affect our decision to give the go-ahead to the new product, but it will take another year or two for that product to come to market, once the funding spigot is turned on. Then it will take another year to gather the sales data. I guarantee that my prediction will be at least three years old by the time the data are available. No one will remember my prediction anymore. Even if they did, and I was way off, I could hedge by explaining how the competitive situation had shifted, or how we had not followed through on the level of advertising I was assuming, or any other type of smoke I choose to blow. So why in the world would I want to spend an extra ounce of energy to improve my accuracy?"

It may be coincidental, but his company ran into financial difficulties a few years later, and wound up being the target of a hostile takeover.

---

if I make good or poor choices. (Chapter 3) If you make more good decisions and fewer poor ones, your overall performance will improve even if people cannot appraise any of your specific decisions. You should deliberately track your decisions to see how they come out. Further, you should start watching your subordinates more carefully to gauge whether they are striving to make good decisions, or are taking the easy route even if it hurts your organization.

6. *The nature of my job changes often, so it's a waste of time to master my current position.* (Chapter 13) On the contrary, with rapid changes in responsibility it becomes even more important to learn how to come up to speed quickly. I am often asked how to speed up the learning curve for new employees, people without much experience or intuition. Their fundamental need is to quickly compile an experience base, through their own explorations, or vicariously by talking with others. The same would hold for someone who moved into a new position and has to exercise authority. We need to help new managers get up to speed quickly for their own sakes as well as for the good of the units they are managing.

7. *The problem of rapid change is that it makes our prior experiences less relevant.* (Chapter 3) The pace of change is much higher than ever before, and we do have to worry about the applicability of precedents and about prior experiences. However, this is not a reason to turn to analytical decision-making techniques, because the rapid pace of change means that all of the base rates and probability data that feed decision analyses are getting obsolete as well. In my opinion, the solution to the issue of rapid change is to equip ourselves with means of quickly building up intuitions that reflect new realities.

8. *You are either born with intuition or not.* (Chapter 2) There is no evidence that intuition is inborn. The types of intuition we have been discussing depend on pattern matching and expertise, and there is no way for people to be born with these capabilities. There is some speculation that individuals differ in how open they are to their intuitions, but that's different from claiming that they differ in the quality of those intuitions. The differences you see primarily come from hard work. For example, in the 1950s, the baseball player George Shuba was regarded as a natural hitter because his swing was so graceful. After he retired, he described his "natural" swing to sportswriter Roger Kahn. He brought Kahn down to his basement, where he still had the

tools he used to develop that natural swing. Although in games he used a 31-ounce bat, in the basement was a bat that weighed about 44 ounces (he had bored a hole in the top of a 34-ounce bat and poured in 10 ounces of lead). He also had a wad of knotted string hanging in a clump from a beam. The wad served as a ball.

> In the winters . . . for 15 years after loading potatoes or anything else, even when I was in the majors, I'd swing at the clump 600 times. Every night, and after 60 I'd make an X. Ten Xs and I had my 600 swings. Then I could go to bed.

That's how a "natural hitter" is made.

9. *Improving intuitive decision-making skills—that is something the human resources department should do, not me.* (Chapter 3) One of the things we know about experts is that they have taken the responsibility for making themselves better from the beginning of their careers to the end. That is how they have turned experiences into expertise.

10. *What's the rush?* If you don't work on intuitive decision-making skills this year, perhaps you can get to it next year. Or the year after. After all, intuition isn't going to go away. Actually, it may go away, like any skill that isn't exercised. This brings us back to the barriers discussed in Chapter 2. Regardless of how much we accept the idea of intuitive decision making there is an array of forces acting to reduce our intuitions. In this book we examined four of them—inability to convey intent, failure to coach subordinates, insensitive use of metrics, and prolonged reliance on information technologies. Add to these the rapid pace of change and high rates of turnover, and the mixture results in an unprecedented assault on our intuitions. If we don't take them seriously and act to preserve and enhance them we may find that they have eroded and become worthless.

The most important attitude is your desire to improve. If you take yourself as seriously as Tiger Woods, Michael Jordan, Jerry Rice, and Tony Gwynn take themselves, then the process of working on your decision skills will not be a burden. It will become the preoccupation found in all experts—continually seeking to hone skills and correct flaws.

Balancing Act

Ultimately, we need to take a balanced position when discussing intuitive decision making, regarding it neither as a defective form of reasoning nor a magical gift. With *Intuition at Work*, I've attempted to strike a balance among the practical, the theoretical, and the experiential.

We have to find a balance between intuition and analysis. Both are important sources of power, and both have weaknesses.

The idea of relying on intuition may initially have struck some readers as an extreme position—it should seem reasonable by now; the criticisms of analysis and metrics that may have caused readers some initial discomfort, should now be appreciated as a healthy skepticism; the criticisms of brainstorming that may have made some people nervous hopefully now appear like worthwhile cautions, even for those readers who remain unconvinced.

Gandhi once mocked the British because "they think they can develop a system of laws that is so perfect that people no longer have to be good." Similarly, we can be skeptical of people who believe that they can come up with a system of procedures that is so perfect that people no longer have to be skilled. Muscular intuition and the tools for intuition skills training take the opposite position—that we can strive for mastery, not through our procedures but through ourselves.

Your growth as an intuitive decision maker will not be easy to gauge because most of the time the changes will be invisible—crises avoided, meetings not needed, confusions averted, bottlenecks prevented. The place to look for changes is in yourself. You will feel less harried, less worried about the need to make changes, more confident in your intuitive judgments.

In fact, you may already be starting to regard yourself differently. You may already be noticing that you are more alert to anomalies, more savvy about types of uncertainty, more apt to consider the big picture, more prepared to adapt, better at directing and coaching others. You may find that you are already more aware of the decision skills you need to work on and you may be seeing more opportunities for discovery around you. If so, congratulations—the balance is already shifting.

Notes

Preface

1. *We have completed more than 100 studies* . . . Many of the research projects performed by my company, Klein Associates, are listed on our website, *www.decision making.com*.
2. *The media, however, somehow noticed* . . . References to G. Klein, *Sources of Power: How People Make Decisions* (Cambridge, MA: MIT Press, 1998), include:

     Breen, Bill. "What's Your Intuition?" *Fast Company*, no. 38 (September 2000): 290–300.

     Lague, Louise. "Decisions, Decisions." *Oprah*. January 2001, 58–59.

     Petzinger, Thomas, Jr. "Gary Klein Studies How Our Minds Dictate Those 'Gut Feelings.' " *Wall Street Journal*, August 7, 1998.

     "A Well-Stocked Library of Business Reading Includes 'Moby Dick.' " *Wall Street Journal*, April 10, 1998.

     Tannenhauser, C. "Making the Most of What You Know." *More*, July–August 1999, 44–49.
3. *Cases such as these show how easy it can be* . . . These examples of skilled decision makers who attributed their ability to recognize patterns to ESP are presented more fully in my book *Sources of Power*.
4. A. M. Hayashi. "When to Trust Your Gut." *Harvard Business Review*. February 2001, 59–65.

Chapter 1: A Case Study of Intuition

1. *One of the nurses has developed* . . . The incident is based on research Klein Associates did for the National Center for Nursing Research under Grant No. 1 R43 NR01992–01: B. Crandall and K. Getchell-Reiter, "Critical Decision Method: A Technique for Eliciting Concrete Assessment Indicators from the Intuition of NICU Nurses," *Advances in Nursing Sciences* 16, 1 (1993): 42–51.

Chapter 2: Where Do Our Hunches Come From?

1. *Where do our hunches come from?* . . . Some of the material in this chapter was presented in greater detail in my 1998 book, *Sources of Power*. If you have read *Sources of Power*, you will only need to skim this chapter. If you want more amplification of the themes in this chapter, you might want to look at that book.

2. *When a new situation occurs* . . . A pattern may stem from a specific experience or, more likely, from an amalgam of related experiences that have fused together.

3. *Some of the leading researchers in psychology* . . . One of the most forceful proponents of the pattern-recognition view was Herbert Simon; for example, see H. A. Simon, "A Behavioral Model of Rational Choice," *Quarterly Journal of Economics* 69 (1955): 99–118, and H. A. Simon, "Rational Choice and the Structure of the Environment," *Psychological Review* 63 (1956): 129–38. Simon's work investigated the importance of pattern recognition in solving problems. In studying skilled chess players, Simon realized that they had accumulated lots and lots of patterns over their years of play and study. He estimated that experts in a field have access to at least 50,000 patterns, and possibly 100,000 or more. To build this large a repertoire takes about ten years of continual preparation.

4. *And the patterns include routines for responding* . . . I am using the term "action scripts" to describe routines for making things happen, as opposed to other types of scripts. An action script is a general course of action, but it is not intended to be carried out as a sequence of steps. For example, a firefighter might have an action script for doing search and rescue in an apartment building, as opposed to conducting an interior attack on the fire. The firefighters will know the general plan of how to conduct the search and rescue operation but they will have to interpret this plan in light of the size of the building, the nature of the fire, the areas where victims may be found, the competence of the crew members, the spatial layout of egress routes. Thus, the adoption of an action script still requires experience in executing that script.

5. *Even today, formal decision analysis is still taught* . . .

   Edwards, W., and B. Fasolo. "Decision Technology." *Annual Review of Psychology* 52 (2001): 581–606.

   Hammond, J. S., R. L. Keeney, and H. Raiffa. *Smart Choices: A Practical Guide to Making Better Decisions*. Boston: Harvard Business School Press, 1999.

   Russo, J. E., and P. J. H. Shoemaker. *Decision Traps: Ten Barriers to Brilliant Decision Making*. Garden City, NY: Doubleday, 1989.

   ———. *Winning Decisions: Getting It Right the First Time*. New York: Doubleday, 2001.

6. L. R. Beach, and T. R. Mitchell. "A Contingency Model for the Selection of Decision Strategies." *Academy of Management Review* 3 (1978): 439–49.

7. *My colleagues and I stumbled on some clues* . . . Most of our early research on decision making in field settings was sponsored by the Army Research Institute. Many of these studies are described in my article "Recognition-Primed Decisions," in *Advances in Man-Machine Systems Research*, edited by W. B. Rouse (Greenwich, CT: JAI Press, Inc, 1989), 47–92.

   The research with firefighters is also described in my book *Sources of Power* and in G. A. Klein, R. Calderwood, and A. Clinton-Cirocco, "Rapid Decision Making on the Fireground," in *Proceedings of the 30th Annual Human Factors Society* (Santa Monica, CA: The Human Factors Society, 1986), 576–80.

Hammond, Hamm, Grassia, and Pearson were exploring the relationship between intuition and analysis in research with highway engineers at the same time (see K. R. Hammond, R. M. Hamm, J. Grassia, and T. Pearson, "Direct Comparison of the Efficacy of Intuitive and Analytical Cognition in Expert Judgment," *Proceedings of IEEE Transactions on Systems, Man, and Cybernetics, SMC-17* [1987]: 753–70). Hammond developed his cognitive continuum theory to explain the interplay between intuition and analysis. See K. R. Hammond, "Naturalistic Decision Making from a Brunswikian Viewpoint: Its Past, Present, Future," in *Decision Making in Action: Models & Methods,* edited by G. A. Klein, J. Orasanu, R. Calderwood, and C. E. Zsambok (Norwood, NJ: Ablex, 1993), 205–27.

Bert and Stuart Dreyfus also explored the shift from analysis to intuition as people achieved mastery of a task. H. L. Dryfus and S. E. Dreyfus, *Mind over Machine: The Power of Human Intuitive Expertise in the Era of the Computer* (New York: The Free Press, 1986). Also see H. L. Dreyfus "Intuitive, deliberative and calculative models of expert performance," in *Naturalistic Decision Making,* edited by C. E. Zsambok and G. Klein (Mahwah, NJ: Lawrence Erlbaum Associates, 1997). I have benefited from collaboration with the Dreyfus brothers as they developed the ideas described in their book.

In 1989, Judith Orasanu at the Army Research Institute sponsored a meeting of a group of investigators interested in these topics. This meeting started the Naturalistic Decision Making movement. I have described some aspects of this movement in my earlier book, *Sources of Power.*

8. *All of their previous experiences (prior to becoming a commander*... In reality, of course, the process is more complex than shown in Figure 2.1. It is not a simple sequence of steps. While it is true that cues allow us to recognize patterns, without some possible pattern already in mind to provide context, a potential cue is just meaningless noise. Likewise, even though it is patterns that activate scripts, sometimes a potential action script can help you recognize a pattern.

9. *"Better is the enemy of good enough"*... Simon distinguished between "optimizing"—finding the absolute best option—with "satisficing"—finding the first workable solution. The firefighters we studied were "satisficing," not optimizing. See Simon, "A Behavioral Model of Rational Choice," 99–118, and Simon, "Rational Choice and the Structure of the Environment." *Psychological Review* 63 (1956): 129–38.

In fact, the concept of optimizing may usually be a fiction; see my article "The Fiction of Optimization," in *Bounded Rationality: The Adaptive Toolbox,* edited by Gerd Gigerenzer and Reinhard Selten (Cambridge, MA: MIT Press, 2001), 103–21.

10. *the firefighters rely on mental simulation*... The process of mental simulation is described in more detail by G. A. Klein and B. W. Crandall in "The Role of Mental Simulation in Naturalistic Decision Making," in *Local Applications of the Ecological Approach to Human-Machine Systems,* edited by P. Hancock, J. Flach,

J. Caird, and K. Vicente (Mahwah, NJ: Lawrence Erlbaum Associates, 1995), 324–58.

11. *If they can't find a way around the problem* . . . We have also tested the recognition-primed decision model in a series of experiments with skilled chess players. First we confirmed that chess masters are able to play at very high levels even under blitz conditions (about 6 seconds per move instead of the 135 seconds per move allowed in regulation games). Next, to explain how they could handle the time pressure, we had medium-strong players think aloud while looking at difficult chess positions. We found that the first move they described was usually acceptable. They were not randomly searching for possibilities. For further information, see:

Calderwood, R., G. A. Klein, and B. W. Crandall. "Time Pressure, Skill, and Move Quality in Chess." *American Journal of Psychology* 101 (1988): 481–93.

Klein, G., S. Wolf, L. Militello, and C. Zsambok. "Characteristics of Skilled Option Generation in Chess." *Organizational Behavior and Human Decision Processes* 62, 1 (1995): 63–69.

12. Figure 2.2 is a streamlined version of the recognition-primed decision model. The detailed version is presented in my book *Sources of Power.*

13. *Other researchers have reported the same results* . . . Studies replicating the finding that skilled decision makers primarily rely on recognition include the following:

Flin, R., G. Slaven, and K. Stewart. "Emergency Decision Making in the Offshore Oil and Gas Industry." *Human Factors* 38, 2 (1996): 262–77.

Mosier, K. L. "Expert Decision Making Strategies." In *Proceedings of the Sixth International Symposium on Aviation Psychology,* edited by P. Jersen (Columbus, OH, 1991), 266–71.

Pascual, R., and S. Henderson. "Evidence of Naturalistic Decision Making in C2." In *Naturalistic Decision Making,* edited by C. Zsambok and G. Klein (Mahwah, NJ: Lawrence Erlbaum Associates, 1997), 217–26.

Randel, J. M., H. L. Pugh, and S. K. Reed. "Methods for Analyzing Cognitive Skills for a Technical Task." *International Journal of Human-Computer Studies* 45 (1996): 579–97.

14. *Back in 1984 Daniel Isenberg studied managers* . . . From D. J. Isenberg, "How Senior Managers Think," *Harvard Business Review* 6 (1984): 80–90. (See also H. Mintzberg, D. Raisinghani, and A. Theoret, "The Structure of Unstructured Decision Processes," *Administrative Science Quarterly* 21 [1976]: 246–75.) Isenberg also asserted that "senior managers . . . seldom think in ways that one might simplistically view as 'rational.' In other words, they rarely systematically formulate goals, assess their worth, evaluate the probabilities of alternative ways of reaching them, and choose the path that maximizes expected return. Rather, managers frequently bypass rigorous, analytical planning altogether, particularly when they face difficult, novel, or extremely entangled problems. When they do use analysis for a prolonged time, it is always in conjunction with intuition" (82).

1. K. A. Ericsson, and N. Charness. "Expert Performance: Its Structure and Acquisition." *American Psychologist* 49, no. 8 (1994): 725–47.

2. *Deliberate practice means not just practicing to practice* . . . Intuition skills training has to be tailored to your job because intuition and expertise are about specific types of judgments and decisions. There's no such thing as a general "expert." I don't believe that there are any tools that teach generic intuition. Your conditioning regimen has to help you become skilled at handling your own challenges at work.

3. *The genesis of the intuition skills training program* . . . Col. Tony Wood, the commander of the Marine Corps Warfighting Laboratory, persuaded me to try to teach intuitive decision making skills to the rifle squad leaders back in 1996. John Schmitt and I worked together to develop the initial training program, assisted by Mike McCloskey and Rebecca Pliske. Others who subsequently contributed to the program are Doug Harrington and Jenni Phillips. See M. J. McCloskey, R. M. Pliske, G. Klein, J. K. Heaton, and B. J. Knight, "Decision Skills Training: Preparing Marine Squad Leaders for Hunter Warrior" (technical report submitted to SYNETICS Corporation for Commandant's Warfighting Laboratory, Special Purpose Marine Air-Ground Task Force under Contract No. N00178–95-D-1008, King George, VA), Fairborn, OH: Klein Associates 1997.

4. *Decision games are a centerpiece of a mental conditioning program.* . . . We generally use the term "decision games." But in some settings people are uncomfortable with the word "games," because that implies a lack of seriousness. We use the term "decision-making exercise" (DMX) as a substitute if we are getting resistance to "decision games." The Marines, who first coined the term "tactical decision game" (TDG), faced the opposite problem. With Marines, lack of seriousness is not a problem, and the term TDG was purposely chosen to imply that the exercises could be enjoyable, as a way of encouraging Marines to participate.

5. *When the military creates decision games* . . . Much of this description is taken from a CD-ROM on Decision Skills Training that we developed for the Army Research Institute. The purpose of the CD-ROM was to show people how to build and facilitate decision games, and how to run decision-making critiques. This program is called IMPACT, which stands for "Improving Performance through Applied Cognitive Training." This effort is described in a technical report: J. Phillips, M. McCloskey, P. L. McDermott, S. Wiggins, D. A. Battaglia, and G. Klein, "Decision Skills Training for Small-Unit Leaders in Military Operations in Urban Terrain" (Alexandria, VA: U.S. Army Research Institute for the Behavioral and Social Sciences, 2001), 109.

6. *John Schmitt and others have developed a concept called "Decision Net"* . . . Keith Holcomb and Scott Fouse also contributed to the development of Decision Net.

7. *Research is very clear that people learn* . . . Outcome feedback, knowledge of results, is important for showing individuals and teams that their performance has to change, but it doesn't give any indication of how to change it, and for some tasks, outcome feedback can actually get in the way of learning. See L. L. Jacoby,

T. Troutman, and A. Kuss, "When Feedback Is Ignored: Disutility of Outcome Feedback, *Journal of Applied Psychology* 69 (1984): 531–45.

Several studies have shown that process feedback is usually more valuable for improving performance than outcome feedback:

Balzer, W. K., M. E. Doherty, and R. O. O'Connor. "The Effects of Cognitive Feedback on Performance." *Psychological Bulletin* 106 (1989): 410–33.

Early, C. P., G. B. Northcraft, C. Lee, and T. R. Lituchy. "Impact of Process and Outcome Feedback on the Relation of Goal Setting to Task Performance." *Academy of Management Journal* 33 (1990): 87–105.

Johnson, D. S., R. Perlow, and K. F. Piper. "Differences in Team Performance as a Function of Type of Feedback: Learning Oriented versus Performance Oriented Feedback." *Journal of Applied Psychology* 23 (1993): 303–20.

8. *And the decision games are a way to practice . . .* The tools described in this chapter can be seen as a way to help decision makers become reflective practitioners, as described in D. A. Schön, *The Reflective Practitioner* (New York: Basic Books, 1983).

Chapter 4: Using Analysis to Support Our Intuitions

1. H. L. Dreyfus and S. E. Dreyfus. *Mind over Machine: The Power of Human Intuitive Expertise in the Era of the Computer* (New York: The Free Press, 1986).

2. *Our intuitions function like our peripheral vision . . .* The contrast between foveal and peripheral vision is a metaphor for contrasting modes of reasoning, such as Steve Sloman's distinction between associative and rule-based reasoning. Sloman has used the concept of two different reasoning systems to explain why we are sometimes torn between what our impulses are telling us to do and what our conscious deliberations are suggesting. While Sloman emphasized the conflict between the two systems, he also appreciated the opportunities of having different reasoning systems that can serve as checks and balances to each other. See S. A. Sloman, "The Empirical Case for Two Systems of Reasoning," *Psychological Bulletin* 119, 1 (1996): 3–22.

Keith Stanovich, at the University of Toronto, also finds compelling evidence for this idea of two reasoning systems, one governed by associations and experiences and intuitions, and the other by rules and analysis and rational deliberations. See K. E. Stanovich, *Who Is Rational?: Studies of Individual Differences in Reasoning* (Mahwah, NJ: Lawrence Erlbaum Associates, 1999).

Robin Hogarth makes the same distinction between a tacit and a deliberate reasoning system. See R. Hogarth, *Educating Intuition* (Chicago: University of Chicago Press, 2001).

Also see the work of S. Epstein, "Cognitive Experiential Self-Theory," in *Advanced Personality*, edited by D. F. Barone, M. Hersen, and V. B. Van Hasselt (New York: Plenum Press, 1998), 211–38.

Ken Hammond points out that the judgments that emerge from intuition are generally in the right ballpark. Most of the answers that come from calculation are exactly correct, but those that miss can show large errors. The trade-off is precision versus the chance of making large errors. Hammond argues for "quasirationality," which blends both intuition and analysis in a form of imperfect reasoning that is robust, adaptive, and useful. See K. R. Hammond, *Human Judgment and Social Policy: Irreducible Uncertainty, Inevitable Error, Unavoidable Injustice* (New York: Oxford University Press, 1996).

The basic source for the notion of tacit knowledge, as distinguished from objective knowledge, is M. Polanyi, *Personal Knowledge: Towards a Post-Critical Philosophy* (Chicago: University of Chicago Press, 1958). Polanyi's ideas about intuition provide an important philosophical support for the approach I have taken.

3. *And if you have made a decision but are pressed* . . . Figure 4.2 suggests that we contrast several options when we want to justify a decision or make an optimal choice. However, in many settings the demonstration of considering several options becomes a charade. We have seen decision makers use their intuition to make the choice, and afterward come up with a few other inadequate options simply to make it appear that they had been meticulous and analytical in considering several candidates.

4. *Why will intuition sometimes prove unreliable?* . . . Although this discussion is about the limitations of intuition we have to distinguish between a healthy acceptance of these types of limitations, versus a phobic dread of intuition. I think this fear of intuition has arisen because it is so easy to devise laboratory tasks that make subjects, usually college students, look stupid. For more than three decades, these types of experiments have shown that people usually did not use analysis, and perhaps could not use analysis even when they needed to. Researchers have been drawing a picture of the typical person, whether educated or not, as a defective reasoner and an unreliable decision maker. Articles and books have been filled with lists of biases that were discovered. Here are three comprehensive reviews of different types of decision biases:

Kahneman, D., P. Slovic, and A. Tversky., eds. *Judgment under Uncertainty: Heuristics and Biases* (Cambridge, MA: Cambridge University Press, 1982).

Russo and Shoemaker. *Decision Traps.*

Sage, A. P. "Behavioral and Organizational Considerations in the Design of Information Systems and Processes for Planning and Decision Support." *IEEE Transactions on Systems, Man, and Cybernetics* 11 (1981): 640–78.

5. *Teams of gamblers have to spend days* . . . R. T. Barnhart, *Beating the Wheel: The System That Has Won over Six Million Dollars from Las Vegas to Monte Carlo* (New York: Carol Publishing Group, 1992).

6. *The stock market is also too complex* . . . A number of researchers have argued that the stock market is basically a random walk with an overall upward trend, therefore defying meaningful forecasting. See B. G. Malkiel, *A Random Walk Down Wall Street* (New York: W. W. Norton & Company, 1999). Another good reference is E. F. Fama, "The Behavior of Stock-Market Prices," *Journal of Business* 38 (1965): 34–105. Others have pointed out that when you look at the professionals, the people who manage mutual funds, only 25 percent match or exceed the S&P 500. The others show performance that is worse than the S&P 500. We would expect that 50 percent of the funds should match or exceed the S&P 500 by chance, so we cannot support notions of competence at this task. See

D. Kadlec, "Your Fund Is Not Up to Par," *Time*, January 27, 1997, 46–47. We can contrast a specialist who tries to predict the behavior of the stock market with a specialist who invests in companies—Warren Buffett. Buffett has been famously quoted as saying that "the only value of stock forecasters is to make fortune tellers look good." Hagstrom does catch Buffett making the prediction, in 1992, that "over the decade of the 1990s, it was unlikely that the S&P 500 Index would post returns similar to the above-average returns it accomplished in the 1980s." This prediction nicely supports Buffett's comment about fortune tellers. See R. G. Hagstrom, Jr., *The Warren Buffett Way: Investment Strategies of the World's Greatest Investor* (New York: John Wiley & Sons, 1994), 51.

7. *In 1970, a study was conducted to examine* . . . The water jar experiment was conducted by A. S. Luchins and E. H. Luchins, *Wertheimer's Seminars Revisited: Problem Solving and Thinking* (Albany: Faculty-Student Association, State University of New York at Albany, Inc., 1970). For a more detailed examination of the ways that experts can become trapped by their own mindsets, see P. J. Feltovich, R. J. Spiro, and R. L. Coulson, "Issues of Expert Flexibility in Contexts Characterized by Complexity and Change," in *Expertise in Context*, edited by P. J. Feltovich, K. M. Ford, and R. R. Hoffman (Cambridge, MA: MIT Press, 1997).

8. Example 4.3 "What Are You Breathing?" is based in part on a newspaper article: Jonas McCartha, "Inman Man Dies in Chemical Tank," *Spartanburg Herald*, January 5, 1975.

9. B. M. Bass, *Organizational Decision Making* (Homewood, IL: Richard D. Irwin, 1983), 77.

10. *But under close scrutiny, analysis, too has its share of drawbacks* . . . In reviewing the literature on decision biases, Judith Orasanu has wondered why the subjects decision researchers ran in their experiments seemed so stupid, while the subjects run in problem solving experiments seemed so insightful. If decision makers were so incompetent, why were computer scientists building expert systems to capture the reasoning processes of experts? See J. Orasanu and C. H. Blumer, "Knowledge-Based Reasoning and Decision Aiding," paper presented at the IEEE Systems, Man and Cybernetics Meeting, Washington, D.C. 1987.

Perhaps the disconnect is that decision research typically compares the performance of subjects against analytical frames dictated by mathematics and statistics and game theory. If people do not use these frames, their performance suffers. But there could be other criteria to use in assessing decision performance.

In 1988, an informal conference was held in Leiden, Germany, to take stock of this situation. (See L. R. Beach, C. Vlek, and W. A. Wagenaar, "Models and Methods for Unique Versus Repeated Decision Making" [Leiden, The Netherlands: Leiden University, Psychology Department, 1988]). The participants concluded that there are many different types of decision tasks, and only a few fit the paradigm of gambles that was imposed by classical decision theory. More troubling, decision makers usually have some control over the events following the decision, but the gambling paradigm does not allow for this. Further, the conference participants felt that the importance of optimal choices—which is emphasized so much in the research—may not be relevant to natural conditions. Worse yet, in natural settings most decision makers are familiar with how the decision task arose, and how it is likely to develop, whereas the laboratory research paradigms often involve stripped-down and unfamiliar situations.

See also:

Cohen, M. S. "The Bottom Line: Naturalistic Decision Aiding." In *Decision Making in Action: Models and Methods*, edited by G. A. Klein, J. Orasanu, R. Calderwood, and C. E. Zsambok (Norwood, NJ: Ablex, 1993), 265–69.

———. "Three Paradigms for Viewing Decision Biases." In *Decision Making in Action: Models and Methods*, edited by G. A. Klein, J. Orasanu, R. Calderwood, and C. E. Zsambok (Norwood, NJ: Ablex, 1993), 36–50.

Lopes has argued that much of the research showing how people make poor decisions relied on tasks where our heuristics will result in the wrong answers. For the purpose of the research, this design makes sense. It produces clear evidence that people rely on heuristics. The flaw is in drawing a conclusion that we cannot trust heuristics for any tasks. See L. L. Lopes, "The Rhetoric of Irrationality," *Theory & Psychology* 1, no. 1 (1991): 65–82.

11. *One of the most common methods taught for analyzing . . .* There are other standard methods for conducting decision analyses besides the one shown in the selection of an automobile. For example, you can work out the consequences of different choices by constructing a decision tree. You can estimate the amount you weight each option (or each path on a decision tree), and the probability of attaining it. Then you multiply the two to get a score for each path. In this way you find the path or option that is best. For more information, see R. Hastie and R. M. Dawes, *Rational Choice in an Uncertain World: The Psychology of Judgement and Decision Making* (Thousand Oaks, CA: Sage Publications, Inc., 2001).

This method will be useful as long as you can make these estimates accurately. People rarely can. It is harder to make judgments about probabilities than to judge which option or path you really prefer.

Decision theorists like this method because they can show how it will lead to optimal choices, as long as the decision makers fill in the data accurately. When the theorists found that the decision makers weren't cooperating, they blamed the decision makers for being biased. In practice, people usually do not have the time, the necessary information, or the cognitive capacity to perform the necessary calculations. Abernathy and Hamm have studied the use of this method by physicians and found that it was usually impractical—it takes too much time to gather the information. In addition, Abernathy and Hamm noted that key data elements are often missing. Further, physicians may not trust the numbers on which the analysis is based. See C. M. Abernathy and R. M. Hamm, *Surgical Intuition: What It Is and How to Get It* (Philadelphia: Hanley & Belfus, Inc., 1995).

12. *the use of analytical methods results in worse decisions . . .* The assertion that rational choice methods can interfere with intuitive decision making has been supported by several lines of research:

Erev, I., G. Bornstein, and T. S. Wallsten. "The Negative Effect of Probability Assessments on Decision Quality." *Organizational Behavior and Human Decision Processes* 51, 1 (June 1993): 79–94.

Johnston, J., J. E. Driskell, and E. Salas. "Vigilant and Hypervigilant Decision Making." *Journal of Applied Psychology* 82, no. 4 (1997).

Schooler, J., S. Ohlsson, and K. Brooks. "Thought Beyond Words: When Language Overshadows Insight." *Journal of Experimental Psychology* 122 (1993): 166–83.

Guy Claxton has also discussed the problems with trying to do all thinking deliberately and analytically. To Claxton, the idea of intuition is inherent in psychology—the appreciation of subconscious influences on thinking and behavior. Attempting to make everything deliberate is the extreme position that is difficult to maintain. See G. Claxton, *Hare Brain, Tortoise Mind: How Intelligence Increases When You Think Less*, 1st ed. (Hopewell, NJ: The Ecco Press, 1999).

Arthur Reber was one of the first to demonstrate the interference created by analytical methods. See A. S. Reber, *Implicit Learning and Tacit Knowledge: An Essay on the Cognitive Unconscious, Oxford Psychology Series* (New York: Oxford University Press, 1993).

In two separate studies, Dan Isenberg and Henry Mintzberg reported that executives do not make formal decisions by using analytical methods:

Isenberg, D. J. "How Senior Managers Think," 80–90.

Mintzberg, H. *The Rise and Fall of Strategic Planning: Reconceiving Roles for Planning, Plans, Planners* (New York: The Free Press, 1994).

13. P. J. Eslinger and A. R. Damasio. "Severe Disturbance of Higher Cognition after Bilateral Frontal Lobe Ablation: Patient EVR." *Neurology* 35 (1985): 1731–41.

14. Benjamin Franklin. "How to Make a Decision." In *A Benjamin Franklin Reader*, edited by Nathan G. Goodman, 786 (New York: Thomas Y. Crowell Company, 1945).

Some decision analysts have followed Franklin's tradition, trying to offer advice that is framed within our thinking patterns. The work of Janis and Mann is a good example. See I. L. Janis and L. Mann, *Decision Making: A Psychological Analysis of Conflict, Choice, and Commitment* (New York: The Free Press, 1977).

Other decision analysts have moved beyond Franklin's perspective. If you want more guidance about these types of strategy, take a look at Hammond, Keeney, and Raiffa, *Smart Choices: A Practical Guide to Making Better Decisions*. I also recommend D. F. Halpern, *Thought and Knowledge: An Introduction to Critical Thinking* (Mahwah, NJ: Lawrence Erlbaum Associates, 1996), and J. E. Russo and P. J. H. Shoemaker, *Winning Decisions: Getting It Right the First Time*.

15. Abernathy, C. M., and R. M. Hamm. *Surgical Intuition: What It Is and How to Get It* (Philadelphia: Hanley & Belfus, Inc., 1995), 30.

Abernathy and Hamm looked at the use of rules and procedures in medicine. They found that "The surgeons who write clinical algorithms do not actually *follow* their algorithms in practice" (ibid., 390). Algorithms work when they are concrete and specific, but that makes them brittle and hard to apply to a range of situations. "Although adding rules may make the algorithm more accurate, at the same time it would make the algorithm more complex and difficult to use—that is, less intuitive" (ibid., 391).

16. K. J. Vicente. *Cognitive Work Analysis: Toward Safe, Productive, and Healthy Computer-Based Work* (Mahwah, NJ: Lawrence Erlbaum Associates, 1999).

17. A. D. deGroot. *Thought and Choice in Chess* (New York: Mouton, 1946/1978).

1. *The second, using the crystal ball technique* . . . The concept of imagining a crystal ball for the PreMortem exercise was based on conversations with Marvin Cohen of Cognitive Technologies, Inc.

2. *In addition, when you offer the PreMortem* . . . I have expressed skepticism about the use of procedures to make decisions but here I am presenting a procedure for running a PreMortem exercise. This seems inconsistent. However, the Pre-Mortem exercise is not a procedure for enabling decision makers to spot problems. It is a way to structure a group meeting and consider the intuitions of all the participants. I think there is a difference. In subsequent chapters I present other procedures for groups to use. These are not procedures that can substitute for intuition in making decisions.

3. The model of problem detection was presented in G. Klein, R. M. Pliske, B. Crandall, and D. Woods, "Features of Problem Detection." *Proceedings of the Human Factors and Ergonomics Society 43rd Annual Meeting* 1 (1999): 133–37.

4. A. Bechara, H. Damasio, D. Tranel, and A. R. Damasio. "Deciding Advantageously Before Knowing the Advantageous Strategy." *Science* 275 (1997): 1293–95.

5. E. S. Katkin, S. Wiens, and A. Öhman. "Nonconscious Fear Conditioning, Visceral Perception, and the Development of Gut Feelings." *Psychological Science* 12, no. 5 (2001): 366–70.

6. *I was just noticing that our meetings* . . . In Example 6.2, "Selling the Company," my awareness of the icy atmosphere created by the manager may be an example of emotional intelligence, which is an aspect of intuition. See D. Goleman, *Emotional Intelligence* (New York: Bantam Books, 1997).

7. *One strategy that some senior executives use* . . . The use of an active stance by senior executives is described by Isenberg, "How Senior Managers Think," 80–90.

8. *If an event occurs that takes them aback* . . . Perrow, C. *Normal Accidents: Living with High-Risk Technologies* (New York: Basic Books, 1984).

9. The account of Project SERENE is taken from J. Morgenstern, "The Fifty-Nine-Story Crisis," *The New Yorker,* May 1999, 45–49.

Chapter 7: How to Manage Uncertainty

1. O. Harari. *The Leadership Secrets of Colin Powell* (New York: McGraw-Hill Professional, 2002), 260.

2. The research on how Marines manage uncertainty is described in J. F. Schmitt and G. Klein, "Fighting in the Fog: Dealing with Battlefield Uncertainty," *Marine Corps Gazette* (1996), 62–69. The sponsor for this research was Lt. Gen. Paul Van Riper (retired).

3. *One research study found that senior executives* . . . The study mentioned with regard to the "shaking the tree" strategy is Isenberg, "How Senior Managers Think," 80–90.

4. P. Schwartz. *The Art of the Long View* (New York: Doubleday, 1991).

5. *One of the most common tactics* . . . The concept of incremental decisions has been

discussed in T. Connolly, "Hedge-Clipping, Tree-Felling, and the Management of Ambiguity: The Need for New Images of Decision-Making," in *Managing the Challenge of Ambiguity and Change*, edited by L. R. Pondy, Jr., R. J. Boland, and H. Thomas (New York: John Wiley & Sons, Inc., 1988), 37–50.

6. *By taking stock of the tactics available* . . . I do not want to get into a lengthy discussion about teamwork issues. However, I will briefly point out that many of the tactics on this list involve the exchange of information between team members. One of the coordination costs faced by teams, as they grow larger, is to develop efficient tactics for the team members to disseminate data and messages in order to reduce each other's uncertainty. Often, too little information is exchanged, leaving the team to operate with lots of uncertainty. The other tendency is to copy everyone on emails and other messages, which just adds to the information explosion. You can see when the information exchange breaks down as people waste more of their workday either just sitting at their desks reading emails, or waiting for materials from others, or wasting their time going in the wrong direction when others have the knowledge that would have prevented this.

7. S. Budner. "Intolerance of Ambiguity as a Personality Variable." *Journal of Personality* 30 (1962): 29–50.

Chapter 8: How to Size Up Situations

1. *These intuitions let us recognize what to do* . . . In our studies of expert and novice decision makers, my colleagues and I found that it's the novices who often jump right in and try to select the best option they can come up with. The skilled decision makers use their energy to make sense of the situation—the problems they have to monitor, the constraints they are facing, the expected flow of events. Recently, this observation was confirmed by a study of the decision making of Marines in a command post scenario. The researchers found that the high-experience group spent much more time than the low-experience group in assessing the situation. However, once the assessment was completed, the high-experience group took much less time to select a course of action from the available options and their accuracy in developing an appropriate course of action was significantly higher. See D. A. Kobus, S. Proctor, and S. Holste, "Effects of Experience and Uncertainty During Dynamic Decision Making," *International Journal of Industrial Ergonomics* 28, no. 5 (2001): 275–90.

2. K. Weick. *Sensemaking in Organizations* (Thousand Oaks, CA: Sage Publications, 1995).

3. *It's this ability that makes it seem that experts* . . . This contrast between experts and novices, shown by John Schmitt and the lance corporal, and by Darlene versus Linda, was described by Abernathy and Hamm, who contrasted physicians at different experience levels. Abernathy and Hamm contrasted first-year residents, third-year residents, and attending physicians, all given the same set of cues and data regarding a patient. They show the same differences in sensemaking as in the "Invisible Adversary" example. See Abernathy and Hamm, *Surgical Intuition: What It Is and How to Get It.*

4. *The Japanese attack at Pearl Harbor provides an example* . . . This account is taken from R. Wohlstetter, *Pearl Harbor: Warning and Decision* (Stanford, CA: Stanford University Press, 1962).

5. *Consider the task of monitoring a nuclear power plant* . . . R. J. Mumaw, E. M. Roth, K. J. Vicente, and C. M. Burns. "There Is More to Monitoring a Nuclear Power Plant Than Meets the Eye." *Human Factors* 42, no. 1 (2000): 36–55.

6. *Accordingly, we expanded the recognition-primed decision (RPD) model* . . . The elaboration of the RPD model was described by G. L. Kaempf, G. Klein, M. L. Thordsen, and S. Wolf, "Decision Making in Complex Command-and-Control Environments," *Human Factors* 38 (1996): 220–31.

7. *In constructing a story, a decision maker tries to connect* . . . The strategy of storybuilding is described in Klein and Crandall, "The Role of Mental Simulation in Naturalistic Decision Making." Also see the chapter "The Power of Stories" in my book *Sources of Power,* 177–96.

   Pennington and Hastie have also demonstrated a storybuilding strategy in their research on jury decision making. See N. Pennington and R. Hastie, "A Theory of Explanation-Based Decision Making," in *Decision Making in Action: Models and Methods,* edited by G. A. Klein, J. Orasanu, R. Calderwood, and C. E. Zsambok (Norwood, NJ: Ablex, 1993), 188–201.

8. *Once the story is constructed* . . . Stories can be experienced as too powerful, particularly for people who distrust intuition and want to rely primarily on analysis. Paul Meehl, a clinical psychologist, wrote an essay, "Why I Do Not Attend Case Conferences," in *Psychodiagnosis: Selected Papers,* edited by P. Meehl (New York: W. W. Norton and Company, 1977). He was worried that the stories and case accounts would be so vivid that they might interfere with his statistical judgments. This seems like an overreaction to me, although Robyn Dawes, a decision researcher, appears to find Meehl's behavior commendable. (See R. M. Dawes, *Everyday Irrationality: How Pseudo-Scientists, Lunatics, and the Rest of Us Systematically Fail to Think Rationally* [Boulder, CO: Westview Press, 2001].) Whether you agree with Meehl or not, the incident does testify to the powerful impact that stories can have. Mental models are also essential to storybuilding. Our mental models are casual accounts for how things work in a situation. Good mental models make it easier to fill gaps by making educated assumptions and they also help us spot expected events that did not occur. The difference between a mental model and a story is that the mental model is a general explanation of how things work, and a story is a specific account, using the mental model to explain the circumstances behind the particular situation.

9. *Sensemaking can go wrong* . . . The risk of being blinded by a mindset was described by Richards Heuer, who has written about how this problem can get in the way of intelligence analysts trying to do their jobs; in R. J. Heuer, Jr. *Psychology of Intelligence Analysis* (Washington, DC: Center for the Study of Intelligence, Central Intelligence Agency, 1999). The growing expertise of intelligence analysts lets them work more efficiently because they know how to direct their attention, but that makes them vulnerable to events that depart from the patterns they are used to seeing. We need to determine the conditions under which events that depart from what we expect are noticed as anomalies, versus conditions where they go unnoticed due to mindset.

10. Perrow, *Normal Accidents*.

11. *Only by actively trying to make sense* . . . The difficulty that physicians have in viewing the data without any presuppositions was reported by A. S. L. Elstein, S. Shulman, and S. A. Sprafka in *Medical Problem Solving: An Analysis of Clinical Reasoning* (Cambridge, MA: Harvard University Press, 1978). More recently, Abernathy and Hamm have confirmed it (see Abernathy and Hamm, *Surgical Intuition*). They have reviewed efforts to get physicians to be more systematic and analytical in the way they size up patients. Despite the best of intentions to turn physicians into scientists, the evidence is not encouraging. Researchers have tried to help physicians to systematically formulate and test hypotheses about what is wrong with the patient, and to prevent themselves from jumping to conclusions. Abernathy and Hamm explain why this doesn't work. It is opposite to the intuitive reasoning that physicians use, and, as a general method, is altogether too weak. Skilled physicians are able to recognize patterns and scripts, to see not only what the diagnosis might be, but at the same time to recognize the available strategies for testing these diagnoses, and also how they manage the patient while the diagnosis is continuing.

Abernathy and Hamm conclude:

"Expert diagnosis is often fast and effortless. The initial hypotheses are available through rapid recognition of patterns, because expert knowledge holds a large number of patterns organized for quick access and the evaluation of the hypotheses within each script is a well-practiced skill. Expert diagnosis is accurate. Because the expert's organized knowledge has been corrected, through experience and objective review by the community of surgeons and the larger medical establishment, the quickly recognized diagnoses are usually quite appropriate. And the experts' judgment allows a flexibility that increases the accuracy even in novel cases that cannot be handled by simple recognition. Finally, the nature of expert knowledge explains why it is difficult for the expert to explain accurately how he or she is able to make a diagnosis (although often a surgeon may volunteer a theory). The knowledge has become highly complex and dense, through a process in which responses become automatic and then are adjusted further, thus its details are inaccessible." (172)

12. *Therefore, the next step is we have to be ready* . . . The issue has been extensively studied in the field of medicine. We'd expect diagnosticians to try to keep an open mind when they examine patients. Yet researchers have found that this doesn't happen. Physicians recognize patterns and build stories and form intuitions while they work, just like the rest of us.

The test for fixation is consistent with the work of Karl Popper on fallibilism. Popper suggested that scientists would make more progress if they accepted the limitations of their theories, and worked to reject and replace them with better theories. Generally, scientists have been unable or unwilling to give up their theoretical commitments. Scientists are usually locked into a mode of trying to support their theories. See K. Popper, *The Logic of Scientific Discovery* (New York: Basic Books, 1959).

For a related perspective, see Y. Xiao, C. F. Mackenzie, and LOTAS Group, "Decision Making in Dynamic Environments: Fixation Errors and Their Causes," *Proceedings of the Human Factors and Ergonomics Society 39th Annual Meeting* (1995): 469–73.

Mike Doherty and others have cautioned us about a confirmation bias—a tendency to seek information that would confirm a hypothesis rather than seeking information that could reject it. See M. E. Doherty, "A Laboratory Scientist's View of Naturalistic Decision Making," in *Decision Making in Action: Models and Methods,* edited by G. A. Klein, J. Orasanu, R. Calderwood, and C. E. Zsambok (Norwood, NJ: Ablex, 1993), 362–88.

My experience had been that experts are usually careful to examine data that might go against their interpretations. For example, firefighters make assumptions about where the seat of the fire is and the experienced captains check other possibilities because they worry about the consequences of being wrong. My concern here is somewhat different from the confirmation bias. I don't think experienced decision makers are necessarily trying to confirm their hypotheses—I think that their hypotheses are guiding the way they search for data and as a result they might miss critical types of information that are unexpected.

13. *Test for Fixation* . . . The test for fixation that I am proposing is described as "Alexander's question" by G. Kolata, in *Flu: The Story of the Great Influenza Pandemic of 1918 and the Search for the Virus That Caused It* (New York: Simon & Schuster, 1999), who attributes this strategy to Neustadt and May, based on an incident that took place during the planning in 1976 to prevent a swine flu epidemic. See R. E. Neustadt, and E. R. May, *Thinking in Time: The Uses of History for Decision-Makers* (New York: The Free Press, 1986).

14. *What you can do is to monitor all the discrepancies* . . . For the strategy of making the strain more visible, my colleagues and I, working on a Navy project, developed a display concept for a decision support system that generated different hypotheses about the intent of an aircraft that might be getting ready to attack a ship. Underneath each hypothesis the display would list all of the information that was inconsistent with that explanation. We expected that the decision makers would explain away the inconsistencies. But we wanted them to have a visual record of how much they were explaining away. We wanted that record to act as a strain gauge, making them aware of the effort it was taking to hold on to their initial explanation. The Navy seemed to appreciate this scorecard—they are continuing to develop it for future displays. See Kaempf et al., "Decision Making in Complex Command-and-Control Environments," 220–31.

15. *Marvin Cohen, the president of Cognitive Technologies* . . .
M. S. Cohen, J. T. Freeman, and S. Wolf. "Meta-Recognition in Time-Stressed Decision Making: Recognizing, Critiquing, and Correcting." *Human Factors* 38 (1996): 206–19.

16. *Failures force us to discard outdated systems* . . . A good example of learning from breakdowns in sensemaking is R. Darnton, *The Great Cat Massacre and Other Episodes in French Cultural History* (New York: Basic Books, Inc., 1985). Darnton argues that it is impossible to really understand a different society, a different culture. However, we can and should strive to improve our understanding. As a

historian, his strategy was to be alert for incomprehensible actions—such as the slaughter of cats by Parisian craftsmen—as points of departure for investigating that society.

Chapter 9: Getting Creative—How to Go Beyond Brainstorming

1. *Then the group builds on another promising idea* . . . For a more recent account of brainstorming, see Roger L. Firestien, *Leading on the Creative Edge: Gaining Competitive Advantage Through the Power of Creative Problem Solving* (Colorado Springs, CO: Piñon Press, 1996). There are suggested rules for brainstorming sessions in A. Osborn, *Applied Imagination*. (New York: Charles Scribner's Sons, 1953).

2. *One research team reviewed a broad range* . . . I expect that this critical appraisal of brainstorming will provoke disagreement among some readers. If you are interested in the topic, there is no shortage of materials that suggest the benefits of the brainstorming method. In fairness to your teams and organization, you should also look at the Mullen et al. and the Kass et al. papers listed below and judge for yourself whether brainstorming works as advertised:

   Kass, S. J., C. M. Inzana, and R. P. Willis. "The Effects of Team Member Distribution and Accountability on a Brainstorming Task." *Proceedings of the Human Factors and Ergonomics Society 39th Annual Meeting* 2 (1995): 882–86.

   Mullen, B., C. Johnson, and E. Salas. "Productivity Loss in Brainstorming Groups: A Meta-Analytic Integration." *Basic and Applied Social Psychology* 12, 1 (1991): 18.

   In addition, Diehl and Stroebe (1987) have provided a different explanation of why brainstorming is so inefficient—production blocking. The need to have everyone in the session thinking about the same idea prevents the parallel processing that makes groups so effective. The single focus of attention becomes a bottleneck. See M. Diehl and W. Stroebe, "Productivity Loss in Brainstorming Groups: Towards the Solution of a Riddle," *Journal of Personality and Social Psychology* 53 (1987): 497–509.

3. *We want that creative energy to result in movement* . . . I am asserting that we usually just need effective solutions, and that creativity has no intrinsic benefit to us. There are exceptions, such as with works of art, where there is a value in having an unusual approach. That is the point of art—to present something people haven't seen before. These works can be inspiring, or they can be trivial. Mere novelty is not necessarily a good thing.

4. *The central premise of directed creativity* . . . I would like to thank Devorah Klein for her useful suggestions in regard to the idea of directed creativity, and for alerting me to the practical benefits of designing creativity approaches that moved beyond brainstorming.

5. *These failures become very instructive* . . . This discussion of the importance of redefining goals is based on some earlier work I did with Julian Weitzenfeld. See G. A. Klein and J. Weitzenfeld, "Improvement of Skills for Solving Ill-Defined Problems," *Educational Psychologist* 13 (1978): 31–41.

6. Isenberg, "How Senior Managers Think," 80–90.

7. *It directs our attention to the high-payoff leverage* . . . This treatment of how people invent options—by spotting leverage points and seeing if they can be formed into solutions—is different from the approach used in many artificial intelligence programs. There, the computer generates a very large problem space of all possible paths between a current state and a desired state. The computer uses predefined evaluation criteria to discard the low-value paths, and to identify the ones with the greatest potential. This strategy fits the mentality of computers, which is to do rapid searching on a well-defined task, with clear evaluation criteria and a nicely structured problem. It does not fit the challenges of working with ill-defined goals, and it does not fit the mentality of people. We are not good at doing massive searches through problem spaces.

The computer metaphor of searching through a problem space has come to dominate our thinking about how to generate new options. I suggest that this is a misleading metaphor. When we try to solve difficult problems we are not creating massive problem spaces to be searched. We are recognizing leverage points, and building from these to construct new options. Steve Wolf and I have described how leverage points can be used to construct new options. See G. Klein and S. Wolf, "The Role of Leverage Points in Option Generation," *IEEE Transactions on Systems, Man and Cybernetics: Applications and Reviews* 28, no. 1 (1998): 157–160.

8. *The concepts behind directed creativity explain* . . . Another process that seems to affect creativity is the way we pay attention to the task we are performing. Guy Claxton, Charles Palus, and David Horth have described the importance of paying attention for supporting creativity:

Claxton, *Hare Brain, Tortoise Mind.*

Palus, C. J., and D. M. Horth. "Leading Creatively." In *Leadership in Action.* Center for Creative Leadership and Jossey-Bass, 1998.

Paying attention can be deliberate, such as truly experiencing a problem instead of categorizing and dismissing it, or taking the time to let your mind drift instead of rushing to figure out a solution. If you are a chess player, it is the difference between playing a game by following move sequences versus overhearing someone say, "He has a checkmate in three," and then scrutinizing the board to see what opportunities it may hold. We cannot pay attention in this way to everything. We have to be selective in using this mental gear. But it is invaluable to have it available when we need it.

Jonathan Schooler and his colleagues have shown that we pay attention differently when we are analyzing and deliberating than when we are experiencing and musing about something. Analysis requires words and propositions, and when we try to fit experience into crisp categories, we lose the aspects of the experience that are not amenable to verbalization. We lose access to the subconscious workings of our minds. See J. Schooler, S. Ohlsson, and K. Brooks, "Thought Beyond Words," 166–83.

9. *Present the dilemma* . . . In the first step of the directed creativity method, you might try to compose your group to include some people who are good at recognizing leverage points and others who are good at connecting them to real problems. You want to get the cross-pollination of engineers who are playing

around with new technology linking to marketing specialists who appreciate the business need that can be satisfied by the technology, to increase the chance for a "great discovery" moment.

10. *Everyone ultimately found the directed creativity session* . . . I emphasize that good subjective reactions to this directed creativity method can never be as convincing to us as solid empirical data showing that the method improves performance. This disclaimer holds for all of the methods described in this section. I have assessed these methods in the workshops I have conducted over the past several years, using participants' subjective reactions. It is difficult to conduct an objective evaluation of methods in the context of field settings.

11. G. Klein and R. Hutton. *The Innovators: High-Impact Researchers at the Armstrong Laboratory Human Engineering Division, Armstrong Laboratory (U)* (AL/CF-FR-1995-0027). Wright-Patterson AFB, OH: United States Air Force Armstrong Laboratory (1995).

    The scientists and engineers we studied either had been or were currently working for the Armstrong Laboratory at Wright-Patterson Air Force Base. Our customer was Ken Boff, the chief of the Human Engineering Division. He wanted to celebrate the fiftieth anniversary of his division by recognizing and studying the intellectual leaders in his organization during the previous half-century.

12. *Creativity depends on selecting the right problems* . . . These findings correspond to field research with business leaders. Dan Isenberg reported the findings of his two-year anthropological study of senior managers. One of Isenberg's observations was that "how managers define and rank problems is heavily influenced by how easy the problems are to solve. Very shortly after perceiving that a problem exists, managers run a quick feasibility check to see if it is solvable. Only if they find it is solvable will they then invest further energy to understand its various ramifications and causes." See Isenberg, "How Senior Managers Think," 86.

13. *They just didn't make enough money* . . . Paragraph (k) stipulates that the top third of the salaried employees can only put in up to 3 percent more than the average percentage of the bottom two-thirds, and no more than twice the amount of the bottom two-thirds. For example, if the bottom two-thirds of employees puts in 2 percent of their pay, the top third can only put in 4 percent of their pay.

14. T. Benna. *401(K) Perspective: Where Did the 401(K) Plan Come From?* www.mpowercafe.com, cited May 31, 2001.

15. *Example 9.3: Flights of Creativity* . . . This account is taken from T. Crouch, *The Bishop's Boys: A Life of Wilbur and Orville Wright* (New York: W. W. Norton, 1989).

16. *For the Wright brothers, the warping of canvas* . . . The Wright brothers had also considered ailerons and described these in their patent. Some inventors at the time added ailerons to their airplanes, but designed these to work automatically so that the airplane would remain stable—to keep the plane straight and level at all times. Today's airplanes rely on ailerons to change the shape of the wings, rather than warping the wings directly.

1. *The adaptation of skilled workers* . . . The treatment of adaptation as akin to jazz improvisation was presented by K. E. Weick, "Tool Retention and Fatalities in Wildland Fire Settings: Conceptualizing the Naturalistic," in *Linking Expertise and Naturalistic Decision Making*, edited by E. Salas and G. Klein (Hillsdale, NJ: Lawrence Erlbaum Associates, 2001), 321–36.

2. K. E. Weick and K. M. Sutcliffe. *Managing the Unexpected: Assuring High Performance in an Age of Complexity* (San Francisco: Jossey-Bass, 2001).

3. *To be adaptable is to respond rapidly and effectively* . . . We can appreciate the ability to adapt by contrasting tasks that require adaptation to those that just depend on coordination. Nicholai Bernstein, a Russian psychologist working fifty years ago, contrasted runners competing on a track to cross-country runners, for whom every step is a problem in handling the challenge of an uneven surface. On a track, you can close your eyes for a few strides, or run backward. On a broken field, this wouldn't be a good idea. The track runners didn't have to worry about adapting. The cross-country runners needed to adapt at every stride.

   For more information, see N. A. Bernstein, "On Dexterity and Its Development." In *Dexterity and Its Development*, edited by M. L. Latash and M. T. Turvey (Mahwah, NJ: Lawrence Erlbaum Associates, 1996).

4. Mintzberg, H. *The Rise and Fall of Strategic Planning.*

5. *Example 10.1: The Japanese Robots* . . . E. Thornton. "Goodbye, Mr. Chips." *Far Eastern Economic Review* (1996): 48–51.

6. The Mann Gulch fire was described by N. Maclean, *Young Men and Fire* (Chicago: University of Chicago Press, 1992).

7. G. A. Jamieson and C. A. Miller. "Exploring the 'Culture of Procedures.'" In *Proceedings of the 5th International Conference on Human Interactions with Complex Systems* (Urbana-Champaign: University of Illinois at Urbana-Champaign, The Beckman Institute; U.S. Army Research Laboratory, Advanced Displays and Interactive Displays, Federated Laboratory Consortium, 2000), 141–45.

8. *Problems arise when we need those operators* . . . The limitations of procedures raise questions about ISO 9000. Many companies need to assure their customers that they are ISO 9000 compliant as a way to show that they have achieved high standards of quality and precision. However, ISO 9000 is primarily about the level of documentation that the company uses, not about the precision of its methods or equipment. The standard examines the thoroughness with which a company documents and verifies and enforces its procedures. Some managers and workers find better ways to do the job but don't mention these, because then they will have to go through the effort and expense of documenting the change. The paradoxical result is that ISO 9000 may be stifling improvement rather than facilitating it because the emphasis on documentation and procedures is incompatible with being adaptive.

1. L. G. Shattuck and D. D. Woods. "Communication of Intent in Military Command and Control Systems." In *The Human in Command: Exploring the Modern Military Experience*, edited by C. McCann and R. Pigeau. New York: Plenum Publishers, 2000, 279–91.
2. This example comes from N. M. Tichy and E. B. Cohen. *The Leadership Engine: How Winning Companies Build Leaders at Every Level*. New York: HarperCollins Publishers, Inc., 1997.
3. *The defining feature of information* . . . The view that information is the reduction of uncertainty comes from the work of Shannon on information theory. See C. E. Shannon, "The Mathematical Theory of Communication," in *The Mathematical Theory of Communication*, edited by C. E. Shannon and W. Weaver. Urbana, IL: University of Illinois Press, 1962.
4. *For executive intent to have an impact* . . . In order to give clear directions, retired Marine Corps Lt. Gen. Paul Van Riper has a formula that is even more succinct than Weick's: "I want you to take Action *A* in order to achieve Purpose *B*." This is nice and snappy. I am using Weick's approach because it captures the types of contextual information that Van Riper's formula assumes have already been provided. (G. Klein, "Why Won't They Follow Simple Directions?" *Across the Board* 37, no. 2, February 2000: 14–19.)

Chapter 13: Coaching Others to Develop Strong Intuitions

1. N. M. Tichy and E. B. Cohen. *The Leadership Engine: How Winning Companies Build Leaders at Every Level*. New York: HarperCollins Publishers, Inc., 1997.
2. Ibid., 45
3. *One estimate is that 70 percent* . . . This estimate is based on a two-year, $1.6 million study by the U.S. Department of Labor and the Massachusetts Center for Workforce Development, Newton, MA: D. Goldwasser, "Me, a Trainer?" *Training* 38, no. 4 (April 2001): 60–66.
4. P. M. Senge. *The Fifth Discipline: The Art and Practice of the Learning Organization*. New York: Doubleday, 1994.
5. For more information about cognitive task analysis, see R. R. Hoffman, B. W. Crandall, and N. R. Shadbolt. "Use of the Critical Decision Method to Elicit Expert Knowledge: A Case Study in Cognitive Task Analysis Methodology," *Human Factors* 40, no. 2 (1998): 254–76.
6. *We may think we are effective coaches* . . . I am frustrated by the inadequacies I see in everyday coaching situations, and I wonder if it all starts with the way that our children are coached. This is particularly true for the appalling practices used to coach children in sports. Parents, mostly fathers, who are continually exposed to televised images of coaching prima donnas in sports such as college basketball, are given free rein to indulge their egotistical fantasies on the soccer field and the baseball diamond and the football field. We all know this is wrong.

We justify it in various ways—it is so hard to get volunteers that we can't alienate the parents who do help us out, or this prepares the kids for the real world, or our spoiled children need to learn some discipline.

I don't buy any of these excuses. We prohibit hazing in colleges and military ranks, so why tolerate it with our six- and seven-year-olds?

If this approach to coaching is what we expose our children to, no wonder that they lack coaching skills when they grow up. We have to break the cycle somewhere, and I suggest that we start with youth sports.

For a discussion of coaching for youth sports, see M. J. McCloskey, "Successful Sports Coaching: Guidelines for Adults in Children's Recreational Activities," *Childhood Education* 75 (1999): 308–9.

7. *For example, some colleagues of mine have studied* . . . The research on instruction given to new drivers is presented in H. A. Klein, E. J. Vincent, and J. J. Isaacson, "Driving Proficiency: The Development of Decision Skills," in *Linking Expertise and Naturalistic Decision Making*, edited by E. Salas and G. Klein (Hillsdale, NJ: Lawrence Erlbaum Associates, 2001), 303–20.

8. The barriers to effective coaching are described in B. W. Crandall, M. Kyne, L. Militello, and G. A. Klein, "Describing Expertise in One-on-One Instruction" (Fairborn, OH: Klein Associates, 1992), and C. E. Zsambok, G. L. Kaempf, B. Crandall, and M. Kyne, "OJT: A Cognitive Model of Prototype Training Program for OJT Providers" (Fairborn, OH: Klein Associates, 1996).

9. *The program that my colleagues designed* . . . The research we performed for the Navy on OJT was sponsored by Kim Smith-Jentsch, and reported in T. Stanard, R. M. Pliske, A. A. Armstrong, S. Green, C. E. Zsambok, D. P. McDonald, and B. W. Crandall, "Collaborative Development of Expertise: Evaluation of an On-the-Job (OJT) Training Program." In *Proceedings of the Human Factors and Ergonomics Society 46th Annual Meeting*. Santa Monica, CA: Human Factors & Ergonomics Society, in press.

Chapter 14: Overcoming the Problems with Metrics

1. *Burger King was growing tired* . . . J. Ordonez. "Crunch Time: How Burger King Got Burned in Quest to Make the Perfect Fry." *The Wall Street Journal*, January 10, 2001, A1, A-8.

2. *At Apple Computer, it was the marginal return* . . . J. Carlton. *Apple: The Inside Story of Intrigue, Egomania, and Business Blunders*. New York: Random House/Times Business, 1997.

3. *Because minor disorders are handled* . . . "The Trouble with Targets." *The Economist*, April 28, 2001, 57–62.

4. *Perverse incentives are the rule* . . . If simple metrics can get us in trouble, then maybe we need to use complex ones, and sacrifice elegance and ease of communication for accuracy. It is harder for subordinates to game several simultaneously applied metrics. By adding more metrics we are hoping to reduce the effects of the distortions introduced by each one.

It will be harder for unscrupulous employees to game multiple metrics than simple ones, but it will also be harder for honorable employees to understand and use multiple metrics.

5. *By getting underneath the aggregated statistics* . . . For an opposing view, see Paul Krugman, "Passing the Buck," *New York Times* (September 3, 2002).

6. *The story and the measures both needed to inform* . . . The Marco Polo story was re-counted by I. Calvino, *Invisible Cities*, W. Weaver, trans. (New York: Harcourt Brace Jovanovich, 1974).

7. *How many of those who test positive* . . . The example of the use of frequency data to estimate the probability of breast cancer comes from G. Gigerenzer, *Calculated Risks: How to Know When Numbers Deceive You* (New York: Simon & Schuster, 2002), 5–6

8. Ibid. The study about the interpretation of 40 percent is on p. 23.

9. *The association between baseball and metrics is not altogether whimsical* . . . For the best example of baseball statistics, and one of the best examples of statistical analy-ses in general, see B. James, *The New Bill James Historical Baseball Abstract* (New York: The Free Press, 2001).

10. For example, consider the debate about why the euro is undervalued against the dollar. The difficulty of assessing the euro is described in "Europe's Economies: Stumbling Yet Again?" *The Economist* (September 16, 2000), 77–78.

11. *As I write this section, the drama of Enron is playing out* . . . I have taken this expla-nation for the fall of Enron from "The Amazing Disintegrating Firm, *The Econ-omist* (December 8, 2001), 61–62.

Chapter 15: Smart Technology Can Make Us Stupid

1. *Hospitals are filled with poisons* . . .

   Brennan, T. A. "The Institute of Medicine Report on Medical Error—Could It Do Harm?" *New England Journal of Medicine* 342 (2000): 1123–25.

   Leape, L. L., T. A. Brennan, N. Laird, and A. G. Lawthers. "The Nature of Adverse Events in Hospitalized Patients: Results of the Harvard Medical Practice Study II." *New England Journal of Medicine* 324 (1991): 377–84.

2. *Only when they are comfortable that they understand* . . . The research on weather forecasting was done by my colleagues Rebecca Pliske, Beth Crandall, Dave Klinger, and Rob Hutton. For more information on this project, see R. M. Pliske, B. Crandall, and G. Klein, "Competence in Weather Forecasting," in *Psy-chological Exploration of Competent Decision Making*, edited by J. Shanteau, P. John-son and K. Smith (Cambridge, MA: Cambridge University Press, in press).

3. *The old-fashioned hand-marked screen* . . . The work with AWACS weapons directors is reported in D. W. Klinger, S. J. Andriole, L. G. Militello, L. Adelman, G. Klein, and M. E. Gomes. *Designing for Performance: A Cognitive Systems Engineering Ap-proach to Modifying an AWACS Human-computer Interface* (Technical Report AL/CF-TR-1993-0093). Wright-Patterson AFB, OH: Department of the Air Force, Armstrong Laboratory, Air Force Materiel Command (1993).

4. *They knew that the difference was statistically significant* . . . Regarding the use of

computers for teaching statistics courses, some experienced teachers still make their students do the problems by hand, even in a roomful of computers, just as I did after the data analysis programs first became available.

5. The accounts of Greenspan's strategies come from several sources, primarily:

Stevenson, R. W. "Inside the Head of the Fed: Alan Greenspan's Journey to the New World economy." *New York Times*, November 15, 1998, B1 and B5.

Woodward, B. *Maestro: Greenspan's Fed and the American Boom.* New York: Simon and Schuster, 2000.

6. *His sight might be restored . . .* O. Sacks. *An Anthropologist on Mars.* New York: Random House, 1995, 117.

7. *Information technologies are exciting . . .* In the section on active search for data I raised the problem of information overload and the question of how much data is "too much." The seriousness of this problem was demonstrated in research that examined the ability of intelligence analysts to handle data overload: The intelligence analysts were asked to quickly sort through a large set of articles describing an accident, to find out what was the likely cause of the accident. When the data rate got too high, and the analysts didn't have the time to read each one, even the experienced intelligence analysts started making errors. They would fail to read the most informative articles and then they would draw the wrong conclusions. (See E. S. Patterson, D. D. Woods, N. B. Sarter, and J. C. Watts-Perotti, "Patterns in Cooperative Cognition," in *Coop '98, Third International Conference on the Design of Cooperative Systems,* Cannes, France, 1998.)

These findings were echoed in the studies of meteorologists mentioned in the text: T. R. Stewart, K. F. Heideman, W. R. Moninger, and P. Reagan-Cirincione, "Effects of Improved Information on the Components of Skill in Weather Forecasting," *Special Issue: Experts and Expert Systems of Organizational Behavior and Human Decision Processes* 53, no. 2 (1992): 107–34.

Similarly, Lusk and Hammond demonstrated that forecast accuracy did not increase with increasing information: C. M. Lusk and K. R. Hammond, "Judgment in a Dynamic Task: Microburst Forecasting," *Journal of Behavioral Decision Making* 41 (1991): 55–73.

Mary Omodei and her colleagues used a simulated exercise to study the impact of information on firefighters. Whenever information resources were made available, the commanders felt compelled to use it, and their performance got worse. Thus, when the commanders were shown only major features of the landscape, given no wind details, and had no fire warnings, they did better than when they had all the landscape features, had the wind details, and got all the fire warnings. The commanders themselves expected that they would do better when they had more data, but they did a better job when they had less information. The explanation given by Omodei, Wearing, McLennan, Elliott, and Clancy was that the commanders had problems prioritizing the information when it was automatically provided, and that they spent more time inspecting the information and less time forming their intentions about what they should try to achieve. With excessive information, the commanders felt they needed to work harder and be more careful with their interpretations. See M. M. Omodei, A. J. Wearing, J. McLennan, G. C. Elliott, and J. M. Clancy, "More Is Better?

Problems of Self-Regulation in Naturalistic Decision Making Settings" in *How Professionals Make Decisions*, edited by B. Brehmer, R. Lipshitz, and H. Montgomery (Mahwah, NJ: Lawrence Erlbaum Associates, in press).

8. *Analysts have been amazed* . . . Kurt Thumlert. *Abandoned Shopping Carts: Enigma or Sloppy E-Commerce?* www.internetday.com [cited August 2, 2001]. Available from http://www.internetday.com/article/0, 1381–785791,00.html.

9. *In commercial aviation, the flight management systems* . . .

Sarter, N. B., and D. D. Woods. "How in the World Did We Ever Get into That Mode? Mode Error and Awareness in Supervisory Control." *Human Factors* 37, no. 1 (1995): 15–19.

Wiener, E. L. "Human Factors of Advanced Technology ('Glass Cockpit') Transport Aircraft." Moffett Field, CA: Ames Research Center, 1989.

10. *In 1995, my colleagues Tom Miller and Laura Militello* . . . T. E. Miller and L. G. Militello (1995). *Increasing the Robustness of AI Generated Plans* (Technical Report No: RL-TR-95–30). Griffiss Air Force Base, NY: Rome Laboratory.

11. R. A. Schmidt and G. Wulf. "Continuous Concurrent Feedback Degrades Skill Learning: Implications for Training and Simulation." *Human Factors* 39, no. 4 (1997): 509–25.

12. *In the world of aviation, this condition* . . . Consider a decision aid that would help us notice important cues. Michelle Yeh and Chris Wickens tried it out. They built an aid that would help decision makers look at a visual scene and notice threatening cues that might be tough to recognize. The threat recognition rate went up. But so did the false alarm rate. These were nonthreats that were mistakenly identified as threats. The chance of a false alarm, which had been 8 percent, increased to 45 percent when the automatic cueing was available to the subjects. And when cueing from the automated decision aid was available, subjects were less likely to detect a threat (one that the aid did not call out) compared to trials where the cueing was not available and the subjects had to scan the scene on their own. The subjects with automatic cueing only noticed 46 percent of the unexpected threats, whereas subjects who didn't have the automatic cueing noticed 59 percent of the same threats.

Even more discouraging is that the better we make the systems, the more they affect us. Yeh and Wickens found that the more realistic they made the visual displays, the more the subjects relied on the automated aids. For further information, see:

Mosier, K. L., L. J. Skitka, S. Heers, and M. D. Burdick. "Automation Bias: Decision Making and Performance in High-Tech Cockpits." *International Journal of Aviation Psychology* 8 (1998): 47–63.

Yeh, M., and C. D. Wickens. "Display Signaling in Augmented Reality: Effects of Cue Reliability and Image Realism on Attention Allocation and Trust Calibration," *Human Factors* (2001): 355–65.

Phil Smith has demonstrated this automation bias with flight dispatchers. In a controlled setting, he gave experienced dispatchers a variety of problems. Smith also had developed a very good (but not perfect) advisory system to recommend solutions. When Smith arranged for the dispatchers to generate their solutions first, and then see the computer's recommendation, the quality of the dispatchers' solutions was significantly higher than when Smith had the dispatchers first see what the computer said, and then try to improve on it. See P. J. Smith, E. McCoy, and C. Layton, "Brittleness in the Design of Cooperative Problem-Solving Systems: The Effects on User Performance," *IEEE Transactions on Systems, Man and Cybernetics* 27 (1997): 360–71.

13. *technology has decided that machines have certain needs . . .*

D. A. Norman. *Things That Make Us Smart: Defending Human Attributes in the Age of the Machine* (Reading, MA: Addison-Wesley, 1993), 223.

David Woods, at Ohio State University, warned us about this back in 1986. He explained that the human-computer interaction was not a true partnership. The operators have to accept or reject the machine solution. There is no reasoning, no back and forth discussion. See D. D. Woods, "Paradigms for Intelligent Decision Support," in *ASI Series: Intelligent Decision Support in Process Environments*, edited by E. Hollnagel, G. Mancini, and D. D. Woods (Berlin: Springer-Verlag, 1986), 230–54.

14. *"at all levels of society computer-type rationality is winning out" . . .* H. L. Dreyfus and S. E. Dreyfus. *Mind Over Machine: The Power of Human Intuitive Expertise in the Era of the Computer* (New York: The Free Press, 1986), 306.

15. *Cognitive engineering begins by determining . . .* The concepts of cognitive engineering are discussed in the following sources:

Rasmussen, J., A. M. Pejterson, and L. P. Goodstein. *Cognitive Systems Engineering* (New York: John Wiley & Sons, Inc., 1994).

Vicente. *Cognitive Work Analysis.*

Woods, D. D., and E. Hollnagel. "Mapping Cognitive Demands in Complex Problem-Solving Worlds." *International Journal of Man-Machine Studies* 26 (1987): 257–75.

For my own approach to a decision-centered design process, see G. Klein, G. Kaempf, S. Wolf, M. Thordsen, and T. E. Miller, "Applying Decision Requirements to User-Centered Design," *International Journal of Human-Computer Studies* 46 (1997): 1–15.

These materials are all written for specialists in the field. One of the best-known and most readable sources is D. A. Norman, *The Psychology of Everyday Things* (New York: HarperCollins Publishers, Inc., 1988).

16. *And we needn't gnash our teeth . . .* There are dissenting views on the victory of Deep Blue. Gulko assets that Kasparov simply played poorly, and that Deep Blue did not exhibit superhuman ability. See B. Gulko, "Deep Blue," *Commentary* 104 (1997): 45–47. Chelminski catalogs all the ways that the match between Kasparov and Deep Blue was rigged in favor of the computer in R. Chelminski, "This Time It's Personal," *Wired* (2001): 98–113.

Chapter 16: Becoming Intuitive Decision Makers

1. *From 1998 to the present, Tiger Woods . . .* I have taken this account of Tiger Woods's efforts to modify his swing from Dan Goodgame, "Tiger Woods: The Game of Risk: How the Best Golfer in the World Got Even Better." *Time*, August 14, 2000, 57–62.

2. *After he retired, he described his "natural" swing . . .* The account of George Shuba

comes from R. Kahn, *The Boys of Summer.* 1st ed. (New York: Harper & Row, 1972).

3. Ibid., 226.

4. *You will feel less harried, less worried* . . . Regarding the concept of muscular intuition, this is a good place to point out that there is almost nothing in this book about personality differences. I included a test of tolerance for ambiguity in Chapter 7 (How to Manage Uncertainty), but that is it. There are lots of tests out there, and lots of speculation about how we differ from each other. Westcott has a test of intuition (M. R. Westcott, *Toward a Contemporary Psychology of Intuition: A Historical, Theoretical, and Empirical Inquiry* [New York: Holt, Rinehart & Winston, 1968]) and so does Agor (W. H. Agor, *The Logic of Intuitive Decision Making: A Research-Based Approach for Top Management* [New York: Quorum Books, 1986]).

One of the four scales of the Myers-Briggs Type Inventory is about openness to intuition. This topic could have been a full section, or even its own book.

I decided not to cover personality differences because a discussion of personality differences would sidetrack the focus of the book on how each of us can improve intuitive decision-making skills. If you discover that you are less intuitive than most people, does that mean that you should not bother trying to build intuitive skills if you probably won't use them? If you are more intuitive than the average person, does that mean you don't have to work on intuitive skills because you are already sensitive? The concept of muscular intuition treats intuitive decision making as a skill to be strengthened, independent of individual differences.

Index

Note: page numbers with *f* and *t* indicate figures and tables; page numbers with *n* indicate endnotes.

fuzzy goals, 148–149, 199–200
goals conflicts, 198
metrics and, 229, 234
revising, 149, 166–167, 175
"Good News" decision game, 124–128
Greenspan, Alan, 238–240, 256–257
groups
directed creativity for, 151–153, 161
group brainstorming sessions, 145–146
Gwynn, Tony, 273, 275

Hamm, Robert, 73, 287n11, 288n15, 290n3, 292n11
Hammond, K. R., 281n7, 284n2
Harrington, Doug, 212–214, 219
Hayashi, Alden, xxiii
Henderson, Simon, 18
Heuer, Richards, 291n9
heuristics, decision makers' reliance on, 287n10
Hutton, Rob, 153

improvisation. See adaptation
incremental decisions and plans, 117, 167
information
defined, 200
See also data
information technologies, 248–269
automation bias, 266, 302n12
as barriers to adaptation, 264–265
as barriers to intuition development, 24
as barriers to pattern recognition and problem detection, 252–254
data overload and, 252, 259, 262, 301n7
design of, 262, 266, 268–269
expertise compromised by, 249, 251
inscrutability of, 253–254, 261–263
mental models weakened by, 259–261, 268
passive vs. active stance and, 252, 255–259, 260–261, 262, 265–266
primacy over users, 267, 303n13
rebellion against, 263
relevant data searches and, 255–259
informative directions, 200
instruction, giving clearly, 203–206
See also executive intent
instructional techniques, 220–221
intelligence analysts, research involving, 291n9, 301n7
intent, communication and interpretation of. See executive intent
Internet decision games, 46
interpreting executive intent. See executive intent
interpreting situations. See sensemaking
intuition
augmenting with analysis, 70–76
barriers to. See metrics
in chess decision making, 75

definitions, xvi, 13
developing, 26, 276. See also intuition skills training
distrust of, xvi, 60, 62–63, 285n4, 286n10
lack of, EVR case, 68–70
limitations of, 56–60
magical vs. muscular, xix–xxi
role in analysis, 64
synthesis with analysis, 54–57, 284n2
intuition skills training, 26–53, 271–272
attitudes that hinder, 273–277
basic elements of, 28f, 29, 52–53, 272
coaching others. See coaching
goals of, 27
identifying and facing uncertainties, 120–123
identifying decision requirements, 29–35
learning to categorize decision types, 79–84
practicing with decision games, 35–46
reviewing decisions, 47–52
intuitive decision making
barriers to, 23–24
in business organizations, xxii–xxiii, 19–23, 24–25
characteristics of intuitive decision makers, 270–271
conditions favoring, 57f
examples of situations requiring, 83
experience as basis of, 26, 271
importance of, 24–25
researchers' views of, 14, 54, 60, 62–63, 70
teaching. See coaching
See also RPD
"Intuitive Landing" example, 212–214
"Invisible Adversary" example, 129
Isenberg, Daniel, 19, 117–118, 148–149, 282n14, 296n12
ISO 9000 compliance, 297n8

Jamieson, Greg, 173–174
Japanese robotics example, 171
job applicant assessment, example involving, 48
job-seeking strategies, research involving, 58–59
Jordan, Michael, 273, 275
justifying decisions, 56–57, 57f

Kahn, Roger, 276
Kasparov, Garry, 269, 303n16
Katkin, Edward, 97–98
"Keeping Your Co-Pilot in the Dark" example, 210–211
"Killing the Customer" example, 130
Kirby, Jerry, 20–22, 228, 234

Leadership Engine, The (Tichy), 208
"Lean Years or Fat Years" example, 49
learning rates, information technologies and, 249, 265
Lehmann, Dave, 175

About the Author

GARY KLEIN is, according to *Fast Company*, a "fearless thinker . . . [who] had the courage to bet his career on the hunch that people have grossly underestimated the power of gut instinct." He is the founder, chairman, and chief scientist of Klein Associates, a twenty-four-year-old research company that studies how people use experience to make decisions and perform tasks in the context of uncertainty, time pressure, conflicting goals, and change. He has studied intuition at work on the front lines of firefighting, aviation, military command and control, and software troubleshooting. Dr. Klein is the author of *Sources of Power: How People Make Decisions*. He lives in Yellow Springs, Ohio.